the indie author guide

the indie author guide

self-publishing strategies anyone can use

April L. Hamilton

WRITER'S DIGEST BOOKS

WritersDigest.com
Cincinnati, Ohio

For more resources for writers, visit www.writersdigest.com/books.

To receive a free weekly e-mail newsletter delivering tips and updates about writing and about Writer's Digest products, register directly at http://newsletters.fwpublications.com.

14 13 12 11 10   5 4 3 2 1

Distributed in Canada by Fraser Direct
100 Armstrong Avenue
Georgetown, Ontario, Canada L7G 5S4
Tel: (905) 877-4411

Distributed in the U.K. and Europe by F+W Media International
Brunel House, Newton Abbot, Devon, TQ12 4PU, England
Tel: (+44) 1626-323200, Fax: (+44) 1626-323319
E-mail: postmaster@davidandcharles.co.uk

Distributed in Australia by Capricorn Link
P.O. Box 704, Windsor, NSW 2756 Australia
Tel: (02) 4577-3555

Library of Congress Cataloging-in-Publication Data
Hamilton, April.
The indie author guide / by April Hamilton. -- 1st ed.
p. cm.
Includes bibliographical references.
ISBN 978-1-58297-994-6 (pbk. : alk. paper)
1. Self-publishing--Handbooks, manuals, etc. 2. Self-publishing--United States. I. Title.
Z285.5.H36 2010
070.5'93--dc22
2010029810

Edited by Melissa Hill
Designed by Terri Woesner
Production coordinated by Debbie Thomas and Mark Griffin

dedication

This book is dedicated to all the indie authors who have poured themselves into the movement, heart and soul. When pundits talk about the revolution that's taking place in trade publishing, they are talking about *you*.

acknowledgments

Jane Friedman, Content and Community Development Director for Writer's Digest, thanks for being the first person at WD to believe in the potential of this book, and for being such a forward-thinking leader in an industry that can sometimes be so stubbornly entrenched in the past.

Melissa Hill, my WD editor, thanks for shepherding this manuscript through the pre-publication process with great professionalism, kindness and aplomb. You were never further away than an email or phone call, your enthusiasm for this book has never wavered, and you've made the entire project a pleasure.

Rita Rosenkranz, my agent, thanks for your input and guidance on this project.

Christina Katz, more widely known as The Writer Mama, thanks for taking me under your wing when I first came to the WD family, introducing me to Rita Rosenkranz, blazing a platform trail for all authors to follow, and most importantly, for being a friend. Thanks too for allowing me to quote from your book, *Get Known Before The Book Deal*.

about the author

April L. Hamilton is an author, blogger, Technorati BlogCritic, leading advocate and speaker for the indie author movement, and founder of Publetariat.com, the premiere online news hub and community for indie authors and small imprints. She's spoken at the O'Reilly Tools of Change conference and the Writer's Digest Business of Getting Published conference, and has also judged self-published books for competitions run by Writer's Digest and the Next Generation Indie Book Awards. She is also on the Board of Directors for the Association of Independent Authors, and works as a freelance editor, designer, and platform/publishing consultant for self-publishers. Find out more at www.aprillhamilton.com

table of contents

one} Indie Authorship: An Introduction

Independence: It's not just for musicians and filmmakers anymore. Plenty of big-name authors, from Anne Rice to Stephen Covey, are self-publishing now; it's just that when such literary luminaries as these do it, few people call it "self-publishing." Reports of Covey's self-publishing endeavors speak of him forming his own publishing company. Stories about Anne Rice's foray into indie authorship tell us she's released an app, or e-book program, for the iPad and iPhone. The names of large publishing houses are absent from these stories, and the activities being undertaken by Rice and Covey are no different than those already undertaken by any number of indie authors. Yet somehow few people reading such stories come away with the impression they're reading about adventures in self-publishing. But make no mistake: That's precisely what they're reading about. A quiet revolution in trade publishing is afoot.

PORTRAIT OF THE INDIE AUTHOR

The active term in "indie authorship" is indie, or independent. An independent filmmaker produces his own films. An independent musician produces his own recordings. Likewise, an independent author produces his own books.

An indie author controls the entire process of creating, publishing, and promoting his book from beginning to end. This doesn't necessarily mean he performs every task along the way himself—he may pay others for specific services like editing, cover art design, or website design—but he's the one calling the shots, he retains all rights to his work, and he keeps all the profit.

Indie authorship demands a certain amount of entrepreneurial spirit, sometimes referred to as a can-do attitude. Working outside the publishing mainstream affords authors complete freedom over their work, but it also places sole responsibility for their careers squarely upon their own shoulders.

The ideal candidate for indie authorship is a writer who's spent years honing her craft and has acquired a basic understanding of how trade publishing and bookselling works, but for whatever reason can't garner the interest of an agent or mainstream publisher. Often the problem lies in the extremely limited parameters of today's highly consolidated, blockbuster-centric trade publishing industry. An author's work may be well-reviewed and might even have won or placed in contests, yet she can't get a nibble from the big boys. On the other hand, she has some computer skills, she's willing to learn, and she wants to redirect her energies toward something productive. As an author, she wants to boldly go where few authors have gone before.

One more thing: The indie author must fervently believe in the indie movement, because she may face episodes of prejudice, ignorance, and possibly even mockery from those in the mainstream who cling to the publishing model of yesteryear. As I'll explain in the next section, prior to Pocket Books' founding, the Stephen Kings, James Pattersons, and Sue Graftons of the world were mocked and dismissed by the establishment, too. In any event, an indie author doesn't need the establishment's approval, or anyone else's. She will market her books directly to the reading public, and history has shown that the public is a pragmatic and open-minded lot.

A HISTORY LESSON

It has never been easy to get an original novel published in the United States. In fact there wasn't even an outlet for most of them prior to the 1940s. In the early 1900s three main types of book publishers existed in America: university presses, small commercial presses, and large commercial presses.

University presses publish books for use in educational, academic, and religious settings. Their domain is the land of textbooks, Bibles, academic tomes, encyclopedias, reprints of classic literature from the past, reference books, and the like.

Small commercial presses, which are largely extinct today, churned out dime novels, the forebears of today's commercial fiction. These presses were entirely profit-driven, and ran very much like the production office of a hit television show today. Every publisher had its various novel series, which were the literary equivalent of today's television series: highly entertaining stories centering on popular characters in interesting or amusing settings. Small commercial publishers hired writers to turn out new volumes in these series, but they weren't interested in publishing any new and original works from those writers. Given that the publishers expected writers to produce new installments at the rate of roughly one 30,000-word novel per week, there was no time to create original works anyway.

Large commercial presses in those days released literary fiction, poetry collections, essay collections, biographies, and other nonfiction: In a word, "important" books. Wealthy philanthropists who typically approached publishing as a family business owned these presses. Such publishers were true patrons of the arts who were thrilled to discover a literary diamond in the rough and willing to invest many years and thousands of dollars to nurture a new talent. Their prime motivation was to enlarge and improve the canon of American literature. Profit was a secondary consideration, and a distant one at that. It was typical for authors to have personal relationships with these publishers, and the relationships were not dependent on profit from book sales.

As you may have noticed, none of the publishers discussed so far had any interest in nonliterary, original novels. University presses didn't publish new novels at all and small presses weren't interested in changing their highly profitable business model. The owners of large presses sought art and wouldn't risk their reputations as arbiters of literary excellence by stooping to publish mere entertainment, nor anything offensive to their high-society sensibilities.

The mainstream commercial novel wasn't born until Robert de Graff founded Pocket Books, the first press to release books in paperback format exclusively, in 1939 with funding from Simon & Schuster. Pocket Books titles sold at lunch counters, newsstands, train stations, grocery stores, and drugstores for just 25 cents each, but ironically bookstores snobbishly refused to carry these popular entertainments until the 1950s. Yet, the mass-market paperback novel became a huge success, thanks to its accessibility, affordability, and portability. Pocket sold over 12 million books in 1941, and due largely to the new format's popularity among WWII soldiers, hit the 40 million book sales mark in 1945.

Big publishers couldn't ignore the sweeping reach of the popular paperback novel. They decided to publish their own paperbacks through subsidiaries or entirely separate imprints so as not to sully the reputations of their flagship literary presses. The postwar paperback market grew even larger with the passage of the GI Bill and subsequent expansion of American universities and colleges. Increasingly profit-minded big publishers introduced the trade paperback at about this time. With a larger format and a higher-quality binding, trade paperback form was reserved for books publishers judged to be a cut above the typical mass-market paperback. Since a hardcover binding was viewed as a mark of artistic legitimacy in the publishing field in those days, commercial novels were entirely excluded from hardcover release for decades.

Through the 1950s and 1960s, book publishing was a booming industry in the United States, though its profit margins remained low:

4 to 6 percent, on average. Gone were the days of the patron publisher, as one by one, big publishers went public and became answerable to shareholders rather than their founders' sensibilities. The 1970s brought merger mania to the publishing industry with CEOs anxious to try out the successful business strategies of their peers in other industries. Mergers and acquisitions may have slashed costs and boosted the bottom line in manufacturing, finance, and the service sectors, but publishing industry margins remained stubbornly narrow. The 1980s saw the birth of the media megaconglomerate: single, huge corporations with national, or even global holdings, in multiple media markets. Not content to dominate film, music, broadcast media, newspapers, and periodicals, the media megas started buying up book publishers.

Thanks to more than three decades of mergers, buyouts, and consolidations, all of which were carried out with the motive of drastically improving profits, the U.S. publishing industry is now dominated by just six media megaconglomerates: Viacom, Time Warner, and News Corp., among them. If these names sound familiar, it's because they also own and operate virtually every television, cable, and radio broadcast network, as well as nearly all major magazines, newspapers, TV shows, movie studios, music labels, video game franchises, cable channels, and Internet service providers in the United States. Media megas are bottom-line focused with a vengeance, and the blockbuster-centric mentality they've used to bring the mainstream film, music, and TV industries to heel is now being applied to book publishing. Priorities have not just shifted, they've completely reversed. Sales forecasts are the primary driver when manuscripts are selected for publication; the quality of the work is now a secondary, far distant consideration.

THE CURRENT STATE OF AFFAIRS

The six major publishing houses are run like movie studios, which means they're increasingly risk-averse, sink most of their attention and resources into a few intended blockbusters, and view profit as the most worthwhile measure of their products' value. One of the first casualties of this new business model was the midlist, the publisher's catalog of books expected to sell only between five thousand and forty thousand copies. Big publishers are no more interested in these relatively small books than their movie studio subsidiaries are interested in relatively small films. Publishers have dropped many former midlist authors, whose books sold reliably for years, on the grounds that while their books may be successful, they're not quite successful *enough*.

Media megas are bringing the movie marketing machine to bear as well. They typically hedge their movie bets by opening new films on as many screens as possible, to sell as many tickets as quickly as they can and keep a step ahead of potentially bad word of mouth for at least a few days. They've found a way to apply a similar scheme to books. By offering booksellers large discounts on certain titles in exchange for maximum display space, reduced retail pricing, and two-for-one deals, they "buy" the prime real estate at the front of bookstores, ensuring their favored titles will monopolize the display racks at the entrance to the store.

To make matters worse, display space in the rest of the store is getting smaller all the time. Anyone who's been to a chain bookstore lately knows that books seem to be taking second billing to other merchandise these days: Next to the incredible shrinking book department in a local store, I recently found DVDs, CDs, stationery, candy, iPod accessories, fashion accessories, games, and even toiletries and cosmetics. Borders, whose United Kingdom operation is already bankrupt, has experimented with a few different strategies in its Ann Arbor, Michigan, store. Chief among them a 5 to 10 percent reduction in book stock. The store no longer carries books that move only one or two copies a month, and the liberated shelf space is being used to display more books "face out" (with the front covers, rather than the spines, facing into the aisle). Books positioned face out do tend to sell better, but face-out shelving requires an overall reduction in stock on the shelves. The bad news for all of us is that Borders reported a spike in book sales since the changes and other booksellers are following their lead. Such changes may not be enough to prevent the brick-and-mortar bookstore chains' ongoing loss of book sales to such outlets as Amazon, supermarkets, discount/big box stores like Target, Walmart, and Costco, where consumers can usually find a better price, more variety in titles offered, or both.

Unless you're a prestige, celebrity, or bestselling author, it's not necessarily good news when you learn a major publisher has decided to buy your manuscript. Advances are shrinking and promotion has turned into a vicious circle for lesser-known authors: They can't get their media megapublisher to spend money on promotion until they've proven their books will sell, but their books won't sell without promotion. Yet, if an author's book doesn't earn enough his current publisher (along with their many imprints) will drop him, and the other major publishers in town will view him as damaged goods. Meanwhile, those publishers lavish money, publicity, book tours, and huge promotion budgets on a few, favored authors. It was once safe to assume that if you were published by a major house, you'd at least get to see your book on the shelf in brick-and-mortar stores, but even this small bit of writer wish fulfillment is no longer a given.

Writers who are not best-selling authors often find they have little choice but to take their meager, long-awaited advances and spend them on makeshift marketing campaigns. It's commonly believed that fewer than two hundred American novelists earn enough to support themselves through book sales alone.

When this type of slow, inexorable crawl toward mediocrity and indifference toward artists came about in film and music, hopefuls jumped at the chance to take their careers into their own hands by going independent. You may wonder, as I have, why writers aren't following suit now that we have affordable tools at our disposal to publish, distribute, and market our books without any help or involvement from mainstream publishers. The two primary reasons, I've come to conclude, are fear and perceived stigma.

INDIE VERSUS VANITY

Before consolidations began, there was some truth in the assumption that the only author who resorts to self-publication is an author whose work isn't good enough to attract a tra-

ditional publisher. Anyone could pay a press to publish a minimum print run of his book, but it was very expensive and bookstores generally refused to carry the finished product. Because the author was assumed to be more or less bribing his way into print, the entire process was viewed as an exercise in vanity, hence the term vanity publishing. The vanity press of yesteryear is a far cry from today's e-books and Print-On-Demand (POD) self-publishing, but the vanity publishing label continues to be broadly, incorrectly affixed to any self-publication endeavor.

Today's self-publishing authors are on much the same path as their peers in independent film and music, choosing to release quality work that may not appeal to a massive enough audience to interest a media megapublisher but may find an appreciative smaller audience. Those former midlist authors whose publishers have dropped them find self-publication a viable option to continue serving their readership, and authors of niche nonfiction, poetry collections, short story collections, or any material deemed to have limited commercial appeal are in the same boat. Even name authors like Piers Anthony, Ian McEwan, and Martin Amis are turning to self-publishing in order to capture higher e-book royalties or to bring out works that didn't interest their publishers or whose rights have reverted to the author following a mainstream release. Such books are the literary equivalent of the independent film, which is generally regarded as the last stronghold of meaning and originality in American cinema. These self-publishing authors are not vanity authors desperate to see their names in print for bragging rights alone. They are indie authors.

Then there's that certain variety of self-publishing author which is best described as an author-businessperson, the best-known and most successful example of which as of this writing is probably Stephen R. Covey (if you are unfamiliar with his books, search Amazon for "7 Habits". Despite his long and profitable relationship with Simon & Schuster, Covey has already self-published two titles in print, e-book, and audiobook editions through his own company, FranklinCovey, and has said he intends to self-publish additional titles in the future. Covey has built a business consulting empire in which publishing is just one more means of spreading his expertise, and just one more revenue stream alongside his consulting, speaking, and business management product offerings. Self-publishing gives him total control over every aspect of his books, from content and design considerations through distribution, marketing, and even setting the retail price. On top of these considerable benefits, Covey enjoys a much higher royalty (profit) on his self-published books than he does on those other companies published because there's no middleman taking a cut of the profits on every sale.

WHY DON'T MORE AUTHORS GO INDIE?

Good question. Why don't *all* established, serially best-selling authors follow Covey's lead? After all, once you've built your name or line of books into a globally recognized and sought-after brand (such as J.K. Rowling with her Harry Potter brand or Stephen King with his Stephen King brand), it doesn't matter who publishes you or how. Readers will actively seek out and buy your work.

As mentioned previously, some established authors already *are* experimenting with self-publishing, and I believe many more will follow in the coming months and years now that the tools needed to match the quality of a mainstream-produced book are so affordable and readily available. However, there is a downside to self-publishing that many authors find so onerous as to cancel out its many benefits: Self-publishing requires the author to become a publisher, and many authors either aren't interested in running a publishing business or fear they lack the skills and knowledge to do so effectively.

In a sense, any author whose work is available for sale is a self-employed small businessperson in that there are profits and expenses to be tracked and reported at tax time. But mainstream-published authors don't have to manage the process of getting their books into print and made available for sale. They don't have to act as producers of their books. Such authors simply deliver a manuscript to a publisher, and the publisher sees to it that the book is properly edited, formatted, and typeset; that review blurbs are collected for the cover; that the cover is designed and printed; that the book is set up through various distribution channels, and so on. None of these tasks would intimidate a business management expert like Covey, but the same can't be said of most authors.

Though it's not all that difficult or complicated to act as your own publisher, as this book will demonstrate, the prospect can seem daunting. This is why so many authors choose e-books as their first venture into self-publishing: Getting an e-book into "print" and made available for sale is easy and requires no up-front investment thanks to such e-book service providers as the Amazon Digital Text Platform, or DTP (for publishing Kindle books), Smashwords, and Scribd.

BIAS AGAINST SELF-PUBLICATION

The characterization of self-published authors as talentless hacks persists in some circles, but it's a perception that's definitely changing now that the trade publishing landscape is in flux. Nevertheless, there are still some literary agents, book consultants, and freelance editors out there who say no major publisher will want to have anything to do with you if you've self-published. Why?

Apart from the assumption that a self-published work won't match the quality of a mainstream book and will therefore tarnish the author's reputation, some publishing professionals believe that in the highly unlikely event you ever manage to sell a manuscript to a big publisher and go on to make the best-seller list, the publisher will want to cash in on any other unpublished manuscripts you may have lying around—even manuscripts they themselves have previously rejected. The anti self-publishing camp also likes to bring up the issue of first publication rights, claiming that once a manuscript has been published in any format and made available to the public, the material is somehow used up and a mainstream publisher can't do anything with it.

These are very dated perceptions. The existence of *this* book, originally self-published but now being offered in a revised and updated edition from Writer's Digest Books, is proof that concerns about first publication rights are groundless. As to the matter of access to an au-thor's full collection of manuscripts, gone forever are the days when hitting *The New York Times* list meant automatic publishing contracts for every other manuscript the author ever wrote. Nowadays, no matter who you are or how many best-sellers you've written, every manuscript must be sold on its own merits—even if its primary merit is the author's popularity, which is often the case with celebrity novels and memoirs. While it's true that a Dan Brown or Mitch Albom may have an easy time selling a publisher on a new manuscript, this is only true to the extent the new manuscript is in keeping with his past successful books. If Albom suddenly decides to write a noir thriller, for example, publishers will know the work may not appeal to the same huge and established audience Albom has built for his previous books, and this makes the project more risky.

Unfortunately, authors and aspiring authors are often the people most vociferously opposed to self-publishing. Many mainstream-published authors view all forms of self-publishing as vanity publishing, and believe it or not, the same opinion is commonplace among unpublished writers, too. These anti-indies believe that mainstream media outlets should exclude self-published books from editorial reviews, as well as from major awards and recognition for writing excellence among published books. They also think that self-published books should be labeled in a specific way in online bookstores as a warning to potential buyers. It's as if there's some sort of bizarre Stockholm syndrome at work, in which writers not only accept the perceived conditions of creative captivity at the hands of media mega-publishers, but have come to believe there's some value inherent in those conditions. Can you imagine anyone seriously remarking to a friend, "Well, I'm just glad we've got the mega-conglomerates deciding what movies and music are produced. If it weren't for the work of those fine people, we might be exposed to just any old thing!" More ludicrous still, can you imagine a filmmaker or musician saying it?

Thankfully, the bias against self-publishing is beginning to crumble. The face of the current crisis in trade publishing coupled with increasing numbers of self-publishing success stories among established and emerging authors have helped. As the history I've provided in this chapter demonstrates, the American publishing industry has a long tradition of elitism and resistance to change. Just as the publishing establishment once looked down its collective nose at the paperback novel, for a very long time it has looked down on the self-published book. When paperback novels gained public acceptance on a scale publishers could no longer afford to ignore, the format became an accepted and respected part of American publishing. Now, as then, public acceptance is the key. Fortunately, readers don't share big publishers' tastes, views, or biases. Readers buy books that appeal to them regardless of where the books came from. In order for indie authors to cross over as the paperback did, enough quality work must be independently released, thereby proving indies' work is as good as that of their mainstream peers—and in some cases, better.

COMMON MISPERCEPTIONS ABOUT INDIE AUTHORSHIP

There's a lot of misinformation out there about what it means, and what it's like, to be an indie author. Let's tackle these old wives' tales one by one, shall we?

I'd never go indie because I'm a writer, not a salesperson.

Any author worth his salt these days knows publishers are all focused on author platform, a topic that's discussed in much greater detail in a later chapter of this book. An author's platform as defined by Christina Katz in her book, *Get Known Before The Book Deal*, "simply describes all the ways you are visible and appealing to your future, potential, or actual readership." Platform covers everything from author websites and blogs to speaking appearances and everything in between. And the job of creating, growing, and maintaining a platform belongs entirely to each author, no matter how obscure or famous, new or established. A publisher might put up a Web page for each of its most popular authors on its own website or in its own online bookstore, but that's a far cry from a true author platform through which authors are expected to actively solicit, and engage with, readers. As Katz goes on to say in her book, "I find it helpful to define a platform as a promise writers make to not only create something to sell (like a book), but also to promote it to the specific readers who will want to purchase it. This takes both time and effort, not to mention considerable focus." Big publishing houses offer promotional services and budgets only to their celebrity, prestige, and best-selling clients. With the exception of authors lucky enough to sign with a small press that treats all its authors equally, *everyone* else is on the hook to promote his own work.

While it's true that only mainstream-published authors have access to the best-known vehicles for mainstream editorial reviews (major magazines, newspapers, and literary journals), the mere fact that you were published by Penguin or Harper doesn't guarantee you'll get mainstream editorial reviews. Thousands of books come out every year, and of course major magazines are much quicker to review the latest book by a name author than a debut from an unknown. Furthermore, a recent *Publishers Weekly* survey demonstrated that word of mouth is a far more effective sales tool for books than professional critic reviews, and this observation appears to be borne out by the popularity of such online reader-reviewer communities as Goodreads, Shelfari, and LibraryThing. Finally, as we all know, newspapers' weekly Books sections are endangered species in newspapers due to its flagging popularity with print advertisers and a perceived lack of reader interest in literary criticism.

Since brick-and-mortar stores won't stock self-published books, indie authors can't ever earn as much as mainstream-published authors.
As explained previously, brick-and-mortar bookstores are struggling as more and more readers turn to the Internet, discount stores, and big box stores like Costco to buy their books. But discount stores and big box stores only carry best-sellers, gift books, and bargain books, so most mainstream authors won't find their books in those outlets. Also, brick-and-mortar bookstores heavily promote each big publisher's favored authors while relegating everything else to the back of the store, and getting your book on the shelves of your local Borders doesn't provide much of a sales boost if the only people who know it exists are you,

your friends, and family. After all, *those* people would've bought your book even if you had to sell it out of the trunk of your car. Moreover, if your mainstream-published book fails to break out (meaning, become a best-seller) within three months of its release, it will be pulled from brick-and-mortar chain bookseller shelves to make room for the next round of contenders, and you'll have to cope with truckloads of returns, all of which are subtracted from your royalty checks.

Online booksellers level the playing field, enabling indie authors to compete as effectively as their mainstream-published peers. In fact, indies actually have an advantage over the mainstream on the Web because mainstreamers, for the most part, have yet to accept the responsibility of promoting their own books and have been slow to acquire the necessary skills. The indie author tends to have a firm grasp of her target audience—she knows who they are and, more than that, is already actively engaged with them via online communities and discussion groups.

Moreover, recall that few authors earn enough to support themselves through sales of their books alone, regardless of who published them. Signing with a big publishing house does not guarantee strong earnings, and the great majority of mainstream-published authors must still work a day job or depend upon the earnings of a spouse or partner. As a savvy indie, you can expect to earn a royalty 10 and 50 percent higher than your mainstream peers, which means you don't need to sell as many books to achieve the same earnings.

My chances of becoming a best-seller are much better with a big publisher.

If you happen to be a favored client of your big publisher, and he intends to put considerable promotional effort and money behind you, then you're absolutely right. Otherwise, not so much. Only about 1 to 2 percent of all books published go on to become best-sellers, so your book isn't *likely* to become a best-seller no matter how good it is or who publishes it. The question shouldn't be one of who's more likely to become a best-seller, but who's more likely to become a favored client. A favored client is one who's presumed to have a built-in audience, which comes down to quality work plus an effective platform, both of which are entirely accessible to indie authors. An indie book is a proven quantity by the time it comes to the attention of a big publisher. This gives the indie author more leverage to negotiate favorable promotion terms. It also gives the big publisher more and better reasons to give the acquired indie book a promotional push.

Indie is fine for publishing one book, but I intend to have a <u>career</u>.

Where a mainstream author has a chance, a very small chance, at career longevity, an indie author chooses for himself how long his career in authorship will last. Recall that a first-time author's book must perform very well very quickly in order to break out, and if it fails to do so, the author will be dropped by his publisher and seen as damaged goods by the other major publishers. With no promotional backing from the publisher, the chances that the author's book will break out are very slim indeed. Even if it does, the literary landscape is strewn with the career wreckage of authors who had one or more best-sellers, only to drop gradually into obscurity thereafter. It is extraordinarily rare for any author to have the kind of career longevity enjoyed by the serially best-selling likes of Michael Crichton or Tom Clancy, and thanks to the death of the midlist, it's only becoming rarer.

While it's virtually unheard of for an indie author to scale those same career heights in terms of consistently high sales, they don't face the performance pressure foisted on mainstream authors. If an indie's book sells modestly, there's no one stopping him from publishing another. Furthermore, because indies earn much higher royalties than mainstreamers (they don't have an agent taking a cut and don't have an advance to pay back), it's entirely possible for an indie author to earn a steady, if modest, income from his writing. There's no analog in the mainstream publishing world, since an author who's earning only modestly for his publisher won't be with that publisher for long. Numerous nonfiction indies earn their entire living off their writing, mostly by serving niche audiences, using their books as cross-promotional tools for their workshops and speaking engagements, and relentlessly promoting.

TOOLS OF THE INDIE AUTHOR TRADE

The tools and skills needed to create and promote a book independently vary according to each author's needs and preferences. For example, an author who intends to hire a publicist doesn't need all the computer and graphics skills required of an author who intends to do all his own promotion.

The tools in the following table will enable you to do everything this book covers, from manuscript formatting to issuing online press releases. The greater your skills and better your tools, the easier it will be to accomplish each task, but even someone with basic skills and a willingness to learn can be successful. Don't worry that you can't possibly afford everything on the list,

ITEM	REQUIRED FOR
Computer	Almost everything in this book
Modern word processing program (e.g., MS Word, OpenOffice Writer)	Manuscript preparation, promotional activities
PDF creator program	Convert your manuscript files and promotional materials to Portable Document Format (PDF), which is the preferred format of many service providers and produces documents which can be read either on- or offline
Graphics or photo editor program (e.g., Microsoft Digital Image Pro, CorelDRAW)	Cover art design, promotional activities, author photo; note that a consumer-level program is usually adequate and you don't need the advanced sort of software used by professional graphic artists and photographers
Clip art and/or stock photos (some will come bundled with graphics/photo editor program, additional collections can be purchased separately)	Cover art design, promotional activities
File archiving program (e.g., WinZip, WinRar, etc.)	Compression of manuscript and cover art files for upload to publisher
Internet access and skills (e.g., email with attachments, ability to post to online discussion groups)	Upload of manuscript and cover art files to service providers, promotional activities, correspondence; ideally, your Internet access should not be dial-up (which requires your computer to be attached to a phone line and place an actual call to a server in order to connect to the Internet), as dial-up is slow and unreliable. If at all possible, upgrade to DSL, satellite, or fiber optic service.
Basic HTML knowledge	Online promotional activities—don't worry, there's an HTML primer in this book

Digital camera	Author photo, photos taken at events to post to author website/blog, etc.
Mini digital video camera	Not strictly required, but a great, easy-to-use tool to have for creating book trailers, YouTube videos, and other promotional material for your author platform

or if some of the things listed are totally unfamiliar to you; there are free or low-cost options for every item, and you will be provided with easy-to-understand, step-by-step directions for using each one in this book.

GOALS IN INDIE AUTHORSHIP

Some authors' definition of career success has more to do with how much readers enjoy their books than it does with how many readers buy their books. Others take the opposite view, using sales as the primary yardstick for measuring their career success. Independence is a viable option for any author, but the former type will be content to remain indie for his entire career in authorship while the latter type will often view indie authorship as a stepping stone to mainstream publication. Either way, the initial goals are the same: to produce quality work and get people to read it.

Given that the mainstream publishing industry has historically looked down on indie authorship, it may seem counterintuitive to use indie authorship as an entrée to that world. However, as with the paperback novel, in the end it all comes down to money. As crossover successes like *The Celestine Prophecy*, *The Lace Reader*, and *Eragon* have repeatedly shown, publishers will welcome commercially successful self-published authors with open arms. Likewise, they will welcome works from authors who've established a large following or generated buzz via their author platform.

In terms of profitability, indie books have the potential to earn much higher royalty percentages for their authors than mainstream books. The fact that so many mainstream-published, big-name authors are beginning to self-publish specifically because of royalty considerations is proof of this. However, regardless of who published a given book, its eventual earnings are a function of sales, and sales are a function of promotion. Promoting your book need not be costly and it need not become a full-time occupation, but it is most definitely a crucial component for success.

Will you get rich as an indie author? Will you earn enough to quit your day job? In most cases, the answer is no. However, it's important to remember that the vast majority of mainstream-published authors aren't rich and can't afford to quit their day jobs, either. At least as an indie author, you can enjoy the benefits of calling your own shots, and controlling your rights and your work while earning higher royalties than your mainstream peers. Best of all, your career in indie authorship isn't over until *you* decide to stop publishing: There are no sales quotas to meet and no fear that your next book won't be published if the current one fails to break out.

two} Getting Organized

Keeping your digital work organized is a critical but often overlooked step in successful authorship. As you work on a manuscript, you need your research, notes, and drafts at your fingertips. When you begin iterations of revision, you need to keep tabs on the feedback you receive and make sure that feedback is available when you need it. After the manuscript is completely polished, proofed, and locked against further changes, you need to maintain separate containers to hold the files for each type of release you intend to make available (POD, e-book, Kindle edition, and others). Finally, you will want to archive all the files related to former works in progress, as you never know when those notes and ideas will come in handy as you work on some future project.

HARD DRIVE HOUSEKEEPING AND ORGANIZATION

An organized filing system is essential for all of the writing-related files on your computer. This will save you a great deal of time and energy in the future, when you can easily locate any file related to any one of your manuscripts with just a few mouse clicks. A well-organized, centrally located filing system also simplifies and speeds the backup process—which of course, you're doing regularly, right?

The question of how to organize your files is a matter of personal preference and what makes sense to you. Most people will have a top-level folder called Writing, Manuscripts, or something similar. Beneath that, some will create a separate folder for each different manuscript, using the manuscript's title as the folder name, and then create subfolders within each manuscript folder to hold rough drafts, notes and research, proofs, and e-book versions. Others will prefer to create folders for each different file type within the main, Manuscripts folder, and then place files for each different manuscript within the file type folders: for example, all final (proof) versions in a Proofs folder, all e-book versions in an E-books folder. My own filing system is a combination of the two, as illustrated below.

Within my Writing folder, shown in Figure 2-1, I have a folder for Articles, Blog, Completed MSs (MS is shorthand for manuscript), Podcasting, Published MSs, Web Presence—Promotion, and WIPs (Works In Progress). The Articles folder contains articles I've written for publication online or elsewhere.

The Blog folder contains all my blog posts, which I create off-line and post when they're finished. This is a good way to manage your blog posts not only because it allows you to take as much time as you like to write and polish your posts without the worry of losing your work due to an Internet crash, but also because it's not unheard of for blogging sites to crash and lose members' content. If you already have a copy of each post stored off-line, reconstructing your blog may be tedious, but it won't be impossible. It's also possible that at some point in the future, you may wish to publish some or all of your blog content in book or e-book form. If so, having all your posts stored in a word processor format will greatly simplify the project.

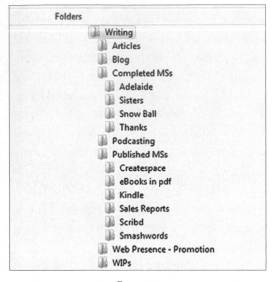

Figure 2-1

The Podcasting folder contains files and documents related to podcasting. If you're podcasting and making your podcasts available through multiple outlets (for example, Podiobooks, the iTunes store), you may wish to set up a subfolder for each outlet and store a copy of each podcast in the associated outlet folder, if for no other reason than to keep track of which podcasts you've made available through which outlets. This is especially helpful for podcasts

of books being released serially (one chapter or section at a time), which is typical on Podiobooks.

The Completed Manuscripts and Published Manuscripts folders are expanded in Figure 2-1 to reveal their subfolders. The Completed Manuscripts and WIPs folders contain one subfolder for each manuscript or book within each of those two categories. All my book-length projects start out in the WIPs folder. When they're complete—and I mean ready-for-the-publisher complete—I move them to the Completed MSs folder. From there, following publication, I move them to the Published MSs folder.

Within the Published MSs folder, the subfolder structure is different. Here, I file my manuscripts according to publisher (or print service provider in the case of CreateSpace). I do this because the final (or proof) manuscript sent to each publisher/provider will differ slightly from each other published version of the manuscript, if only in terms of the copyright page. The copyright page for each published version should indicate the edition, such as, "Smashwords edition published May 2010" or "Kindle edition published May 2010." If I ever need to revise and rerelease a given manuscript for a given publisher/provider, the manuscript will be easy to locate and I will avoid accidentally editing and uploading the wrong version: It's less likely that I'll edit and upload a Kindle version of the manuscript to Smashwords, for example.

Within the Published MSs folder, there's also an e-books in PDF subfolder for my own PDF copies of any manuscripts or documents I offer directly from my website or blog, and

THE INDIE AUTHOR GUIDE

a Sales Reports subfolder. You may prefer to keep a separate Sales Reports subfolder within each publisher's folder; I just have the one folder to save myself the trouble of having to combine all the different reports at the end of the year for tax reporting.

The Web Presence Promotion folder contains subfolders to store all documents, notes, and information related to my websites and promotional activities.

Figure 2-2 shows how my work is organized within each manuscript folder in the Completed MSs and WIPs folders. There are subfolders for Correspondence, Current Version (for the most recent version of the manuscript or, in the case of published manuscripts, the final version), Drafts, Excerpts, Graphics (for cover art or any images appearing in the manuscript), Notes (for workshop feedback), and Research.

Figure 2-2

E-MAIL HOUSEKEEPING AND ORGANIZATION

Just as on your hard drive, a logical, tidy e-mail filing system will save you a lot of time and headaches when you're desperate to locate a specific note, name, or contact information. Just as with your hard drive filing system, your e-mail filing system should be organized in a way that makes sense to you, but there are some overall guidelines that will probably make sense for everyone.

Typically, you correspond with many of the same people about all your different works and it may initially seem like a good idea to set up a separate folder for each of those people, containing all e-mails you send to and receive from each individual. However, if you set up your e-mail files this way, when you need to find a specific e-mail from Susan Editor about your My Super Fantastic Career manuscript, it may not be easy to locate among all the other emails from Susan Editor pertaining to all your other manuscripts. I suggest creating a separate folder for each manuscript and storing all relevant correspondence accordingly. Separate folders can also be created for correspondence not specifically related to any particular manuscript. And don't forget, you need to periodically archive and back up your e-mail, too.

three} Creating Your Brand

A NOTE ABOUT IMPRINT BRANDING VERSUS AUTHOR BRANDING

While many of the concepts and considerations introduced in this chapter can be applied to imprint/publisher branding, this chapter is intended only to address author branding, which is separate from imprint branding.

Neil Gaiman the author brand is both separate and different from the brands of the many imprints under which he's been published. For example, Vertigo released his Sandman graphic novels, but the HarperTrophy imprint of HarperCollins released the mass-market paperback edition of his book, *Coraline*. Where Vertigo is known for its edgy, gritty graphic novels typically aimed at older teens and adults, the HarperTrophy imprint is known for its children's/independent reader and children's/chapter book offerings. Gaiman's author brand encompasses both types of books but is not limited to being exclusively edgy nor exclusively kid-friendly. Gaiman the author is multifaceted.

You may have been told that in order to self-publish, for legal and business reasons you must form your own imprint, or separate publishing company. While I can't address the accuracy of this statement around the world, in the United States, it's not true. As an indie author working with a print services provider,

you are the publisher. In the United States, you can list your legal name as the publisher of record, and report your publishing-related earnings and expenses to tax authorities as a "Sole Proprietor," or individual conducting business on your own. If you form an imprint however, the imprint is the publisher; you must list the imprint name as the publisher of record and report all publishing-related income and expenses to U.S. tax authorities under that imprint business name.

The question of whether you might *want* to form your own imprint comes down to factors that are pretty much the same as those in the decision to form any small business entity. First, presenting a company name to the public can bestow a greater sense of legitimacy on your publishing endeavor. Second, if you want to enjoy the U.S. tax and regulatory benefits of incorporation—and to learn what those benefits are, consult a professional tax preparer—you will need to form a separate business entity and incorporate it according to U.S. regulations. Third, if you expect to publish the works of other authors in addition to your own, setting up a separate business entity will keep your publishing record and bookkeeping segregated from your personal financial matters. Finally, if you incorporate in the United States, the corporation shoulders all matters of liability rather than you as an individual.

This protects your personal income and assets from legal judgments, which may be important to you if you're publishing nonfiction books on subjects in which there's the possibility that readers could injure themselves, others, or physical property. If a lawsuit should ever be brought, it will be against the corporation, not you, and any judgments awarded will be limited to the assets of the corporation, not your personal assets. Note that in the United States, you do not have to incorporate in order to form a small business entity, but there are specific situations in which it makes the most financial and legal sense to do so.

This is a decision with long-term financial and legal ramifications, and I strongly recommend you consult a professional tax preparer and an attorney before making the decision. All you need is a half-hour consultation with each, each of which should cost you $50 or less. It may turn out to be the smartest $100 or less you spend across your entire self-publishing undertaking. If this is too great a strain on your budget, call your local city hall to see if your community offers free or low-cost accounting and legal clinics. If they don't, do an Internet search on "free legal help" and "free accounting help." Be prepared to explain the intended content of your books, as well as your publishing plans, both near-term and long-term, in detail, to get the best-informed advice. If you ultimately opt to form your own imprint, whether incorporated or not, you can find plenty of books on the subject of how to do so. Just search Amazon or Google Books for books with the keyword "publishing" or the phrase "form your own imprint" to find a large selection.

OVERVIEW OF AUTHOR BRANDING

In the context of authorship, what is a brand, and why do you need one? Your brand is the name that stands for the public image encompassing both you, the author, and the body of work affiliated with that name. For most writers the brand name will be the same as that listed on their books as author, but it can also be an alias or company/imprint name. Establishing a known, consistent, and reliable brand is key to marketing success, regardless of what you're selling, and it's a big mistake to think marketing products like detergent and soda pop is all that different from marketing books and authors.

A brand becomes a placeholder in the consciousness of the customer, a bucket containing all the good or bad associations, opinions, and factual observations the customer has come to connect with a given product line.

Consider Ben & Jerry's ice cream. The Ben and Jerry's name typically calls to mind premium ingredients, wild flavor combinations, and socially conscious executives. Ben and Jerry's products are also known to be more expensive than supermarket ice creams, but this is an acceptable trade-off for fans of the brand.

Now take the example of author Terry Pratchett. Common ideas about his work, and by extension about Mr. Pratchett himself, are fantasy, dark humor, imagination, whimsy, and a touch of the philosophical. These associations are so strong that many people will buy Pratchett's books they've not yet read without having any idea of the plot or characters, on the strength of the Pratchett reputation alone. Each book that delivers on the promise of that reputation further solidifies the brand and serves as cross-promotion for every other Pratchett book.

Conversely, readers who don't care for dark humor and whimsy in their fantasy books know to avoid Pratchett's work. It seems counterintuitive, but this helps the author as well. Readers whose tastes don't align well with Pratchett's brand will not enjoy his books, and if they buy one with unrealistic expectations, they will go on to become dissatisfied customers. Dissatisfied customers tend to share their dissatisfaction with everyone they know, and bad word of mouth has a way of spreading.

SHOULD YOUR NAME BE YOUR BRAND?

The answer to this question is, "It depends." It depends on you, your work, your past history, your current life situation, and the life situation you hope to have in the future.

The *you* part of the equation comes down to your tolerance for fame, however small or large that fame may be. Remember that if you use your real name as your brand name, not only you, but your relatives, friends, and even hometown may one day come to national media attention. For many writers this is entirely welcome, and in fact the ultimate goal. For others, it's far preferable to have one persona for public consumption and another for private life.

If you're writing a tell-all type of book or a fictionalized memoir in which your thinly veiled characters are based on real people who may be recognized by readers (regardless of their phony names and the way you altered their physical descriptions), using a pen name

is your safest bet. If you're writing such a book, however, using a pen name is not the sum total of protection you'll need: Consult an attorney to be certain you aren't making libelous—and therefore illegal—statements in your book. Outside these narrow circumstances, the *your work* part of the equation comes into play primarily when there's something about it that could be controversial, as you'll see in the following examples.

For instance, suppose a former child star from a squeaky-clean family sitcom now writes gory crime thrillers. If he wants to leave his former child-star persona intact, or if he worries people may not take him seriously as a writer because they've pigeonholed him as an actor, the author should consider publishing under a different name. However, if he wants to capitalize on his fame and create buzz from the shock value of turning his former image on its ear, publishing under his celebrity name will accomplish his goals.

Also consider any existing body of work. Having a series of finance books in print under your real name may nudge you in the direction of taking a pen name for publication of fiction. Conversely, if you've got a few volumes of arty poetry in print and now want to turn your efforts toward writing books about tax law, establishing a separate brand for your new line may be a good idea because people don't generally look to poets for advice about tax law.

Look at your current circumstances as well. If you're a school teacher whose students are minors, publishing a series of steamy, borderline erotica romances under your real name is a bad idea. Similarly, if you live in a very small community where everyone knows everyone else, you may not welcome the notoriety that comes with having published anything provocative or controversial. Consider the general character of your community, and whether your friends and neighbors might feel what you've written reflects negatively on them or the community in any way. If you have children, consider any possible impact your work may have on them.

Finally, think about your future. If you hope to someday occupy a spot in the public eye for anything other than your writing (for example, public office, acting, singing) or hold a position of authority over children (for example, Boy Scout leader, cheerleading coach, middle school teacher), consider how your published work will be viewed in the future.

If you've already published, it's too late to make a branding decision on any work that's already out there. The de facto brand for that work is the name (or names) under which you've published. However, you will want to be brand aware going forward, and you may elect to publish future works under a different brand after reading through this lesson and giving the subject further thought in light of the information here.

YOU VERSUS YOUR BRAND NAME

First, the usual caveat: I am not, nor have I ever been, a lawyer, and nothing in this book should be construed as professional legal advice. If you have any questions or concerns about publishing under a name other than your legal name, please consult an attorney.

However, one thing I can tell you is this: If you choose to publish under a brand name that is not the same as your legal name, which

is also known as taking a pen name, you are still required to conduct all financial and legal business under your real, legal name. In other words, when Sting files his taxes, signs contracts, applies for a passport, receives his earnings from the record label, or reports his earnings to the government, he does so under his legal name, Gordon Sumner. Likewise, the man known to readers as Mark Twain was known to the U.S. government as Samuel Clemens.

If you attempt to conduct financial or legal business of any sort under a pen name, you will run afoul of the authorities. The name listed as author on your books need not be the same as your legal name, but when you set up accounts with author or print services companies (such as Lightning Source, Lulu, CreateSpace), provide payee information for receipt of royalties from booksellers, and set up a business entity to form an imprint, you must do so under your legal name. You'll notice that when you work with author and print service providers, they'll have a set of data entry fields for you to use in entering your legal name and contact information, and a separate field for author name(s). They understand that many authors use pen names.

CHOOSING YOUR AUTHOR BRAND: WHAT'S IN A NAME

There are many things to consider in choosing your brand name, even if you've elected to go with your legal name or some variation of it.

When marketing types come up with new brand names, they try to convey some sense of the product line or some favorable associations through that name. For example, Mr. Clean evokes the image of an efficient and polite cleaning expert who's very serious about his job. An author's brand name doesn't have to convey anything about the content of her books, but it shouldn't clash with them, either. If your name naturally evokes certain feelings or ideas, think about how well those feelings or ideas mesh with the work you intend to publish. Bambi Waverly would be a good fit for romance, children's books, or fantasy, and is probably fine for general fiction as well, but may not convey the necessary authority desirable in nonfiction reference nor the sobriety the author may be aiming for in literary fiction. In such a case, if the author doesn't want to use a pen name, she can go with a variation of her real name, such as B. Waverly.

CONSISTENCY IS KEY

Consumers know the Big Mac and Quarter Pounder are both McDonald's products; likewise, you want to make it easy for readers to find all your various works and know they came from the same source. You don't want to publish one book under the brand Joe Blow, a second under Joseph B. Blow, a third under J.B. Blow, and so on. In bookseller listings and library card catalogs, it won't be at all clear that the books were all written by the same person. If you already have books in print and want readers of your new books to know you are also the author of those prior works, you pretty much have to go with the name you used previously.

Exception to the Consistency Rule

There is one exception to the consistency rule: Authors who have more than one product line. Gothic fiction author Anne Rice has written erotica under the pen name of A.N. Roquelaure for example, to keep the two bodies of work separate and distinct from one another. Some authors use one version of their name for nonfiction and another for fiction, so that their reputation as a writer of fiction doesn't dilute their authority in the world of nonfiction. The respected author of highly technical computer manuals risks being viewed as little more than a goofy fanboy if word gets out that he writes sci-fi novellas on the side.

Think very carefully about what you stand to gain or lose in choosing separate brands for separate product lines, however. An author with ten books in print under the same brand has ten promotional tools at his disposal, all of which build up his reputation, with each book acting as a cross-promotional vehicle for every other book in the line. If that same author published five books under one brand and five under a second brand, he has two separate avenues of promotion but each is only half as powerful than it would be had they been combined into a single line.

And don't forget, that author has easily twice as much work in keeping the marketing fires stoked for two separate product lines because he must cultivate and maintain two separate brands, and possibly even two separate identities if he intends to give interviews, blog, or otherwise communicate with his readership.

KEEP YOUR OPTIONS OPEN

Never forget, your brand will be a constant throughout your career and life; it should not be based on fads, the content of a specific book, or specific reader age demographics. As a twentysomething author of gossipy chick lit, you may find a name like Snark E. Gurl very clever and so will your intended audience. But if you hope to have some career longevity as a writer, flash forward another twenty years and see if that name doesn't sound ridiculous hanging over the head of a fortysomething author of hen lit, mysteries, or literary fiction. When the day you must switch to a more mature-sounding name inevitably comes, poof! All the promotional and brand-loyalty equity you've built up will vanish.

Also remember, your brand name will be used as a single point of reference to stand for you and your body of work in every venue. Your chosen name will not only appear on book covers, but also in interviews, on websites and pages, press releases, merchandise related to your books, publicity materials, and so forth. If you absolutely hate your middle name, don't make it part of your brand name because you'll have to hear people say that name for the rest of your career.

BEWARE OF THE COMMON NAME

Common names like John Miller, Susan Wilson, and the like can be easy for your readers to forget because more often than not, they will only remember that the name was "something common like Smith or Jones." If you want to stand in for the Everyman or Everywoman in your writing, John Smith or Joan Smith may be a good pen name. Otherwise, you can either choose a pen name totally different from your real name or choose a variant of your real name. John Miller could be J. Lee Miller and Susan Wilson could be Susan Nicole Wilson, for example.

THE SAME NAME GAME

When you've settled on a few options for your brand name, do some research to ensure no one else is publishing, or doing anything you find objectionable, under your chosen name. Ideally, you want to be the only one using your chosen brand name in a noticeable way.

First, do a Google search. In my own case, a Google search of April Hamilton turned up nearly five thousand hits, with everyone from an interior designer to a professional soccer player among them. The same search on April L. Hamilton returned only references to me, so I chose that variant of my name as my brand name.

You don't have to rule out your chosen name if your search turns up just a small number of references to people other than yourself, on two conditions: First, none of them are authors, and second, none of them are doing anything you find objectionable under that name. For example, if you find only one other person listed with your desired brand name but that person is on the FBI's most wanted list, you don't want to risk having people confuse you with that other person when they go looking for you online. Likewise, if one of the same-name people is prominently featured on an adults-only website or in embarrassing YouTube videos, it's probably best to go with a variation or a completely different name.

Just to cover all the bases, also do a search on the name at Amazon.com. On the off chance that someone else is publishing under your chosen brand name and it has escaped Google's attention, you'll find out about it at Amazon.

BECOME THE MASTER OF YOUR DOMAIN

Once you have your name, and you're confident that you're the only one using it in much of a public way, check its availability as a Web address or Internet domain. Go to any domain registration site (such as Network Solutions [www.networksolutions.com], GoDaddy [www.godaddy.com], Tucows [www.tucows.com], Register.com [www.register.com]) and do a domain search on the name you've chosen with a .com extension, as shown in Figure 3-1.

Figure 3-1

If the Internet gods are smiling on you, your brand name will be available as a .com domain name, and if it is, immediately reserve that domain name before someone else grabs it. Even if you don't have the time, skills, or funds to set up a website for the foreseeable future, you should still reserve the domain and keep it. Remember how carefully you chose your brand name, how you searched the Net to make sure your good name wouldn't become wrongly affiliated with some other person? It's a safe bet there's an exotic dancer, drunk frat boy, or crazy shut-in out there in the world with your chosen name, and there's nothing stopping any of them from reserving your .com and building a website that will unravel all your due diligence the day their site goes live.

Some domain registrars offer low domain registration prices on the condition that you allow them to advertise their services on your site(s), which is something you'll want to avoid.

So be sure to check the fine print on any discounted domain registration deals. Still, it can be worthwhile to shop around for the best price if you're on a budget.

Registering your domain through a hosting service such as HostGator, GoDaddy can get you the domain name reservation for free, but you must sign up for fee-based monthly hosting services. You may want to check out some hosting providers and shop around for the best deal, even if you don't intend to build a full-fledged website. If you know anyone who has a website, ask which service he or she uses for hosting, how much it costs, and whether or not the service is satisfactory. If not, you can look for service provider reviews online by searching phrases like "Web host reviews." Again, be on the lookout for any hosting deals that require you to accept advertising from the hosting company on your site(s), and avoid them!

Don't be too quick to assume you're not ready to set up a website. Most hosting providers offer simple fill-in-the-blanks creation tools, so you may find you can set up your own website without any technical skills whatsoever. More details on setting up an author Web presence are provided in the Author Platform and Promotion chapters.

If Your Domain Is Already Taken

If your chosen brand name is not available as a .com, I strongly recommend you choose a different brand name. The existence of a .com website is taken as a sign of realness and professionalism in the eyes of the public. Think about it: If you hear about a hot new toy company called Whoozit, you'll tend to assume you can go online to the Whoozit.com website to learn more about their products or even order something from them. If there is no Whoozit.com website, or if the Whoozit company site address is something like Whoozit.wackypages.cc.net, suddenly Whoozit Corp. starts looking a little fly-by-night to you, doesn't it? Don't risk making the same bad impression.

Also, if you've reserved a .net or other domain when someone else owns the same domain with a .com extension, many of those who go online looking for you will end up at that other person's website. This will annoy the people who are looking for you, as well as the owner of that other domain when he starts getting confused e-mails from people who think he's you, demanding to know why there's nothing about your books on his site. The general public isn't used to entering .net, .tv, and other extensions in Web browsers as regularly as they do .com Web addresses.

You may need to tweak your author brand name to find an available .com web address, but it's worthwhile to do so in such a case if you're just starting out and have not yet published under your first-choice author brand name. Otherwise, you might want to opt for a slogan, title, or nickname strongly associated with you or your work. For example, if Poe were setting up a website today he might consider something like theraven.com, since that's probably his best-known work and a title many Web surfers will search on.

Another option to consider when your first choice Web address is taken is to do a WHOIS search on the Web address to find out who owns it currently and how soon the current registration will expire. If it will expire soon, it may

be worth waiting for. To do a WHOIS search, go to any domain registrar site and look for a link that says "WHOIS," "WHOIS Search," "WHOIS Lookup," or something similar. In Figure 3-2, this link is shown in the box of links at the bottom of the GoDaddy site and is indicated by an arrow. Other domain registrar sites put the WHOIS Search link in this location as well.

Figure 3-2

When you click on the link, you'll be taken to a form where you can enter the URL of the Web address you're after. A registration record will be shown for the URL, including the date the current registration is set to expire. The full name and contact information for the current registrant will also be shown, unless the registrant has paid extra for a private registration. In that case, contact information for a secured registrations company will be shown. If the registration will expire soon, you may want to simply mark your calendar and grab the domain as soon as the current registration expires; note that it may take up to six weeks following the current registration's expiration date for the domain to be released for sale to a new party, so you may have to check its availability every day for weeks.

To be even more certain you'll get the domain as soon as it's released, you can pay for a domain back order, in which the domain registrar automatically watches for, and registers, the desired domain for you as soon as it becomes available. Many domain registrars offer this service. On GoDaddy it's called DomainAlert Pro. On Network Solutions, it's simply called back ordering an expired domain, though the service allows you to place a back order for Web addresses set to expire within the coming year, as well. If you're using a different domain registrar, search its site for "back order" and if any relevant pages come up, follow the directions provided to set up a back order. If not, you can use the service on another registrar's site. In that case the new domain will automatically be registered with the service that has your back order set up, but you can always switch the domain to a preferred hosting service later if you wish. More detailed information about how to do this is provided in the Promotion chapter, in the Author website section.

four} Publishing Options

The terms *self-publishing*, *subsidy publishing*, *vanity publishing*, and Print on Demand (POD) are often used interchangeably when people speak of self-publishing, but these terms aren't synonymous. Rather, they describe different self-publishing options or processes.

SELF-PUBLISHING

In common usage, *self-publishing* has become a catchall term. People using it may be talking about subsidy publishing, vanity publishing, or POD, but they're rarely talking about true self-publishing.

In the strictest sense, self-publishing is exactly what it sounds like: producing your own documents and making them available to an audience. This is also known as *desktop publishing*, since it's generally done with an ordinary computer, also called a desktop computer.

Typical self-publishing projects include club or family newsletters, brochures, booklets, and research papers, any of which can be created using a standard word processor. There are also dedicated desktop publishing computer programs that enable the user to create more sophisticated and lengthier publications. Either way, desktop publishing isn't a workable solution for book manuscripts because binding options are severely limited.

Office supply stores and print shops offer several types of binding and can generally bind up to three hundred pages with no difficulty. However, their binding options are more fitting for reports or business documents than books. The pages may be hole punched and placed between two report covers, or drilled for comb or spiral binding. The finished product will have a binding, but even if you customize the report covers with artwork and a book title, it won't look like a book. You won't be able to duplicate the look of a real book, which has pages glued or sewn into a wraparound cover at the spine. Furthermore, having manuscripts bound individually is very expensive.

VANITY PUBLISHING

As described previously, vanity publishing is the process whereby an author pays a publishing service to format, print, and bind a minimum number of copies of his book. The publisher usually offers related services on a fee basis, from editing to cover art design and even promotion. The author is essentially paying to have his book produced, and so long as he's willing to pay the required fee, the vanity publisher will not turn him away. It is because of this that as a group, books from vanity publishers are presumed to be of poor quality.

This bias is one downside to vanity publishing, but expense is the primary reason vanity publishing isn't advisable for most authors. An author who chooses to go with a vanity publisher must pay all production costs for a minimum print run of her book, generally at least two hundred copies. Cost per book goes down as quantity ordered goes up, but in most cases the author can expect to pay anywhere from $6 to $10 per copy for a trade paperback edition and between $12 to $16 for a hardcover. Multiply those figures by two hundred, then add hundreds more dollars in flat fees for project setup, optional ISBN assignment, proof corrections, project management, and delivery. Add another thousand or two if the author pays for related services. Vanity publishers tend to offer only bundled packages of services, which in most cases forces the author to pay for some services she doesn't necessarily want or need.

The third downside to vanity publishing is distribution, or lack thereof. When the print run is finished, all the books are delivered to the author and it's up to him to store them, sell them, give them away, or otherwise dispose of them. With few exceptions, brick-and-mortar bookstores won't stock *any* type of self-published book. They're particularly leery of books from vanity publishers, all of whose names are widely known in the publishing and bookselling industries.

More recently, vanity publishers have begun addressing the distribution problem by setting up online bookstores to stock their clients' work, but the sites don't get much traffic because they only stock the vanity publisher's books, and again, most people assume those books aren't very good. In addition, there's little reason to go book shopping on a vanity press's website, which offers only its own titles,

when you can go to a larger online bookseller to get access to both indie *and* mainstream titles in a single location.

Enterprising authors can turn a profit selling their books themselves, on their own website, at community fairs, through direct mail, and so on. Occasionally one will even do well enough to attract the attention of a mainstream publisher, but this is very rare.

Lastly, even though vanity publishers are only providing book production services, they act like conventional publishers when it comes to contracts and rights. As part of the publishing arrangement, the author will be required to sign a contract granting certain exclusive rights to the publisher. The contract may stipulate the author cannot publish the same work in the same format, or any other format, for a set period of years. In this way, the publisher ensures the author must come back to it to order additional print runs if the book is successful enough to sell out its first print run. The contract will also specify whether the author can buy his way out of the contract before the term is up, and if so, what it will cost to do so. This stipulation lines the vanity publisher's pockets in the event a mainstream publisher wants to publish the book.

SUBSIDY PUBLISHING

Subsidy publishing is virtually identical to vanity publishing, except that subsidy publishers will not publish every manuscript submitted to them. Instead, they accept submissions (sometimes for a fee) and choose the manuscripts they wish to publish. Subsidy publishers sprang up as a legitimate self-publication alternative to vanity publishing, but subsidy

THE INDIE AUTHOR GUIDE

publishers aren't all created equal. Some are hardly more discerning than vanity publishers, while others are so selective as to rival mainstream publishers.

The worst subsidy publishers are rip-off artists par excellence, assuring every prospective client her manuscript is a diamond in the rough that is practically guaranteed to become a best-seller if she will only pay for professional editing, artwork, promotion, and other services—all of which the publisher (or a company the publisher refers) just happens to offer.

The best subsidy publishers truly strive to distinguish themselves by putting out quality books and dealing fairly with authors, but even in that case the author must contend with all the same downsides she would face with a vanity publisher. She must pay for a minimum print run and related services, she must sign over at least some of her publication rights in a contract, and she faces all the same distribution challenges as a vanity-published author.

PRINT SERVICE PROVIDER

A print service provider is like a vanity publisher in that it will publish any manuscript submitted to it for a fee. Also, as with vanity and subsidy publishers, print service providers may offer related services for a fee, and the books they produce aren't likely to be carried by brick-and-mortar stores. That's where the similarities end, however.

Print service providers typically allow authors to choose between ordering a minimum print run or going with a POD fulfillment model, which is more fully described in the next section. Some providers require payment of a project setup fee, while others charge no up-front fees whatsoever. Print service providers may offer book preparation services for a fee, but they are also prepared to accept print-ready files from authors. This is where the author can save thousands of dollars by using the information in this book to do all those related tasks himself. Many print service providers don't charge a setup fee, and some even throw in an ISBN and EAN, which will be described in more detail later, for free. Often, the only expense shouldered by the author is the cost of proof copies, which the author reviews before approving the book for release.

With a print services provider, the author retains all rights to her work. If there's any contract at all, its terms are limited to the details of fees, royalty payment, services provided, and the responsibilities of each party. With a print service provider, it's made perfectly clear that the *author* is the publisher and therefore retains all rights to her work. If the company you deal with requires you to order a minimum print run or sign over any of your publication rights, it's a vanity or subsidy publisher, *not* a print service provider.

Most print service providers have distribution relationships with major online booksellers such as Amazon and Barnes & Noble, through which the bookseller agrees to sell the service provider's books on its website. Some providers offer this only as an optional service, for a fee. Another service some offer, always for a fee, is called "guaranteed returns," whereby brick-and-mortar stores are allowed to return any unsold copies of books to the author. This is supposed to encourage brick-and-mortar stores to carry self-published books, since many cite "un-returnability" as a reason not to carry them, but in reality the centralized purchasing departments and computerized inventory systems of chain bookstores present obstacles at least equal to concerns about money lost on unsold copies.

All print service providers can print paperback books in various standard sizes, both in black and white and full color, but only some of them can print books in hardcover editions. When the hardcover option is available, the production cost for it is much higher than that charged for paperbacks.

Since an author who goes the print service provider route can still opt to pay for certain related services as desired, vanity and subsidy publishers have no advantages to offer the typical indie author. Why pay stiff fees upfront, warehouse your books, and sign away your publication rights if you don't have to?

PRINT ON DEMAND

POD is not truly a type of publishing but a book production method. As such, it may be employed by a vanity publisher, subsidy publisher, or print service provider, so don't assume that a company calling itself a POD Publisher is *not* a vanity or subsidy publisher.

With POD, individual copies of the book are printed and bound by automated systems on demand, meaning each time an order for the book is received. The author doesn't pay to have on-demand copies produced. Instead, the print service provider keeps a share of the book's cover price to cover its production costs and pays the remainder to the author as a royalty.

While the minimum print run model is fine for a book with a built-in customer base, such as a textbook published by a college professor

for use in his class, POD is the better way to go for an indie author who intends to sell her book to the general public.

RIGHTS, ROYALTIES, AND ADVANCES

In a traditional publishing scenario, an author grants a publisher the right to package, publish, promote, and distribute his content for commercial sale for a set time period, in exchange for a percentage of the profit from those sales. The details of the exchange are laid out in a contract, which is negotiable and therefore unique for each manuscript sold.

Mainstream Rights

Publication rights are many and varied, covering all the different ways the manuscript's content can be published for distribution to the public. Rights to publication of the entire manuscript in different formats include hardcover, softcover, trade paperback, mass-market paperback, audiobook on CD or tape, audiobook digital download, and e-books in various formats. Rights to portions of the manuscript include excerpts to be distributed for promotional purposes at no cost to consumers, reprints of entire chapters to be sold as stand-alone articles or short stories, reprints of art or text from the manuscript for reproduction and sale in a different product format (for example, calendars), and reprints of excerpts to be included in subsequently published anthologies.

Other content rights include screenplay rights, broadcast rights, and licensing rights. Licensing rights govern the terms under which manuscript text, artwork, or character likenesses

THE INDIE AUTHOR GUIDE

can be printed on T-shirts, mugs, or other merchandise offered for sale. Broadcast rights pertain to the terms under which the manuscript (or portions thereof) may be broadcast over television, satellite, or radio waves, and usually pertain to broadcast of audiobook editions or live readings. Screenplay rights cover situations where someone wants to make a film or television show based on content from the manuscript.

Mainstream publishing contracts grant the publisher any or all of the above rights for a certain number of years in exchange for a percentage of profit from sales. Megaconglomerate publishers may negotiate for publication, broadcast, licensing, and screenplay rights simultaneously, offering a flat-fee payment or profit-sharing terms for nonpublication rights in addition to the royalties offered on book sales.

Smaller publishers will typically sign on only for publication rights, leaving the author free to sell the remaining rights to other parties. In that case, the author's agent or manager may attempt to sell the remaining rights on the author's behalf.

Indie Rights

Indies who go the vanity or subsidy route are subject to rights contracts just like mainstream authors, but the contracts are usually limited to publication rights and the author doesn't get royalties or advances in return. In a basic vanity or subsidy publisher situation the author sets her own price and sells her own books, so her earnings are a function of how many books she sells and how she prices them. If she manages to get them into a bookstore, she'll be subject to the same 40 percent bookseller fee (see next section) as any other author.

Indies who go the print service provider route retain all rights to their work, leaving them free to negotiate for the sale of those rights with whomever they wish, under whatever terms they wish.

Mainstream Royalties

The percentage of the profit from those sales to be paid to an author in exchange for rights is called the author royalty. Among mainstream publishers, author royalties are somewhat standard according to the type of book and publication format, but are open to negotiation before the contract is signed. Best-selling and prestige authors can demand higher royalties than other authors, and usually get them. For everyone else, royalties are usually figured either as a percentage of the book's list price or as a percentage of the net profit from the book.

Consider a manuscript to be published as a trade paperback book with a list price of $14. Typical royalties offered on ordinary trade paperbacks are 8 to 10 percent of the list price, or alternatively, 15 to 25 percent of the net amount from each sale.

The list price is the suggested retail price. An 8 percent royalty based on the cover price of $14 is $1.12 and a 10 percent royalty based on cover price is $1.40, which makes the net option look a whole lot more attractive at first blush, but the net calculation isn't yet complete. Net royalty is calculated as list price minus production costs minus bookseller fee.

Production costs for a typical mainstream-produced black-and-white trade paperback book of average length run anywhere from $2 to $4 per copy, depending on the quantity of books in the print run (as quantity goes up, cost per copy goes down), and paper and binding quality. Let's say our sample book's production cost is at the low end, at $2 per copy.

The standard bookseller fee is 40 percent of the list price, meaning that every time you buy a book in a store, whether in person or online, the seller keeps 40 percent of the list price. On our $14 book, the bookseller fee is $5.60. This leaves a net of $14 - $2 - $5.60, or $6.40. Fifteen percent of $6.40 = 96¢, and the higher end net royalty of 25 percent of $6.40 = $1.60. As you can see, royalties calculated from net can vary widely based on the author's negotiated royalty percentage, as well as the size of the print run due to the associated variance in production costs.

Royalty percentages for hardcover, mass-market paperback, e-book, and audiobook formats are calculated in a similar way, though standard percentages vary for each different format. Also, it's typical to reward the author with a higher royalty percentage on additional print runs after the first run sells out, but best-selling authors are usually the only ones in a position to collect that reward.

Any way you slice it, less than $2 per copy sold is not a lot of money. At $2 per copy you'd need to sell fifteen thousand copies to earn $30,000, and that's *before* taxes and fees for professional services have been deducted.

Royalty Advances

The contract may require the publisher to pay the author an advance, or up-front lump-sum payment. The advance is not a free-and-clear payment, such as a professional athlete's signing bonus, however. It's actually a loan against future royalties. When an advance is paid, the publisher enters it into the author's royalty account as a negative amount, indicating the author owes the publisher that much money. The publisher keeps track of sales, calculates the author's royalty on each sale, and deposits the funds into the author's royalty account. No royalties are paid to the author until the advance loan is paid off.

Since it takes time for earnings to cancel out the advance, it's not unusual for authors to wait many months after their book is published to see that first royalty check. In the majority of cases, the book doesn't ultimately sell enough copies to pay back the advance. The publisher won't make the author pay back the difference, but he will not want to publish the author again, either. The larger the advance, the bigger the author's risk of committing career suicide.

Paying the Piper(s)

If the author has contracted with a manager, agent, or attorney for services, each of them will take a percentage of the author's advance, flat fees, profit-sharing proceeds, and royalties. It's easy to see why so few authors actually make a living on their writing, regardless of who published their books.

Indie Royalties

Indie authors don't earn royalties; they earn net profit. However, self-publishing companies tend to refer to the author's net profit on each book sold as a royalty, thereby mimicking the terminology of the mainstream. Indie net profits are calculated according to list price, production costs, and bookseller fees, just like mainstream author royalties.

The Production Cost Problem

Production costs for indic books tend to run about two to three times higher than mainstream books due to economies of scale. Recall that production costs go down as quantity of books printed goes up. Big publishers order print runs in the tens of thousands. Vanity and subsidy publishers order print runs in the hundreds, or occasionally, the low thousands. POD service providers produce one book at a time.

This problem can be a major stumbling block for indie authors, since they may be forced to set their books' list prices higher than comparable mainstream books to earn as much per book as a mainstream author. This situation can feed the bias against self-published books since customers are being asked to pay more for untested self-published books than they would for a best-seller.

The Production Cost Solution

Print service providers realize the production cost problem alone can be enough to deter authors, so some now offer reduced production costs in exchange for flat fees, annual dues, or a combination of both. Authors who opt for reduced production costs can set their books' pricing equal to comparable mainstream books and still earn royalties three to five times higher than the authors of those books.

Such fees range widely from provider to provider, so authors should do some what-if calculations to figure out what their net profit will be at various list price points, both with and without the production cost discount, and how many books they must sell at each price point to cover the cost of the fee.

Another consideration is author copies. Authors can buy copies of their self-published books for the cost of production alone, so reduced production cost means less money spent when ordering author copies. If the author intends to order twenty or more copies of his book to give to friends and family, he may find the savings on author copies alone are enough to cover the fees. Authors who buy larger quantities of their books to sell at signings, appearances, and through bookstores (see chapter 11) will almost certainly find the savings in author copies makes it worth paying for reduced production costs.

WHAT'S THE DEAL WITH ISBNS?

Any commercially sold physical book must have a unique International Standard Book Number, or ISBN, and each different edition of a given book—hardcover, paperback, or audiobook) must have its own ISBN. E-books, which are essentially digital files, don't require an ISBN. The ISBN is a unique identifier consisting of a ten- to thirteen-digit number and associated barcode. Bowker (www.bowker.com) is the only agency allowed to distribute U.S. ISBNs. Bowker sells ISBNs to publishers and authors in blocks of 10 or more or individually. It's not unusual for self-published authors to purchase their own ISBN blocks, though unless you're very prolific or issue your books in multiple editions, you may never use all the numbers.

Some publishers/service providers require authors to obtain their own ISBNs at their own expense, some will provide ISBNs to authors for a separate fee, and still others include ISBN assignment as part of their standard publishing package. If you buy your own block of ISBNs, each ISBN in the block can be used only once, and only for a specific edition of your book.

For example, let's say you use the first ISBN in your block for a paperback edition of Novel A, the second for a hardcover edition of Novel A, and the third for an audiobook edition of Novel A. A couple of years later, when you're ready to publish Novel B, you must assign ISBNs to all of its editions beginning with the fourth ISBN in your block. Once assigned, an ISBN can never be reused, not even if the book to which it was assigned goes out of print.

In Europe, books are tracked with a European Article Number, or EAN. Some publishers can assign an EAN to your book, so be sure to check with your publisher if you intend to sell your book in Europe—or through online vendors that accept international orders.

WHAT ABOUT BOOKSTORES?

You may be wondering how you can sell significant quantities of your books when it's nearly impossible to get brick-and-mortar stores to stock them. The answer is, you don't *need* brick-and-mortar bookstores to stock them.

Until fairly recently, brick-and-mortar bookstores were the biggest sellers of books. Now that books are sold in discount stores, grocery stores, big box retailers and online, this is no longer the case. As of this writing, Amazon is the number one seller of books worldwide and number two in North America. Barnes and Noble is the number one bookseller in North America, with that rank including both its brick-and-mortar and online stores.

Recall from the introduction, how major publishers have bought up all the prime real estate in the store, and the fact that your book most likely *won't* land on a prominent shelf. An exception to this is the bookstore with a local authors display, but that's only one display in one store. Getting a brick-and-mortar chain store to stock your book does not guarantee an increase in sales.

Another consideration is the fact that you must provide copies of your books to brick-and-mortar stores willing to stock them. While author copies are sold at a much lower price than retail copies, you still have to pay for production and shipping (to you). Then you have to deliver or ship them to the bookseller, who isn't likely to stock more than two or three copies at a time, and work out an arrangement for collecting your net profit, if your books sell.

Recall that the standard cut for any bookseller, be it Amazon or a local mom-and-pop store, is 40 percent of the book's list price. If the list price for your book is $14, the bookseller's cut for each sale is $5.60. Assuming the author copy price is $6, you will earn only $2.40 per book sold in the store. Granted, this is a much higher royalty percentage than mainstream authors earn on the same book, but even if all three copies of your book sell, it's an awful lot of up-front trouble and expense for a measly $7.20 profit. If you had to ship your books to the store, or pay for gas to deliver them yourself, your net profit is even less.

While it's true that Amazon or any other online bookseller will take the same 40 percent as a brick-and-mortar store, the advantage of working with an online seller and POD print service provider is that you won't have to order, pay for, or deliver any books up front. Most major online booksellers can list your book on their sites, and when a customer orders your book, send an electronic order to a POD service provider. In such a scenario, the book is printed and sent directly to the customer with no involvement from the author whatsoever. The online seller gets its 40 percent, thereby reducing the amount of royalty paid to you, but you haven't incurred any expense or hassle in the process.

These order/fulfillment agreements vary from bookseller to bookseller however, so an author who wants this kind of arrangement must make sure his chosen POD service provider has an ordering/fulfillment relationship established with the bookseller(s) through which he intends to make his book available for sale.

CHOOSING A SERVICE PROVIDER

Your choice of service provider depends on your goals as an indie author and the resources you're prepared to expend in the endeavor—not just money, but time and skills as well. As with so many things, the best way to find a good service provider in this area is on the basis of a recommendation from a trusted third party. If you know any self-published authors, get their input.

If you don't know any self-published authors, or the ones you know recommend *against* the service providers they used, do an Internet search for "self publish" or "POD" to find other providers and what people are saying about them. Narrow the field to just two or three candidates, then review each one's terms of service (sometimes called a "membership agreement"), submission guidelines, and FAQ sections to determine which will be the easiest for you to work with according to your specific needs and priorities.

For example, if you intend to minimize costs by doing as much as possible yourself, it doesn't make sense to go with a publisher whose most basic package charges up-front fees for providing services you don't need. If you want your book to be made available for sale on Amazon's United States site, you'll want to be sure your intended provider has a sales and order fulfillment relationship with Amazon in the United States. Similarly, if international sales are important to you, you'll need to verify your intended provider has a global distribution option which will ensure your book is listed in all the various wholesale book catalogs used by booksellers around the world.

Look at the trade-offs. One service may have excellent tech support and customer service through the setup and publication process, but charge stiff setup fees or production costs. In contrast, a different service may offer tech support and customer service via e-mail only but charge much lower fees. Remember that the eventual buyers of your book won't care how easy or hard your service provider was to work with, they only care about the physical quality of the book, how good it is in terms of content, and how much it costs. If going with the first provider requires you to set the list price for your 6" × 9" (15cm × 23cm) trade paperback at $16 just to net $1 in profit (when mainstream books of the same type and dimensions are selling for $14 or less), in the final analysis it won't matter how great the service provider is: Your book will be hard to sell.

Rights will be a primary concern if your goal is to attract a mainstream publisher. You won't be able to negotiate with any other publishers if you've already locked up publishing rights with a subsidy or vanity publisher. However, as discussed previously, subsidy and vanity publishing don't offer any advantages over POD publishing these days, so there's no reason for an indie author to sign away her publication rights in the first place.

Another factor to take into consideration is the service provider's level of author support. Providers like CreateSpace and Lulu are very supportive of individual self-publishing authors and provide extensive online help, user community forums, and detailed step-by-step guides and templates for properly formatting your manuscript and book cover and using their services. In contrast, Lightning Source Inc., (LSI) was originally set up as a print services provider for midsized to large mainstream publishers and therefore doesn't offer as much in the way of author hand holding. LSI has online tutorials for formatting your files, uploading them, and ordering copies of the completed book, as well as templates for manuscript and cover formatting, but they assume that anyone using these items is already pretty knowledgeable about the publishing process. If you run into trouble with manuscript or cover formatting, LSI's customer support will likely suggest you seek a freelance consultant.

However, LSI is a subsidiary of book wholesale distributor/catalog company Ingram, and offers much broader distribution options than Createspace does. Lulu offers distribution outside their own online store for a fee, but Lulu's production costs are considerably higher than either Createspace or LSI. There are trade-offs no matter which service provider you choose, so comparison shopping is key.

Finally, consider how you intend to sell your books. The online bookstores some print service providers run typically charge a bookseller fee substantially lower than the standard 40 percent, but those stores also get a lot less traffic than say, Amazon. You can link to your books in the publisher's store from your website or elsewhere, but you won't get as many sales from customers browsing the virtual shelves since Amazon has far more customers than a print service provider's bookstore. I feel that an Amazon store listing is critical if you hope to turn a profit on your self-published books, not only because Amazon has an overall huge market share, but also because of the greater promotional opportunities available for products listed on Amazon's site (see chapter 11). Verify that the service providers you're considering can do this, and if they charge a fee to do so, that the cost isn't prohibitive.

If you have all the tools recommended in the first chapter and are willing to put in the necessary time and effort to become proficient with them, this book will provide all the help and information needed to do everything from formatting your manuscript to promoting the finished book by yourself, so don't make any hasty decisions when it comes to paying for related services until you've thoroughly perused the remaining chapters.

CRUNCH THE NUMBERS

When deciding amongst print/POD service providers, it's important to do some what-if calculations based on your specific book before you commit to a provider. In the table on the next page, I've provided sample pricing from three different service providers for a three hundred, page book that will have a full-color perfect-bound trade paperback binding and a black-and-white interior. As you look at the table, consider what a mistake it would be to choose your provider based only on whether or not the provider charges a setup fee, or what the provider charges per copy or per page alone. It isn't until you take all three factors into account that you get an accurate picture.

At first glance, you might reject Provider C out of hand simply because Provider C charges an up-front fee whereas Providers A and B do not. However, as you go down the table, you can see that in exchange for your setup fee, Provider C will give you much lower per-copy production costs. The lower your per-copy production costs, the more you stand to earn per copy sold, as you will see in the next section.

Yet another consideration is author copies. If you're already planning to buy twenty author copies for family, friends, reviewers, and promotional giveaways, Provider C's up-front fee will be more than covered by your savings in author copies alone because the next-closest provider would've charged you $5 more per author copy. $5 x 20 = $100.

If you're hoping to make a profit selling your books online, crunch the numbers for various service providers. Compare the setup costs, production costs, and provider fees for production of the same book. If a provider's production costs will force you to price your book higher than a comparable mainstream book just to break even after taking the 40 percent bookseller fee into account, find out if they offer any programs or membership upgrades that will reduce production costs. If not, cross that name off your list of candidates. Working with a list price that's typical for a mainstream-published book of the same type, see what you will earn per book for sales through booksellers and through each publisher's online store (if applicable).

So, as you can see, being indie does not mean having to price your books higher than mainstream books, nor having to sell them out of the trunk of your car. Today, there are more ways of getting your book into print at a competitive price—and in front of the book-buying public—than ever before.

1. Setup fee	$0	$0	$50.00
2. Per-copy fee	$.85	$1.25	$.45
3. Per-page fee	$.035	$.030	$.02
4. Shipping, per book	$5.60	$7.00	$5.50
Production cost per copy = #2 + (300 x #3)	$.85 + 10.50 = $11.35	$1.25 + 9.00 = $10.25	$.45 + 6.00 = $6.45
Cost per author copy = #2 + (300 x #3) + #4	$.85 + 10.50 + 5.60 = $16.95	$1.25 + 9.00 + 7.00 = $17.25	$.45 + 6.00 + 5.50 = $11.95

five} DIY Formatting for POD

If you're using a vanity or subsidy publisher, you don't need these formatting instructions because your publisher will either do the formatting for you or provide its own, very specific formatting requirements. This chapter explains how to format your book for print through a POD service provider or e-book producer. You may be familiar with standard formatting conventions for submitting manuscripts to an agent or editor, but formatting for POD is entirely different.

The manuscript you submit for print must be formatted as print galleys, that is, pages that look *exactly* how they should look in the published book. Therefore, it's up to you to ensure everything from page dimensions to headers and footers are properly formatted before sending your manuscript off for print.

The keys to success with formatting a proof manuscript are minimalism and consistency. Use as few different formatting options as possible and apply them consistently. Ideally, you should start with a preformatted document "shell" so that your pages will be properly formatted as you write. However, if this was not done, you can also set up a shell and then copy text from your existing manuscript and paste it into the shell as unformatted text so that it acquires the correct formatting from the shell.

In this chapter, I'll demonstrate how to build and use a manuscript shell in Microsoft Word 2003 (MS Word). All the program features and options shown should be available in any word processing program from that year or later, and since MS Word has been the leading word processing program for decades, most other word processors are designed to mimic Word's interface and layout. If your word processor is substantially different, you'll have to consult your program's menus and help files to locate the features shown and learn how to use them. If you don't already have a word processing program that provides all the functions described in this chapter, you can download OpenOffice for free at www.openoffice.org. OpenOffice includes a very sophisticated yet easy-to-use word processor that looks and operates very much like MS Word, and despite being free, the software is entirely legal and legitimate.

STYLES

Every modern word processing program has Style functions built into it. Styles are a way of storing formatting options, such as font size, line spacing, and so on, so you can easily apply all the same options to other sections of text with a single click. In MS Word, Style functions are accessed under the Format menu. (See Figure 5-1.)

When you open a new document in your word processor, certain default styles are already assigned to the document. If you start typing into your document, the default styles specify what font face and font size will be used, among other things. Clicking on the Styles and Formatting menu item in MS Word will display a list of all styles currently available for use in the document. The default styles for a new document in MS Word are shown on the right in Figure 5-2.

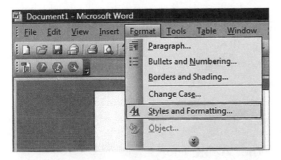

Figure 5-1

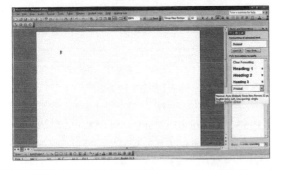

Figure 5-2

Mousing over a style in the list pops up a little box displaying all the formatting options being used in that style. As shown in Figure 5-2, the Normal Style is defined as Times New Roman, 12-point text, using English language conventions (that is, no umlauts or Chinese characters will be needed), with text left-aligned, lines single-spaced, and widow/orphan control (explained later in this chapter) turned on. Notice that style names are displayed with their respective formatting options applied, to give you a preview of how your text will look when

each style is used. For example, the heading style names are all displayed in boldface because each of those styles applies boldface to text.

Three heading styles are available in the default list; headings are formatted differently from ordinary text and are intended for use as chapter and section headings in a document's table of contents. In Word, when you insert a table of contents (demonstrated later in this chapter) the program locates every piece of text with a heading style applied to it and includes that text in the table of contents. The Clear Formatting command appears above the listed styles.

Using Styles in Word is simple: Just highlight the text you want formatted, then click the style that has the formatting options you want. However, it's obvious that this only works if there's an applicable style containing all your desired formatting options in the list.

People who don't know how to use Styles apply formatting changes to the text in their documents on the fly, meaning as they go, by selecting the text they want to change and applying their desired formatting manually through use of the toolbar (shown in Figure 5-3).

Figure 5-3

Each time the user does this, Word stores the chosen formatting options as a new style and adds that Style to the list. The newly created style is named in the list like this:

[name of style before changes] + [list of changes applied, in order applied]

For example, if you select text formatted as the default, Normal Style and apply boldface and italics to it using toolbar buttons, the new style will be named:

> Normal + bold + italics

If you applied the italics first, then the bold-face, the new style would be named:

> Normal + italics + bold

As you can imagine, it's easy to quickly build up a huge number of differently named styles, many of which are duplicate in terms of the formatting changes they apply. The on-the-fly approach is fine for personal documents, letters, notes to yourself, and the like, but not for a word processing file to be submitted to a print service provider. This is because the provider must convert word processing files into a format that their printing programs and equipment can read.

You probably know that some computer programs place a limit on how many characters you can use for a file name; similarly, service providers' conversion tools have internal limits on how many characters of a style name they can read. If a given document has four different styles that all begin with "Normal + bold + italics," each of which goes on to set different options for line spacing, indenting, font face, or anything else, the service provider's file converter may not read beyond *italics* in the style names. It will assume that all four styles are the same, ignore the latter three duplicates, and apply only the first instance of "Normal + bold + italics" to all the text that was originally formatted using four *different* styles. It will still apply all the formatting options specified by that first style, but any formatting changes applied by the latter three styles will be lost and you'll get an unpleasant surprise in the proof copy.

It's far better to determine all the different formatting required in your manuscript ahead of time and create different style names for each. Note that if you only intend to publish in e-book formats *other* than PDF (such as PRC, PDB, LRF, HTML, and Kindle), you should keep the number of styles you use to a minimum and keep them very simple, because when you're done formatting you will have to convert your finished document into the desired e-book file format(s) and all but the most basic formatting options will be lost. See the Publishing in E-Book Formats chapter for more details.

What About PDF Files?

Some print service providers accept PDF file submissions in addition to, or instead of, word processing files (for example, DOC, TXT, and RTF). In that case, no file conversion is needed at the service provider's end. Their processing programs and equipment print the PDF file exactly as is, so you can feel confident your published book will look exactly like the PDF file you submitted. This is one reason I include a PDF-maker program in the indie author's required tools of the trade.

However, turning a word processing file into a PDF is also a file conversion process. A PDF file is essentially a series of images; it's as if the PDF-maker program takes a photograph of each page in the source document and assembles all those pictures into a single file. The PDF file looks just like the word processing source file, but you can't edit it with a word processor. The PDF file is also a lot smaller than the source file in terms of file size, because it doesn't contain all the behind-the-scenes formatting details and instructions that were present in the source file.

There are many PDF-maker programs, and some of them are available online as a free download. Do an Internet search for "pdf maker" + "free" to find them. OpenOffice includes PDF-maker functionality with all its programs, as does the Mac computer operating system. The granddaddy of them all is Adobe Acrobat, the first PDF maker invented. Adobe distributes its Acrobat Reader software free of charge, but that program can only *read* PDF files. The full Acrobat program is needed to *create* PDF files. Many other free and low-cost options are available for download online, just do an Internet search for "pdf maker" or "free pdf maker."

One caveat: If you opt for a free, downloadable PDF creator program, I recommend you go with the free stripped-down edition that the manufacturer of a full-featured PDF-maker program offered for sale at a price. This ensures you're getting the download from a reputable company that has a vested interest in insuring their products—even the free ones—are virus free and functioning properly, because they're hoping users of the free version will eventually upgrade to the paid version. Paid versions generally include more advanced document proofing, format conversion, and editing tools, but these are options you won't need for purposes of manuscript preparation or any other aspect of self-publishing. A couple of options to check out are PrimoPDF and CutePDF Writer, either of which is easily located online with an Internet search on its name.

Every PDF-maker program creates PDF files, but they don't all use the same file conversion process. Some don't take source file Styles into account, but those that include a feature enabling the user to convert PDF files back into word processing files usually do. Adobe Acrobat's conversion engine generally disregards Styles, but it sometimes falters with heavily formatted documents due to the large amount of data in the file. This isn't necessarily a problem with the Acrobat program itself, but with the demands it makes on your computer's processing power. Formatting your word processing document through the use of a small number of consistently applied Styles keeps file size to a minimum, which prevents this problem.

Creating Custom Styles

Open a new blank document and open the Format feature and select Style. Click the New Style button (shown in Figure 5-4). The New Style dialog box is displayed.

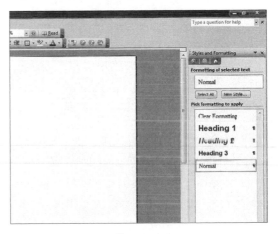

Figure 5-4

Begin by specifying a name for your Style. Custom Style names must be different than any of the Style names already included with your word processing program, so you can't name your Style "Normal," for instance. The name will appear in the Styles list box, so choose something that will be easily recognizable to you in the list.

The style name I chose for normal body text in Figure 5-5 is IAG Normal Body Text. Consider beginning your custom style names with a specific designation so they will all appear together in the alphabetical Styles list. For example, the names of all the custom styles I created for use in this book begin with "IAG," which is a designation for *Indie Author Guide*.

Next is Style type. As shown in Figure 5-6, there are only four choices. The only ones you're likely to ever need are Paragraph and List. If your style will be applied to blocks of text, choose Paragraph. If it will be applied to numbered or bulleted lists, choose List.

The Style Based On box (shown in Figure 5-7) lists every style that comes preinstalled in your word processing program. Select any style from the list to see its formatting options. The goal is to find the preexisting style whose formatting options are closest to the custom style you're creating. For example, for the main title on the title page of this book, I selected Title for Style Based On, then merely changed the font face and font type. All the other preselected formatting options were fine as is.

In Figure 5-8, I've selected Title. The Formatting section is updated to reflect all the options applicable to the chosen style, and the display box shows an example of how text formatted with the style will look.

The most commonly used formatting options are right there on the New Style dialog box, and all other options are accessible through the Format button, located in the lower left-hand corner of the dialog box. Click the button to access a pop-up menu of choices (see Figure 5-9).

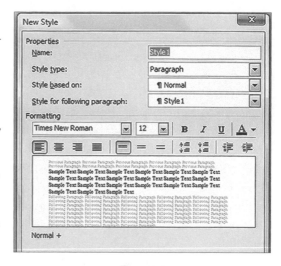

Figure 5-5

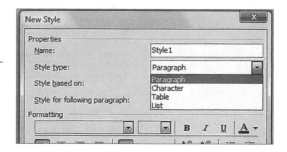

Figure 5-6

Figure 5-7

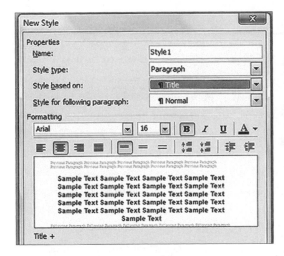

Figure 5-8

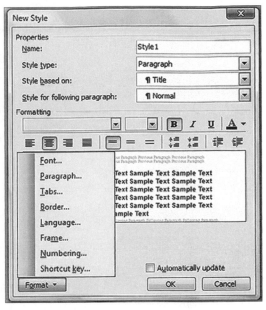

Figure 5-9

Each list item links to the same formatting dialog boxes that are accessible from the main toolbar under Format (see Figure 5-10).

A whole chapter could be written on each option item in the pop-up menu, but this chapter assumes you are already versed in at least the basic use of each one. If not, refer to your word processing program's help files and tutorials for further detail. If you write novels, the options you will use most often are Font and Paragraph. In a nonfiction book (like this one), you may also need styles that incorporate settings for Tabs, Border, and Numbering.

When creating a chapter heading style be sure to check the options set for Paragraph, because that's where you specify an outline level for heading styles to ensure they will show up as you want them to in your table of contents. In the New Style dialog, click the Format button at the lower left and select Paragraph from the pop-up list. The Paragraph Formatting dialog opens, as shown in Figure 5-11; use the drop-down list to select an outline level for each header you create.

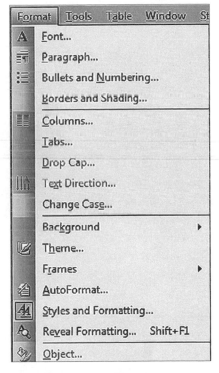

Figure 5-10

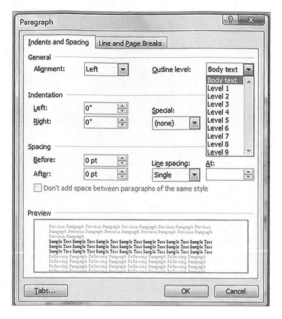

Figure 5-11

Styles with an outline level of Body Text won't appear in the table of contents. Outline level 1 styles will appear as left-aligned text in the table of contents. This is the level you'll select for your chapter headings, and it's most likely the only level you'll need for a novel. Outline level 2 styles will appear in the table of contents as text indented five spaces in from the left-aligned Outline level 1 styles. This is the level to choose for chapter subheadings. Outline level 3 styles will appear in the table of contents as text indented five spaces in from the indented level 2 styles. This is the level to use for headings beneath subheadings. The pattern continues from there, but for the sake of easy readability it's a good idea to limit your table of contents to just three outline levels. The table of contents for this book shows three levels.

Set your desired formatting options in each applicable dialog box and return to the main New Style dialog to see an updated preview of how your custom style will look. Return to the various formatting dialogs to make any needed changes.

Make a selection in the Style For Following Paragraph drop-down box, specifying the default style to apply to paragraphs beginning immediately after the style you're creating. For example, when working with a Header Style, the Style For Following Paragraph is generally normal body text (or your custom style version of it). This setting can save you a lot of time and hassle as you work on your chapters by automatically applying your desired style to the text immediately following any style, so make good use of it.

For example, you probably want to set the Style For Following Paragraph for your customized body text to the customized body text style itself, so you won't have to manually apply that style to every single body text paragraph you come across. You also probably want to set Style For Following Paragraph on your chapter heading styles to your customized body text style, so *that* style will automatically be applied to any paragraph immediately following a chapter heading. Note that the Style For Following Paragraph setting merely sets a default style, you can override it at any time on any paragraph by highlighting the paragraph and selecting a different Style from the Styles list box.

When you're happy with your style, click on the Add to Template check box above the Format button to select it, and click the OK button to save the style. When the New Style dialog box closes, you'll see your custom style has been added to the Style list.

What Styles Are Needed?

To figure out how many custom styles you need to create for your book, and how they should be formatted, look through the pages of a book that's the same genre as yours (novel, user guide, software manual, textbook, reference book, nonfiction, for example). You will notice that the book employs different styles for different types of text. For example, main body text, footer text, header text, title page text, and the table of contents will all probably employ different formatting options. Some text may be printed in a different font, different size, or indented to set it apart from blocks of normal body text. The following table lists the styles most commonly used for different types of books.

STYLE TYPE	NEEDED FOR	FICTION, POETRY OR NONFICTION PROSE	GENERAL NONFICTION
copyright	copyright info page	√	√
title	title page, main title	√	√
subtitle	title page, subtitle	√	√
byline	title page, author name	√	√
dedication	dedication page	√	√
TOC heading	table of contents page, table of contents heading	√	√
TOC body	body of table of contents	√	√
header	headers—usually contains book or chapter name	√	√
footer	footers—usually contains page numbers	√	√
body text, normal	within chapters	√	√
body text, italics	within chapters	√	√
body text, bold	within chapters	√	√
chapter heading	start of each chapter	√	√

chapter subheadings	within chapters, one for each 'level' of subheading		√
index	index		√

The table is just a starting point. You may not need all the styles in it for your book, or your book may require additional styles for things like captions to describe illustrations, indented text blocks, or bulleted or numbered lists.

About Industry Standards

You may have noticed that a lot of published books look alike in terms of layout and the styles they employ, and this is due to industry standard formatting. Each imprint, or subsidiary, of a mainstream publisher will have its standard font, layout, and sometimes even cover design. Rules and guidelines dictate everything from line spacing to header and footer height. The only place you find variety in the look of published books these days is in the children's book lists, where more creative layouts and unusual fonts are still acceptable.

Plenty of how-to books and articles admonish indie authors to school themselves on industry standards and strictly apply those standards to their self-published books in order to avoid an amateurish look. Not surprisingly, I do not share this viewpoint.

First of all, nobody but publishing professionals know the industry standards for book formatting. The general public may be aware that books from a given imprint all look sort of the same, but they don't know or care why. The general public judges the professionalism of a book by the quality of its binding and cover, and the readability of its content. The average reader will not discard a book in disgust, exclaiming, "Verdana isn't an industry standard font!"

Secondly, industry standards were established around mechanical typesetting, before the digital age began. In those days, each letter and character of text was carved into a tiny metal or wooden block, and the blocks were all laid out in a frame to create a massive stamp of each page of text to be printed. The entire frame could be inked and then stamped onto a page. Publishers and typesetters didn't think of fonts as design elements, or experiment with different fonts, because the process of creating a whole new set of those tiny blocks was very expensive and time-consuming. Similarly, in the old days line spacing was built into the frames used to hold the tiny character blocks. Access to a variety of line-spacing options required a variety of different frames, and this was another expense to be avoided. When digital design came along, a whole plethora of fonts and page layout options followed. Still, the moldy oldies dominate mainstream publishing—not because of any inherent superiority but because mainstream publishers are used to them and loathe to incur the hassles and expense of change.

Finally, as any graphic designer will tell you, one can use fonts and layout to convey something about their content. Anyone who's ever chosen a font for a sign, greeting card, banner, or scrapbook knows this is true. Look at the various fonts in the following table, and see if each one doesn't inspire a different mood.

ALGERIAN	Comic Sans MS	Goudy Old Style	Modern No. 20
Andy	Curlz MT	Jokerman	Papyrus
Bauhaus 93	Euphemia	Kristen ITC	Segoe Print
Beesknees ITC	Garamond	Maiandra GD	Tempus Sans ITC

Not all of the examples in the table are appropriate for use in a book, they're shown to illustrate a point. However, if you want to use Euphemia for your futuristic sci-fi book, Garamond for your romance, or Goudy Old Style for your circa 1880s mystery, why shouldn't you? If you want to use Bauhaus 93 just for the chapter headings of your 1970s era chick lit, why not?

Where your mainstream-published peers are stuck with a limited number of font options and don't get to choose which font will be used in their books, as an indie author you can utilize fonts to enhance the reader's overall experience. As long as the font is easy to read and not so busy or design-heavy that it will fatigue the eyes when laid out in paragraphs (like Algerian, Bauhaus 93, and Beesknees ITC would), there's no reason *not* to choose a font that evokes the mood you're after.

Similarly, your chosen font may be too small in a standard 10-point size, or easier to read with line spacing slightly greater than industry standards dictate. Many readers find the typical 10-point narrowly spaced lines of the mass-market paperback hard on the eyes, but don't really need a large-print edition. I generally work with non-standard fonts in a size larger than industry standard with one and a half line spacing, and readers have specifically complimented the superior readability of my books.

Here's an important caveat: If you will publish your manuscript in an e-book format other than PDF, you should only use HTML-compliant fonts (see HTML Primer appendix).

BUILD A MANUSCRIPT SHELL

A manuscript shell is to your manuscript what framing is to a house: It provides a consistent structure to the overall project. The shell is where you set up all the necessary formatting options for text and the manuscript in general. Setting up the manuscript shell is a lot of work, but you only have to do it once and any manuscript created in the shell will automatically be properly formatted for print publication as you work. After the shell is created, save it for use as a template: Each time you begin a manuscript, open the shell and Save As under a new file name.

Begin by opening a new blank document and doing a Save As with your desired file name. Save frequently as you work on setting up the shell.

Create Custom Styles

Make a list of the styles you will need, select a name for each one, and create them as described previously.

Modify Page Setup

Go to File > Page Setup to access the Page Setup dialog. The screenshot in Figure 5-12 shows how the dialog looks when you first open it, with default values filled in.

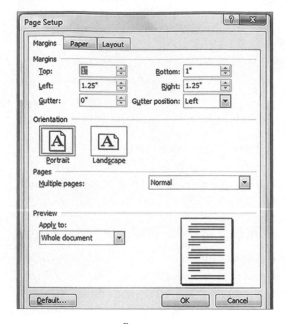

Figure 5-12

The dialog has three tabs: Margins, Paper, and Layout. When setting your top and bottom margins, bear headers and footers in mind. If you will have headers and footers—and most books do, even if only for page numbering—be sure to make headers and footers wide enough to allow for spacing between the header/footer and adjacent text. Your text should not butt right up against your headers or footers.

Before changing anything else, in the Pages section select Mirror Margins (highlighted in screen shot in Figure 5-13). Doing so makes the margins on facing pages mirror images of one another. It also alters some options in the dialog. Left and Right margin names are changed to Inside and Outside respectively, the gutter position drop-down is

locked, and instead of one page, the dialog displays two facing pages at the bottom (see Figure 5-14).

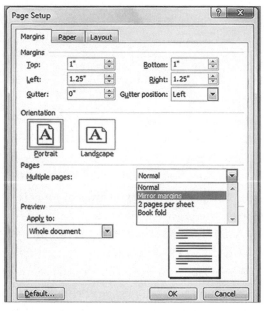

Figure 5-13

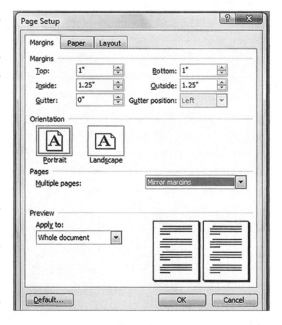

Figure 5-14

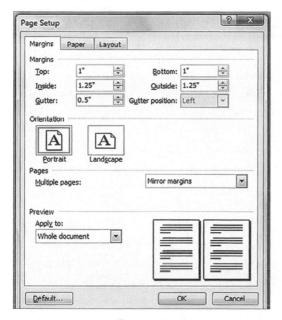

Figure 5-15

Now you can set your inside and outside margins. Take a book of the same dimensions and genre as your intended book (trade paperback novel, training manual, how-to) and measure its margins. Note that margins are sized up or down incrementally for different page sizes. A workbook-type nonfiction or reference book may have 1" (25 mm) margins, but that would be much too wide for a mass-market paperback book. For trade paperbacks, I set margins of ½" (13mm). (See Figure 5-15.)

Inside and outside margins should be set to the same width. Don't worry about making the inside margin wider to account for the binding, because the gutter setting will handle that.

Because hardcover and paperback books do not lie flat when they're opened, a certain amount of empty space is needed between the book's spine and the text on each page, to account for the part of the page the binding hides.

The gutter setting allows you to specify how much empty space you want in that area of each page, between the spine and the inside margin.

The dimensions, page count, and purpose of your book will determine the appropriate gutter width. A large-format book will open a bit wider than a small-format book, exposing more of the gutter area to the reader. A thin book will open wider than a thick one, also exposing more of the gutter.

Get a book of the same approximate size and thickness as your intended book and open it to a page somewhere near the middle, as if to read. Tilt the top of the book down so you can see the top edge of the spine, and measure the distance between the spine and visible inner edge of the printed pages. In other words, measure how much of each page is invisible because it's curved inward, toward the spine. That distance is the width of the gutter, and in mainstream books with glued bindings, it's often too narrow.

If you've ever had to forcibly flatten an open book in order to more easily see the text closest to the spine, you know how annoying it is to the reader when gutters are too narrow. Moreover, flattening a book in such a way can crack a glued binding, resulting in loose or even lost pages. If you want to make the reader comfortable and increase the chance your book will survive its first reading, be generous with your gutters.

The purpose of your book comes into play when you imagine how the book is most likely to be positioned when the buyer is reading it. Books that are read for pleasure will be held in the reader's hands. A how-to book, however, will frequently lay open on a desk or table and the reader will refer to it as she follows a step-by-step procedure. If yours is this type of book, you may want to set the gutter to 1" (25mm). This, to-gether with a 1" (25mm) inner margin, makes the distance from the spine to the inner edge of the text a whopping 2" (5cm). A hardcover or pa-perback book formatted this way still won't lay flat on a desk or table, but the reader should have no difficulty reading right up to the inner margin when she glances up from her work to look at it.

In the example shown in Figure 5-15, the gutter has been set to .5, or ½". Notice that the Facing Pages image at the bottom of the dialog displays the gutter as shaded margins along the inner edge of each page.

In the Preview section at the bottom of the dialog, leave the Apply To dialog box set to its default value of Whole Document. Click the Paper tab to open the Paper options dialog, as shown in Figure 5-16.

All you need to set on this tab is Paper size, at the top of the dialog, by manually entering your desired page height and width. If your book will be a perfect-bound paperback, in which the pages of the book are flush with the edges of the cover, set the paper size to your intended book's dimensions (for example, 6" × 9" (15cm × 23cm) for trade paperback).

If your book will be a hardcover, you will need to consult your publisher to learn the cor-rect paper size for your book's dimensions.

The Facing Pages preview at the bottom of the dialog will display a rough approximation of how your margin and gutter options will be applied to pages of the size you've specified, so if something looks askew in that little picture you may need to go back to the Margins tab and make adjustments. When you're satisfied with the preview image, click the Layout tab (shown in Figure 5-17).

For most books, the only settings to be altered here are in the Headers and Footers section.

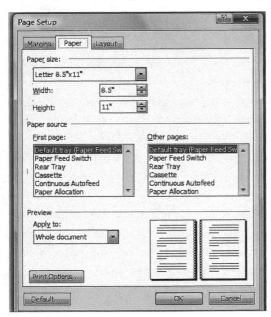

Figure 5-16

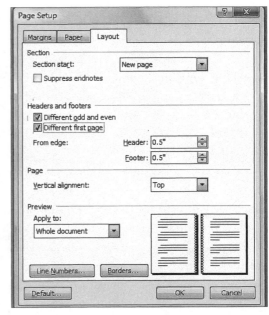

Figure 5-17

THE INDIE AUTHOR GUIDE

Click on the check boxes next to Different Odd and Even and Different First Page to select them.

If yours is a poetry book, cartoon collection, or other type of book with alternative page layout, you may want to set Vertical Alignment in the Page section to Center instead of its default value of Top.

Click the OK button, and you're done with the Page Setup dialog.

Set Up Front Section

Your book should have all the same front matter as a mainstream-published book. That means a copyright page, dedication page, title page, and table of contents. The page facing the reader when he opens the front cover should be blank. Set a placeholder on the first page of your word processing document for this page, followed by some carriage returns and a page break, as shown in Figure 5-18.

To insert the page break, under the Insert menu on the toolbar, select Break. In the Insert Break dialog (see Figure 5-19), select Page Break and click OK. To insert a page break using the keyboard shortcut, hold down the Ctrl key while pressing the Enter key.

This brings you to page 2 of your word processing file, which is actually the reverse of that blank page the reader sees when he opens the cover of the book. This is where you will put your copyright information, in the format shown in Figure 5-20.

You will notice that the left-hand margin on the copyright page in Figure 5-20 is much narrower than the left-hand margin on the page shown in Figure 5-18. This is because the left-hand margin on the Figure 5-18 page

Figure 5-18

Figure 5-19

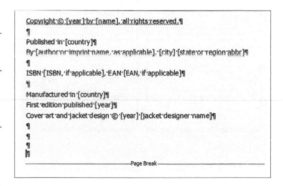

Figure 5-20

consisted of a gutter plus a margin, since on that page the left-hand side is where the page will be glued or sewn into the book's spine. On the copyright page, which will be the reverse of the first page in the printed book, the gutter is on the right-hand side.

The effect can be jarring when viewed on screen. Remember that each page of the finished book will consist of two pages from your word processing document. The blank page directly beneath the front cover is page 1 of the book, an odd-numbered page. Its reverse is page 2 of the book, an even-numbered page. When the book is open, pages on the left will always be even-numbered (because they are always the backs of odd-numbered pages) and pages on the right will always be odd.

Recall the facing-pages preview in the Page Setup dialog box, shown in Figure 5-21. If these were two facing pages bound into a book, the one on the left side would be even-numbered and the one on the right would be odd-numbered. The gutter will always appear on the left on odd-numbered pages and on the right on even-numbered pages.

Figure 5-21

If you do not have all of the information needed for your copyright page (the ISBN, EAN, etc.), leave placeholders as necessary. Just don't forget to go back and update your copyright page when all the needed information is available. If your book mentions brand names of products or services, add copyright and trademark information about those items to your copyright page,

following the format shown on the copyright page of this book. Finally, select all the text on the page and apply your custom copyright style to it. Insert a few carriage returns and another page break.

Now you're on page 3 of your word processing file, which is the front of the second page in the book. This will be your title page. Enter your title, subtitle (if applicable), and author byline as desired, then apply the correct custom Style to each item. Enter a few carriage returns and a page break.

This brings you to page 4 of your file, which will be the reverse of the title page in your book, shown in Figure 5-22. It may be blank or display titles of your other published books in an Also By [author name] list, according to your preference. Enter a placeholder, carriage returns, and page break as shown.

Figure 5-22

Now you're on page 5 of your word processing file, or the front of the third page in your eventual book. This is your dedication page. Enter your dedication message about one-third of the way down from the top of the page, then select all of its text and apply your custom dedication style to it. Enter a few carriage returns and a page break.

Page 6 of your word processing file is the back of the dedication page in your book and should generally be blank. Enter a placeholder, carriage returns, and a page break, following the prior examples of blank pages.

The next page, page 7 of your word processing file, is where the table of contents goes. Enter a Table of Contents header and apply your custom formatting style to it, then the usual carriage returns and page break. The actual table of contents will be inserted much later, when the book is being prepared for print.

Now you've reached page 8, the reverse of your table of contents page. This page may or may not have text on it in the printed book, depending on the length of your table of contents. For now, set it up like the other blank placeholder pages, but instead of inserting a page break after the carriage returns, insert a Next Page Section Break.

This is done via the Break menu, as described previously. You're inserting a section break instead of a page break to create a new section for chapter one of your book (see Figure 5-23). This is necessary because headers, footers, and page numbers aren't typically displayed on front matter pages (copyright page, title page, dedication page, table of contents) but *are* displayed on the pages making up the main body of the book.

Figure 5-23

Since headers and footers are applied on a per-section basis, if you want headers and footers on some pages but not others, you must set up separate document sections for each instance of changed formatting. Going forward, each chapter will be set up as a new section in the document.

A Note About Copyright

Per the United States Copyright Office, "Your work is under copyright protection the moment it is created and fixed in a tangible form that it is perceptible either directly or with the aid of a machine or device."

In response to the question of whether or not copyright registration with the U.S. Copyright Office is mandatory in order to receive copyright protection in the United States, the Office responds, "No. In general, registration is voluntary. Copyright exists from the moment the work is created. You will have to register, however, if you wish to bring a lawsuit for infringement of a U.S. work."

In response to the question of why a copyright should be registered at all if copyright already exists, the Office answers, "Registration is recommended for a number of reasons. Many choose to register their works because they wish to have the facts of their copyright on the public record and have a certificate of registration. Registered works may be eligible for statutory damages and attorney's fees in successful litigation. Finally, if registration occurs within five years of publication, it is considered prima facie evidence in a court of law."

In other words, a registered copyright affords an author maximum protection in a court of law if he or she should ever need to bring a case of copyright infringement.

Having said that, legal matters are outside the scope of this book and nothing herein should be construed as legal advice. If you are uncertain whether or not to obtain a registered copyright for your work in the United States, I encourage you to obtain Circular 1 - Copyright Basics, from the U.S. Copyright Office website (www.copyright.gov), and confer with an attorney for further guidance. For information about copyright law and enforcement outside the United States, confer with an attorney versed in international copyright law.

Set Up Headers And Footers

Headers and footers will appear on your chapter pages but not on the first page of each chapter. This is why you selected the Different First Page option for headers and footers in the Page Setup section.

In this book, text in the header is right-aligned on odd-numbered pages and left-aligned on even-numbered pages. This ensures the header is always aligned to the outer margin of each page, not the inner margin, near the gutter. Likewise, in the footer, page numbers are right-aligned on odd-numbered pages and left-aligned on even-numbered pages. This is why the Different Odd

and Even option exists for headers and footers in the Page Setup section.

If you want the text and page numbers in your headers *or* footers to be differently aligned on odd- and even-numbered pages, as they are in many mainstream books, you need to insert four placeholder pages in your manuscript shell, as shown in the table on the following page. If your header *and* footer content will be centered on every page, you still need to insert one placeholder page for the first page of the chapter (which won't have a header) and a second placeholder page to represent how headers and footers should be formatted on every other page of the chapter. In that event, you can go back and deselect the Different Odd and Even check box in the Page Setup dialog. (See the table below.)

Begin by inserting placeholder pages, without headers or footers. Page 9 is the first page of your first chapter. Enter the name or number of the chapter and apply your custom chapter heading style to it. Enter a few carriage returns and a page break.

For header and footer formatting with differently aligned odd- and even-numbered pages, you must set up three more placeholder pages. On pages 10 and 11, enter a few carriage

CHAPTER PAGE	HEADER CONTENT	FOOTER CONTENT
1	No header	Right-aligned page number
2	Left-aligned header text	Left-aligned page number
3	Right-aligned header text	Right-aligned page number
4	Left-aligned header text	Left-aligned page number

returns and a page break. On page 12, enter a few carriage returns and a Next Page Section Break, as described previously. For books with identically aligned headers and footers, you only need to have one additional placeholder page (page 10) with a few carriage returns and a Next Page Section Break on it.

Set Up Headers

Go back to page 9 and select the Header and Footer option of the View menu, shown in Figure 5-24.

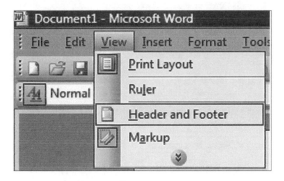

Figure 5-24

The cursor jumps up into the header section, and the Header and Footer toolbar is displayed, as shown in Figure 5-25.

Notice the highlighted button on the toolbar shown in Figure 5-26 (you can also mouse over the toolbar to see each button's name).

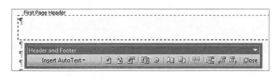

Figure 5-25

Figure 5-26

That's the Link to Previous button, and it's always selected at the start of a new section by default. Its current setting is displayed in the header or footer onscreen as well. This option should never be selected for your headers, even if you intend to use centered headers, because the first page of each chapter won't have a header but subsequent pages will.

You don't want a header on the first page of any chapter. Leave the header blank. The far right button, next to the Close button, is the Show Next button. Click it to go to the header on the second page of your chapter.

The second page of your chapter is an even-numbered page. If the Link to Previous button is selected, click it to deselect it. In a book with centered headers, the header on this page should be center aligned. In a book with headers aligned along opposite outside margins, the header on this page should be left-aligned so it will appear near the outside margin of the page. Enter your desired text (book title or chapter title) in the header. Apply formatting options as desired, including desired text alignment. Click the Show Next button.

If your page headers are all center-aligned, you don't have any more page headers to set up. Click the Previous button to get back to page 9 of your manuscript, then skip ahead to the Set Up Footers section on the following page. Otherwise, read on to complete your header formatting.

The third page of your chapter is an odd-numbered page, which means its header should be right-aligned. Deselect the Link to Previous button if applicable. Enter the same header text as on the previous page and apply the same formatting, but make the text right-aligned. Click the Show Next button.

The fourth page of your chapter is an even-numbered page, which means its header should be left-aligned. If the Link to Previous button is selected, click it to deselect it. Enter the same header text as on the previous page and apply the same formatting, but make the text right-aligned.

Instead of the Show Next button, this time click the Show Previous button, located immediately left of the Show Next button. Click it two more times to get back to the blank header on the first page of your chapter.

Set Up Footers

Click the Switch Between Header and Footer button, to the immediate right of the Link to Previous button, to switch to the footer.

Again, by default, the Same as Next button is selected. Click it to deselect it. Insert the page number (and any other desired text) in the footer. Apply desired formatting, including desired alignment. Page numbers will be either centered or right-aligned.

By default, page numbering will display the actual page number of the word processing document. If you want page numbering to begin with *1*, click the Format Page Number button (highlighted in Figure 5-27) to display the Page Number Format dialog box.

Figure 5-27

In the Page Number Format dialog box, shown in Figure 5-28, click the Start At option to select it and accept the default number setting of *1*. Leave all other options in the dialog set to their defaults and click OK.

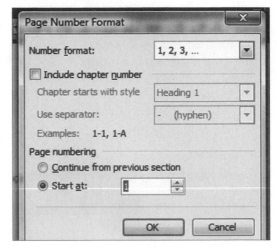

Figure 5-28

On the Header and Footer toolbar, click the Show Next button to go to the footer on the second page of your chapter. Insert the page number (and other desired text, if applicable) and apply desired formatting, including left-alignment of the page number.

That's all there is to footer setup, regardless of whether your footers will be differently aligned on odd and even pages. Since all chapter pages will have footers, all even-page footers will be formatted the same as one another, all odd-page footers will be formatted the same as one another, and Link to Previous is always selected for a new section by default. You don't need to do any footer setup for subsequent chapters/sections. Word will automatically continue inserting the correct odd- and even-page footers as pages are added to the manuscript. If your word processor doesn't apply this Link to Previous option by default, you will have to manually set up your footers at the start of each section following the directions provided above.

As for headers, Word will continue to insert the correct odd- and even-page headers as you add pages to your chapter, but because you don't want a header on the first page of any subsequent chapters/sections you will have to repeat the header setup steps for each chapter/section in your manuscript. Again, if your word processor doesn't apply this Link to Previous option by default, you will have to manually set up your headers at the start of each section following the directions provided above.

An even number of pages (two or four, depending on whether or not you want differently aligned headers and/or footers) are inserted as placeholders for each chapter/section to ensure the first page of each *new* chapter/section will always be an odd-numbered, or right-hand, page. This is pretty standard in mainstream-published books, and while I don't generally kowtow to mainstream conventions this is one case where I do, simply because it's what readers are used to and have come to expect. Later on, as you type or paste chapter text into your manuscript, you may find the chapter/section ends on an odd-numbered page. If that's the case, insert a page break to create a blank even-numbered page at the end of the chapter.

The last page of each chapter/section should always be an even-numbered page and should always end with a Next Page Section Break. After you're finished typing or pasting in chapter text, if you find some of your original placeholder pages are still there at the end of the chapter/section, delete any extra blank pages—but again, make sure the last page of the chapter is an even-numbered page and that it ends with a Next Page Section Break.

Set up a second chapter/section as you did the first one, inserting and formatting desired headers and footers the same as for the first chapter/section. Two placeholder chapters are enough for the manuscript shell, so let's move on to the back matter of the book.

Set Up Back Section

The last page of your manuscript shell is the beginning of a new section, but instead of setting it up as another chapter you'll be using it for back matter. The back matter of a book consists of all the pages at the end of the book that have nothing to do with the contents of the book. An About the Author page, and an Also From [author name] page containing cross-sell descriptions of the author's other books are two typical examples. Definitely add an About the Author page in every one of your books, and include a link to your author website or blog. Keep the bio brief, as you'll want to use it online as well and most websites place limitations on the About Me or Biography section in member profiles. See my bio at the end of this book for an example.

If you have other books similar to the one you're working on already in print, include descriptions for one or two of them on a cross-sell page. If the book is part of a series, you can include cross-sell descriptions for every other book in the series that's available for purchase. Otherwise, more than two cross-sell descriptions may seem tacky.

Just as with the front matter section, the back matter section doesn't typically include headers or footers.

CREATE A SEPARATE CHAPTER SHELL

You should now have a complete manuscript shell with all your custom styles, a front matter section, two chapter sections and a back matter section. Save it with your desired manuscript shell name.

The manuscript shell will be used to assemble your final manuscript, but as you work through drafts of chapters it's best to store, and work on, each chapter as a separate file. This is because you want to be able to make full use of your word processor's spell-check and grammar check tools (see Editing chapter). These tools run in the background as you work, constantly scanning every word on every page for errors. As page count increases, performance gets more and more sluggish. Eventually you'll hit the point where the file is so large it crashes your word processor altogether, and from then on you won't be able to open the file at all. That's why you need to create a separate chapter shell.

Do a Save As to create a copy of the manuscript shell, saving it with a name specific to a chapter shell. Delete the front matter section, the second chapter section, and the back matter section, and save again. There you have it, your chapter shell is complete.

Using the Chapter Shell

To write a new chapter, open the chapter shell and do a Save As to create a copy. Type the chapter into the word processing file as you normally would but apply your custom styles from the Style list.

Don't Fake It

You went through all the trouble of setting up a shell so that formatting would be applied consistently using the word processor's formatting tools and so there will be no unpleasant surprises after file conversion. Don't undermine all that effort with fake formatting tricks (for example, indenting paragraphs with the space bar instead of using the actual indent function, manually creating a numbered list instead of using the numbered list style) while using the shell.

If indents aren't already set up in your Styles list (they should be), use the tab key to indent at the beginning of a new paragraph if an indent is desired, *not* the space bar. Use the left and right indent tools to inset blocks of text, *not* the space bar. Use the borders and shading tool to insert horizontal lines, *not* a row of dashes. When creating a long dash in a sentence for emphasis—like this—insert an em dash (accessed via Insert > Symbol > Special Characters, or Alt+Ctrl+[minus sign]) instead of typing three short dashes from the keyboard.

What About Preexisting Chapters?

If you already have a chapter written, copy its contents and paste it into a copy of the chapter shell as unformatted text. This feature is accessed via the Paste Special option under the Edit menu on the main toolbar, shown in Figure 5-29.

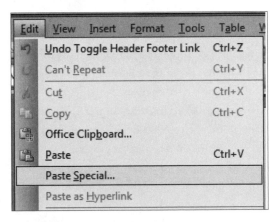

Figure 5-29

In the Paste Special dialog, select Unformatted Text. When your text is added to the chapter shell document, it will acquire the custom styles you've set up in the shell.

Note that you can leave the chapter heading out, since it will already be in place in the manuscript shell when you're ready to assemble all your chapters into a single document.

USING THE MANUSCRIPT SHELL

Open the manuscript shell and do a Save As to create a copy. Under the Tools menu, shown in Figure 5-30, select Options.

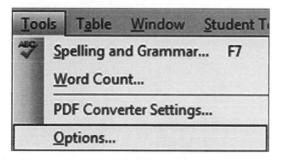

Figure 5-30

Figure 5-31

In the Options dialog, select the Spelling and Grammar tab (shown in Figure 5-31). In the Spelling section, deselect Check Spelling As You Type. In the Grammar section, deselect Check Grammar As You Type. Click OK to save your changes.

Copy and paste the contents of your separate chapters into the document, creating new chapter sections as needed. If you're copying and pasting from a corresponding chapter shell, you don't have to use the Paste Special command because the text should already be formatted with the same styles as those in the manuscript shell. If you're copying and pasting from a different source, use the Paste Special function, as described in the previous section.

When all your content is present in the manuscript, go to the placeholder page for the table of contents. Delete the placeholder text. Place your cursor where you want the table of contents to begin, a line or two beneath the table of contents header, and select Index and Tables from the Reference list under the Insert menu on the main toolbar, as shown in Figure 5-32.

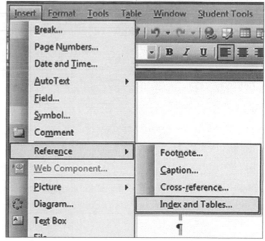

Figure 5-32

In the Index and Tables dialog, shown in Figure 5-33, click the Table of Contents tab. Deselect the Use Hyperlinks Instead of Page Numbers option on the right-hand side.

Set other options as desired and click OK to insert the table of contents on your page. Its font most likely will not match the rest of your document. If this is the case, select all the text contained in the table of contents and manually change the font and point size according to your preference by applying your previously created TOC body style. If your table of contents is longer than one page, make sure the last page of the front matter section is still an even-numbered page ending in a Next Page Section Break. Insert a blank page with placeholders after the table of contents to accomplish this, if necessary.

Do a Final Review

Update the copyright information page if needed to eliminate any placeholders remaining there. Delete placeholder text on pages that will be blank in the printed book. Go through the completed manuscript to verify your headers are correct, any extraneous placeholder pages have been removed, page numbering is correct, and graphics are properly positioned (if applicable).

If you've moved chapters around or inserted new chapters or sections between preexisting ones in the manuscript shell, you may find the relocated or inserted sections have inherited the same headers as the sections preceding them due to that pesky Link to Previous default. Edit such headers as needed. Also note, since the back of the last page in a printed book

is an even-numbered page, the manuscript file must end with an even-numbered page. Insert a blank page at the end if necessary.

READY FOR THE PRINTER

When you're done, you'll have a manuscript that's properly formatted to meet the basic requirements of any POD print service provider, though you should check your own provider's specific formatting guidelines (available on the provider's website) to see if there are any additional requirements specific to that provider.

If your provider will accept a PDF file, I strongly recommend you convert the file to PDF format instead of submitting a word processor document. A PDF file won't require further conversion or manipulation at the publisher's end, so you can feel confident that the file you send them is exactly what you'll see in print when you receive your proof copy of the book. Be sure to do a thorough review of the PDF file before you send it to the publisher, since PDF converters don't work perfectly every time, or for every file.

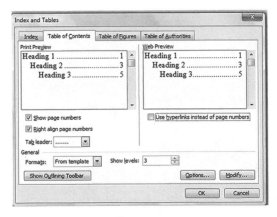

Figure 5-33

six} Editing and Revising

Under the general heading of *editing*, there are actually three types: developmental editing, copyediting, and content editing. Developmental editing deals with the broad strokes of your manuscript: structure, organization, character plotting, and tone. As such, this type of editing is best performed early in the manuscript outlining or drafting process, and must generally be done by a professional editor or skilled creative writing instructor. Copyediting concerns itself with the nuts and bolts of correct language: grammar, spelling, and punctuation. Content editing is about flow, readability, and showing stylistic choices in their best light.

Consider an example in which three sentences in a row begin with the phrase, "He was all alone." Because there's nothing grammatically wrong with the three sentences, a copy editor would sign off on them. As to the other editor, his response depends on whether the three appear to reflect a purposeful, stylistic choice on the part of the author, or seem merely to be an oversight. In the following passage, the usage seems purposeful:

> He was all alone, he sensed it. He was all alone, he felt it. He was all alone, he knew it.

Clearly, the author intended to repeat the opening phrase for effect, to achieve a certain rhythm. Now look at this passage:

> He was all alone, so now it would be up to him to complete the mission. He was all alone, Harold and Jessica wouldn't be there to show him the way anymore. He was all alone, and the next week was looking like it would be a lot harder than he first imagined.

In this case, it doesn't seem as if the repetitive usage of the phrase was a purposeful stylistic choice, and even if it was, it's not effective. An editor would likely suggest these changes:

> He was all alone, now it would be up to him to complete the mission. Harold and Jessica wouldn't be there to show him the way anymore. The next week was looking like it would be a lot harder than he first imagined.

You can see that deleting the second and third usages of the phrase punches up the prose considerably. Even so, notice that I said the editor would *suggest* deleting the phrases. When editors mark up your manuscript, they are suggesting changes, not actually making changes.

While grammar, spelling, and punctuation rules are fairly constant, sometimes authors make the stylistic choice to go with usage that's technically incorrect but works for the sentence or passage in question. The word *library* may be purposely misspelled as *liberry* to convey a character's mispronunciation of the word, for example. In the second "he was all alone" passage above, the suggested edits seem to improve the flow of the prose, however, it's ultimately a matter of taste and opinion. Therefore, the editor makes the suggestion but it's up to the author to decide. Likewise, treat the contents of this chapter as a guide, not a set of rules. In the end it will be up to you to decide what's right for your book.

DIY COPYEDITING

If you are the sort of writer who's a stickler for proper grammar, spelling, and punctuation when reading nonfiction (books, articles, even e-mails), you can probably catch 80 to 90 percent of your spelling and grammar errors with the proper use of the tools and techniques in this chapter. You can't expect to do the job as completely or thoroughly as a professional copy editor, but even so, an 80 to 90 percent copyedited draft probably does not require the services of a professional copy editor because that last 10 to −20 percent of errors will likely be caught in your workshopping rounds, if you undertake them properly and seriously (explained later in this chapter). Moreover, hiring a copy editor after most of the work is done doesn't make financial sense because they charge by the page, the word, or the hour, regardless of error count.

On the other hand, if you know grammar, spelling, and punctuation aren't your strong suits, and you don't have anyone with whom to swap drafts who *is* strong in these areas, you're probably best served by hiring a pro. You may think the occasional typo, misspelling, or bit of incorrect grammar should be easily overlooked, but there are two problems with this attitude. The first is

that it betrays a lack of pride in your work, and if even *you* can't be bothered to care that much about your work, why should anyone else? The second is that, among the general public, there's a reasonable presumption that anyone who offers his writing for sale has a mastery of the language in which he's writing. Language is the primary tool of the writer's trade, and people tend to think of authors as educated intellectuals endowed with linguistic skills over and above those of the general public. This characterization isn't accurate for many, many terrific authors, but just as you expect the guy you hire to fix your computer to know a great deal more about computers than you do, people expect authors to have a much greater mastery of grammar, spelling, and punctuation than they do. If you fail this test, your "author" status is summarily revoked in the mind of the reader.

Still, a certain amount of editing is required just to get a draft in good enough shape for workshopping, and your editing task is not limited to copyediting, so whether you intend to hire a pro or not you'll find a lot of valuable tips and techniques in this chapter.

There are numerous editing software programs available, but I don't recommend them, for three reasons. First, I've yet to find one with a features list that exceeds what you can already get in a quality word processing program. Second, no matter how great such a program may be, there will always be a need to have at least one human being review your manuscript to catch all the errors and proposed edits an automated program can't. Finally, all the available programs I've investigated are pretty costly, some scarcely less expensive than hiring a human copy editor.

If you're using Microsoft Word 2003 or higher, or any comparable word processor from that year or later, you should be able to manage most of your copyediting simply by using your word processor's built-in copyediting tools. If you're not using such a word processor, you can buy one for the same or less than what you'd typically pay a professional copy editor to do the job for you. Even if you're totally broke, you can download a free copy of OpenOffice, as I mentioned previously.

The tools are very robust, but they use a lot of system resources and memory. The larger your file is, the more resources and memory are required. For that reason, you will want to save each chapter of your manuscript in a separate file as you work, then combine them into a single file when you're confident you're finished copyediting.

In MS Word, click on Tools > Spelling and Grammar > Options to access the Spelling and Grammar options dialog box, shown in Figure 6-1. The location for this tool varies with the version of MS Word and with different word processors. If you don't know how to access it in your program, consult the help files and search for "spelling and grammar" or "spelling" + "grammar."

Figure 6-1

In Figure 6-1, the most commonly used options are selected.

"Check spelling as you type" means the program will check your spelling on the fly, as you type, and immediately provide visual or auditory feedback to let you know when it detects a misspelled word.

"Always suggest corrections" means that when you run a spell-check and/or grammar check, the program will suggest corrections for any items it has found to be misspelled or grammatically incorrect.

"Suggest from main dictionary only" means spelling will be checked only against the main dictionary, not any custom or user-populated dictionary files. The dictionary is discussed further below.

Leave "Hide spelling errors in this document" unselected, to display spelling errors.

"Ignore words in UPPERCASE" ensures the spell-check will ignore acronyms. "Ignore words with numbers" makes the spell-check ignore special words you may have made up as part of the world of your story, for instance, a nightclub called Area61. "Ignore internet and file addresses" is self-explanatory.

In the Grammar section, "Check grammar as you type" and "Hide grammatical errors in this document" work the same way they work for spelling.

If "Check grammar with spelling" is selected, when you run a spell-check your program will also check your grammar.

"Display readability statistics" is an option to display the calculated reading level of the writing after the spell-check and grammar check are complete. This is a useful tool for authors writing books aimed at a specific reader grade level.

Under Writing Style you can select "Grammar only" (shown in Figure 6-2) or "Grammar and style" (shown in Figure 6-3), and then click the Settings button to specify what types of things you want corrected.

Now let's look at how these tools work. As you type, the program highlights the errors you've selected under Options and Settings. Look at Figure 6-4.

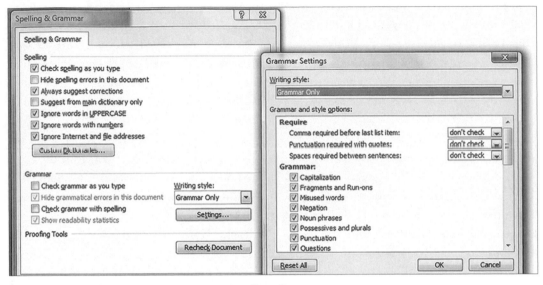

Figure 6-2

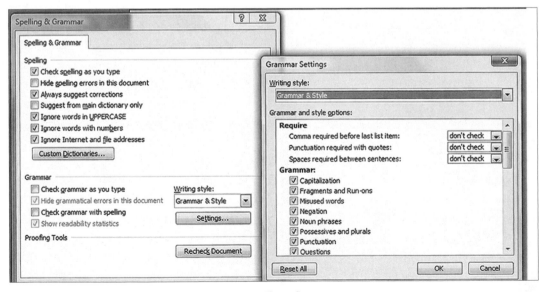

Figure 6-3

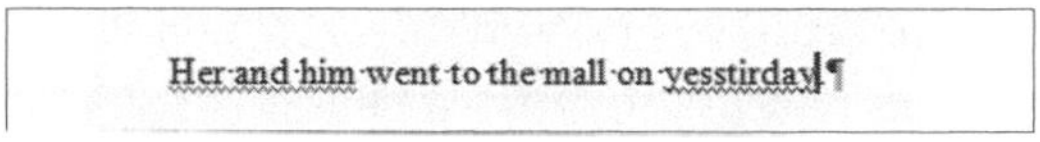

Her and him went to the mall on yesstirday ¶

Figure 6-4

Red squiggly underlining means the word processor has detected a misspelling. Green squiggly underlining means the word processor has detected a grammar error. When I select the text and run a spelling and grammar check, I see what's shown in Figure 6-5.

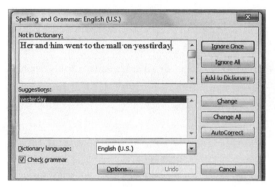

Figure 6-5

First, the spell-checker will go through each misspelled word one at a time and suggest corrections.

I won't go into detail about how spell-checkers work since their specific use varies from program to program. I assume anyone reading this already knows how to use them, but I do want to highlight the Add to Dictionary button. Your word processor may allow access to the dictionary elsewhere; if you don't know where it is, go to your program's help files and search for "dictionary."

Use the Add to Dictionary function to add any proper names, made-up words, and words not already included in your word processor to the program's dictionary so it will ignore them in future spell-checks. Writers of fantasy, science

fiction, and possibly literary fiction will find this feature to be very useful. You can also choose to Ignore specific instances of misspelling.

When all misspellings have been reviewed, the grammar check shows its suggestions (see Figure 6-6). Note that while you can calibrate the grammar checker's rules and sensitivity with the Settings check boxes, it will never catch every single mistake simply because the English language is so complex. In this case, it caught the incorrect pronoun usage but did not indicate that on yesterday is also incorrect.

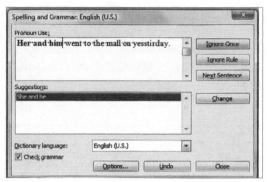

Figure 6-6

Most word processors have an autocorrect feature, which automatically corrects common typographical errors on the fly (for example, changing *teh* to *the*). In MS Word, autocorrect is accessed via Tools > AutoCorrect Options. There, you can specify the things you want the program to correct on the fly, and how you want them corrected.

When exposing the manuscript to a workshop later on, you can ask your readers to mark any errors they find as they read, confident that there shouldn't be many grammatical or spelling errors as to interfere with the read overall.

Fresh eyes—eyes other than your own—are the only way you'll catch misspellings that result in different words that are correctly spelled, and therefore overlooked by your spell-checker. For example, you want your character to *read* a book, but due to misspelling he will *reed* a book.

DIY EDITING

Your manuscript should now be pretty clean in terms of grammar and usage, but there are still some problems you most likely won't have picked up on yet. This is where you hit the finer points.

Overused Words and Phrases

Use your word processor's search function to locate and eliminate overused words and expressions. You are probably aware of certain words or phrases you tend to use as transition crutches or standby openers, but there are plenty of other go-to words and expressions you may not even realize you're using too often. Your workshopping readers will probably pick up on some of them, particularly if you ask your readers to be on the lookout for any repetitive speech patterns as they read. While you may know you're supposed to avoid overreliance on *–ly, –ing,* and *–tion* words, it's easy to lose track of how often they find their way into your prose while you're concentrating on plot and characterization.

As you do a search for the upcoming words, make note of their frequency. If it's low, the words may be fine as is. But if you're seeing the same word or expression more than once in the same page or even the same ten pages, it's time to do some ruthless editing. Since overuse of certain words also exposes overuse of certain sentence structures, the best tack when eliminating those words is to rework the sentence. Turn to the thesaurus as a last resort. The al-

ternatives found there will rarely match the tone or flow of your specific bit of prose, will frequently sound stilted, and will therefore tend to draw attention to themselves.

An excellent resource for this type of copy-editing is *The Dimwit's Dictionary: More Than 5,000 Overused Words and Phrases and Alternatives to Them* by Robert Hartwell Fiske. Look for:

Tricky Grammar and Punctuation

There are many instances of incorrect grammar and punctuation that your word processor's grammar check will miss because they're areas of nuance, or situations in which correct usage is dictated by context. Unless you intend to become a career grammarian, the best cure is prevention.

First, get a copy of the book *Eats, Shoots and Leaves: The Zero Tolerance Approach to Punctuation* by Lynne Truss. It's a small book, not very expensive or time-consuming, and surprisingly entertaining. Read through it to acquaint yourself with the most common punctuation mistakes, then go on a search-and-destroy mission through your manuscript just as you did with overused words and phrases.

Next, when in doubt about grammar, try some online research. The following sites are excellent free resources for grammar help:

Grammar Girl: http://grammar.quick anddirtytips.com

Using English: www.usingenglish.com

Guide to Grammar & Writing: http:// grammar.ccc.commnet.edu/grammar/

Finally, when in doubt, cut it out. If you can't find adequate clarification on your grammar

The real evils, indeed, of Emma's situation were the power of having rather too much her own way, and a disposition to think a little too well of herself; these were the disadvantages which threatened alloy to her many enjoyments.

The danger, however, was at present so unperceived, that they did not by any means rank as

misfortunes with her.

widow
Sorrow came - a gentle sorrow - but not at all in the shape of any disagreeable consciousness.

Miss Taylor married.

It was Miss Taylor's loss which first brought grief.

orphan
It was on the wedding-day of this

beloved friend that Emma first sat in mournful thought of any continuance.

The wedding over, and the bride-people gone, her father and herself were left to dine together, with no prospect of a third to cheer a long evening.

Her father composed himself to sleep after dinner, as usual, and

Figure 6-7

or punctuation quandary, change the sentence to eliminate the questionable thing(s).

Check Your Jargon

If your manuscript uses a lot of technical, historical, or idiomatic jargon, you need to be sure you're using that language properly. Inevitably, there will be someone out there reading your book who just happens to be an expert in whatever it is you're writing about, and when the time comes he won't hesitate to criticize your ignorance in his Amazon review.

For specific terms, try www.glossarist.com. For more general inquiries on a specific subject or time period (human anatomy, for instance, or twelfth-century foods), do an Internet search.

Improve Readability

View your manuscript in full-page, or facing-pages, print preview mode to spot lengthy blocks of unbroken text and awkward page transitions.

Break up paragraphs to improve readability. In general, no paragraph should take up more than half a standard trade paperback (6" × 9" [15cm x 23 cm]) page; ideally, none should take up more than one third of a page.

Look for instances of only one or two words on a line at the end of a paragraph, and see if you can't rework the sentences to eliminate these danglers.

Do some widow and orphan control. In copyediting, the term *widow* is used to describe the last line of a paragraph which appears at the top of a new page. An *orphan* is the first line of a new paragraph that appears at the bottom of the previous page. Widows and orphans tend to break up the author's intended flow of text, thereby reducing readability. Look at the example shown in Figure 6-7, which is from the now-defunct site, www.textcontrol.com.

If you really don't want to alter your sentences to eliminate widows and orphans, consider judicious application of page breaks only where doing so will improve readability.

CONTENT RIGHTS

If your manuscript quotes commercial material originated by another person, living or dead, unless that material is in the public domain you cannot include it in your manuscript without securing the rights to do so first. Common examples are song lyrics, bits of poetry, excerpts from essays, and product jingles from advertising.

Song Lyrics

If you have a character singing along to a song and you feel their singing is an important action on the part of that character, make sure you have the right to use those lyrics. The easiest solution is use a song that's in public domain. If you wrote the passages with a non-public domain song, you can switch whatever lyrics you've got for lyrics to a song in the public domain that has a similar theme or structure—or whatever it needs to make the scene work. Do an Internet search on "public domain lyrics" and "public domain songs" to find alternatives.

If the song in question is not in the public domain but isn't a current hit, it may be worthwhile to contact whoever owns the rights and ask permission to quote from the lyrics. In many cases, owners of older lyrics will allow you to use them at no charge so long as you provide proper credit on your copyright page or in the notes section of your book. If permission is only given for a fee, you will have to decide if use of the lyric is worth the asking price. Go to the American Society of Composers, Authors, and Performers website (www.ascap.com) and run a search of their ACE database for the song by title, composer, or performer at www.ascap.com/ace/search.cfm?mode=search

The search results will provide contact information for the current owner. Politely ask if you may quote the lyrics in question, and specify that when the book is printed, you will provide a copy of it to the rights owner at no charge; this is a standard condition of rights permissions. Also provide the full context in which the quotation will appear.

If the quotation serves as a chapter opener, specify that the quotation will stand alone and will not take the form of character dialog. Conversely, if the quotation will take the form of a character quoting or singing the lyrics, provide a description of the character, a brief description of the setting and circumstances in which the lyric will be quoted, and an excerpt from the manuscript containing the proposed lyric quotation in the context of the scene in which it appears. This is important because the rights owner may give permission for a hero character to sing along to the song as he's rushing in to rescue the fair maiden, but she might feel very differently about the story's villain singing along to the song as he's committing murders.

Published Material

You can quote from public domain published material without securing rights. To locate public domain material, search for "public domain _____" on the Internet, filling in the blank with the type of material for which you're searching (poetry, books, stories, plays, essays, or what have you). You can also search sites that contain nothing but public domain material, such as Project Gutenberg (www.gutenberg.org).

In cases where the copyright has not expired, you will have to contact the publisher who currently holds the rights to the material and ask for permission to quote from it. As with the song lyric example above, you will want to provide as much information as possible about how the quoted material will be used, and you must be prepared to send a free copy of the published book to the rights holder. Again, if permission can only be had for a fee, you'll have to decide whether it's worth the cost.

Commercial Jingles

Generally, jingles for companies and products that no longer exist are safe to quote without permission, simply because there is no longer anyone to provide that permission. Otherwise, you will need to contact the public relations department of the company in question or the company that manufactures the product in question.

Public Figure Names and Likenesses

As a rule, it's a bad idea to make references to contemporary public figures by name in your manuscript if you intend to have a character or narrator voice any opinion whatsoever. Apart from the risk of being slapped with a libel lawsuit, the more practical reason is that such references will date your manuscript.

In the case of historical fiction you still must tread lightly around living public figures, as well as deceased public figures with surviving relatives. It's fine to say, "Joe was looking forward to the debate between Gore and Bush," because you're only making reference to the fact that such a debate took place, a fact this is already a matter of public record. However, it's very risky to say, "Joe was hoping [blank] would win the debate, because he knew the other guy had always been a two-bit lying hustler in a designer suit." In the latter sentence, your character is expressing an opinion about a public figure which that public figure or his living relatives may find offensive.

Believe it or not, even a reference you think is highly complimentary may not pass muster with the public figure in question, or his surviving relatives. There could be a pop singer who's particularly well-known for her eight-octave range, but if your narrator or one of your characters speaks of admiring that facet of the singer it's possible the singer (or her surviving relatives) could be miffed that you didn't also mention the singer's ability to compose her own songs. When in doubt, ask permission. When you can't get (or can't afford) permission, eliminate the reference completely.

WORKSHOPPING

It's somewhat misleading to use the term *DIY* in reference to revising, because the truth is, you cannot fully revise your manuscript on your own. Obviously, if you had noticed the areas where your pages could be improved, you would've improved them. You need an unbiased outsider's opinion, but this doesn't mean you must fork over the big bucks to a professional editor or book doctor. In fact, paying for such services will not necessarily get the best results.

Seasoned professional editors and book doctors are used to editing toward the goal of pleasing a major publisher. But that isn't *your* goal, since you're an independent. Your goal is to please the eventual reader. To that end, collection and consideration of input from multiple, informed readers can serve your needs as well, or even better, than the opinion of a single paid professional.

Can You Handle the Truth?

Before going on, you need to be brutally honest with yourself in answering this question: Can you receive constructive criticism gracefully? I'm sure you just answered yes as a reflex, but really stop and think about it because this is a crucial juncture for the independent author, even more so than for mainstream authors. A mainstream author's agent or manager will solicit feedback from a professional editor and then share that feedback with the author in the most tactful, sensitive manner possible. When you solicit feedback, those notes and comments will be coming back to you in a raw, unfiltered form.

Imagine your most beloved, carefully crafted character. Now imagine an incoming note that says the reader especially disliked that character or found that character to be poorly written. How will you react to this news? Think about a cherished scene or dialog exchange in your manuscript. Will you go ballistic if your reader suggests you summarily drop the passage because it doesn't add significantly to the plot or tone?

Finally, no matter how ill-advised or even downright crazy a given note seems to you, are you capable of simply absorbing it, appreciating the time and effort your reader has given, and sincerely thanking him or her? Can you resist the overwhelming urge to correct the reader or defend the choices you made to which the reader took exception? Books are a matter of taste, but you must also remember that very often, if you have to explain something to the reader it's a sign that you didn't write it well enough in the first place. After all, you won't be sitting there next to each person who will someday buy your finished book, ready to explain and defend every questionable item.

However careful you are in selecting readers, occasionally you will still find yourself the victim of someone who doesn't know how to give truly constructive criticism, and may even seem to get a bit of a thrill from hurling insults at your work in the most personal and inappropriate terms possible. Even in this extreme situation, you must be able to politely thank the reader for her time and effort, and make no further attempt to respond to the notes; it's pointless to try to reason with an unreasonable person. Do remove that reader's name from consideration in any future rounds of note collecting.

If you can't maintain an air of detachment when the notes come rolling in, your best option is to pay for the services of a professional editor or book doctor. You can be certain a professional editor or book doctor has no personal investment in your success or failure, because you are paying for his services and the price doesn't go up or down based on opinion. Therefore, you will be much more likely to accept the notes given in the impersonal, dispassionate tone they are intended.

Finding Feedback

Many aspiring writers will turn to their writing group at this point, to exchange manuscripts and share notes with one another. There is some value in that approach, but in my opinion it's primarily value is based in bonding and mutual support. When you agree to such an exchange, you don't necessarily know the other authors' level of skill or style of writing. Notes from someone who's just written the first chapter of a first manuscript probably won't be as useful to you as notes from a more-seasoned writer. Likewise, if you write sensitive, coming-of-age dramas, notes from a writer of gory horror stories probably won't be too meaningful to you. Carefully targeted readers will yield much more useful feedback.

THE INDIE AUTHOR GUIDE

You need to find three writers whose work you admire, whose preferred styles and genres are in line with your own, and who are working at a level of the craft either at or above your level—preferably *above*. Ideally, at least one of them will be a stickler for grammar and spelling, too. These people do not have to be professional writers, though. You want three so the vote on a given note will never be split.

Start your search on the Internet. Many, many aspiring authors have blogs and websites with excerpts of their work on display, and you can find some to match your needs by using keyword searches. For example, if you want to find authors of comic fiction, search "writer" + "comic fiction." You can search for writers in other genres the same way. Also try searching for writers' groups, as many of them include a showcase area for members' work.

When you find some likely candidates, e-mail three of them. Briefly introduce yourself (just your name, rough location in the world, and the fact that you're an aspiring writer is enough), then explain where you found their work and what you liked about it. Finally, ask each writer if she would be willing to do a manuscript exchange for notes with you, and if not, whether she could suggest someone else for the task. Very clearly state your desire for constructive criticism, and MEAN it. Include a link to a brief excerpt from the work for which you're seeking help (see the Promotion chapter for details), so that the candidate will have some idea of what he is getting into before agreeing to the arrangement. And remember that manuscript exchange means you are offering to provide the same service to each author you contact.

If the answer is no, graciously accept it and write back to thank the writer for responding to your message anyway. You never know when your paths may cross again, and you can't know for certain why the person turned you down. It may be that they didn't like your excerpt, but it could also be that they do exchanges only within their writing group, or they're simply too busy at the moment to help you.

If the answer is yes, when submitting your manuscript for notes you may want to highlight the type(s) of feedback you're seeking. Leaving the door wide open for whatever the reader wishes to bring to your attention is the best approach for early rounds of revision, but as you get into later rounds you will probably feel pretty confident that certain aspects of the draft are more or less done. At that point, you'll probably seek more specific feedback only on those areas about which you still have some doubts. For example, you may feel your plot and pacing have been massaged to near perfection but sense your dialog still needs work. Letting readers know what you're looking for ahead of time both simplifies their task and makes their feedback more valuable.

I guarantee if you keep trying you will eventually succeed in finding three like-minded writers with whom to exchange manuscripts. One of the advantages of this approach is that the writers with whom you connect will be virtual strangers, so you don't need to worry too much that they'll hold back on their constructive criticisms for the sake of your feelings.

What to Do With the Feedback

You've solicited feedback and graciously, profusely thanked everyone who's given it. Now, what do you do with it? Above all other considerations are the facts that it will ultimately be your name on the cover, and the finished book should reflect your unique sensibilities and writer's voice. Having said that, I have a few rules of thumb for deciding what to change and what to leave alone.

First, when you sent the manuscript out, there were undoubtedly some things about which you yourself felt a bit iffy. If two or more of your three readers are likewise iffy on them, those things probably need to be changed.

Second, let the majority guide you. If the same change is suggested by two out of three of my readers, I seriously consider making the change. If it's suggested by all three readers, I make that change without much further consideration. Remember, these are all writers whose work you admire; their opinions are not to be dismissed lightly.

Third, anytime a change is suggested which strongly resonates with me, I make that change even if only one reader made the suggestion.

Beyond this, there are no other easy-to-follow, all-inclusive rules I can suggest. Even the three rules of thumb are entirely up to your discretion.

If you write the sort of material that tends to divide readers, eliciting only very positive or very negative reactions, your task is much harder because something one reader found particularly objectionable could be the exact thing another reader particularly loves about the work. Typically, this is the constructive criticism experience for authors of literary fiction; if you write literary fiction that will likely polarize readers, you're probably best served by a paid, professional book editor or book doctor.

Otherwise, you want to incorporate all the revisions that make sense to you, and then go out for the next round of constructive criticism. One or two of your readers may have expressed interest in reading the revised copy, but you will need to contact all of them and politely ask if they are willing to read it again. If not, you will need to solicit as many new readers as necessary to get your group of three. Repeat through additional iterations of review until you, and the majority of your readers, feel the manuscript is ready for a wider audience.

Then seek out three new readers who've never seen a single draft of the work. If their reaction is substantially positive, you're ready to mark that draft *final*. This is where connecting with like-minded writers pays off: At this final point, there should be some consistency across the feedback. Nevertheless, remember that even published best-sellers are not uniformly liked, so it's not reasonable to expect to reach a point where every reader loves the draft. You can reach a point where virtually every reader agrees the draft is well-written, however.

If this sounds like a lengthy and challenging process, that's because it is. Remember that as an indie author, you're facing the bias that all self-published books are dreck. It's not fair, but your book must be a whole lot better than not dreck to overcome that bias.

seven} Designing Your Own Book Cover

It may not be possible to accurately or fairly judge a book by its cover, but that doesn't mean potential book buyers won't try. An unattractive or amateurish cover will do even more damage to your book's prospects than poor (or non-existent) editing can, because people who don't bother to pick up your book in the first place will never have an opportunity to judge the quality of its edit. However, this doesn't mean that the only way to get an appealing cover is to pay thousands of dollars to a professional cover design artist. It's entirely possible for most indie authors to get a quality result when designing their own covers, provided they take the task seriously and factor in all the different aspects of a typical book cover: not just the image on the cover, but the font(s), layout, brief description and blurbs for the back cover, and even ISBN/bar code placement.

Before designing your book cover, you'll need to get a rough idea of what you want the cover to look like, write a book description, and gather blurbs.

Begin with a trip to the bookstore, and take a pad and pencil with you. Go to the section of the store where books of the same genre or type as yours are shelved, and start looking at covers. Make a rough sketch of any that appeal to you, blocking out the major shapes, text areas, and title locations from both the front and the back of the book. If you're very uncomfort-able sketching the covers, simply write down the titles and then refer to the covers online at Amazon.

You'll use your sketches (or the covers viewed on Amazon) for inspiration, but the goal is *not* simply to copy a design you've seen. Rather, it's to get an idea of what a typical cover looks like on a mainstream-produced book of the same genre as yours.

WRITE A BOOK DESCRIPTION

You will need a description of your book, to appear on its back cover as well as for use in marketing materials and on product pages when the book is released. You're going for a summary that says enough about the story to lure a reader in, but doesn't give away too much. Keep it brief because you'll need to use this description wherever the book is eventually sold, and booksellers and catalogs have strict word limits. The book description field on Amazon is limited to two hundred words or less, so this is a good number to shoot for. Create a separate word processor or .txt document for the description, and work and rework it until it's exactly what you want. You can look at the brief descriptions provided on the back covers of books similar to yours to get a better idea of what works.

For each book, I set up a single .txt file containing my description/back cover text, any one-liner reviews I may want to quote on the book, my brief About the Author biography, and a cross-sell one-liner for another of my books. I can copy and paste from this .txt file as needed when editing the book cover template or creating promotional materials like posters or press releases.

GATHER BLURBS

Remember, you want your finished book to be indistinguishable from a professionally produced book. Professionally produced books tend to have review blurbs on their back covers, and so should yours.

You can quote a blurb from anyone who has given you permission to do so. That means people from your writing group, a college professor, a blogger, or anyone else who has read your book and has something nice to say about it. Even on mainstream books, blurbs don't always come from famous critics or well-known publications.

To the person perusing your book jacket, assuming that person isn't familiar with either of the two critics quoted, either of these two blurbs will accomplish the same degree of sell as the blurbs on mainstream book covers:

> Don't buy this book unless you can stay up all night reading it, with the lights on!
>
> —Candace Meyers, Bookish
>
> Creepy and atmospheric...a page-turner.
>
> —Trent Willoughby, *Times Herald*

It's not apparent in the first blurb that Bookish is the name of Candace Meyers' blog, nor is it apparent in the second blurb that the *Times Herald*

is a small quarterly distributed only within a local community. Nevertheless, there's nothing dishonest or misleading about the blurbs, so long as you are accurately quoting your sources and have obtained their permission to do so.

Solicit for manuscript reviews, and if those requests net you some complimentary quotable one-liners, ask the reviewer if you may quote him on your book cover. Most are flattered by the request and will happily agree.

Many Amazon Top Reviewers accept review requests, so long as you're willing to send them a free review copy of your book. An electronic version is acceptable to many prior to your book's publication, but they will still want a copy of the actual book as soon it's available. First you'll need to check each reviewer's profile to see if she provides a contact e-mail address, and whether she accepts review requests. Also, you'll want to determine whether your work will suit her tastes. If you get a good one-liner from your efforts, you can credit the blurb as: [Name], Amazon Top [number] Reviewer, that is, Amazon Top 10 Reviewer or Amazon Top 50 Reviewer.

To find a list of Amazon Top Reviewers, go to any product page with reviews and click on the user name of any reviewer to get to his profile page. Scroll down the profile page to the bottom of the Reviews section and click on the View Top Reviewers link, indicated by an arrow in Figure 7-1.

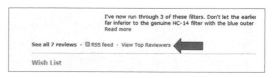

Figure 7-1

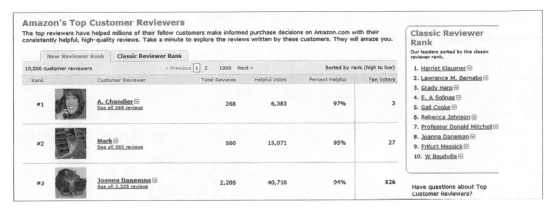

Figure 7-2

That link will take you to the current version of the Amazon Top Reviewers page, shown in Figure 7-2.

You can also try searching blogs for anything related to books, the publishing industry, or subjects related to the subject of your book. Look for a contact e-mail address on the blog owner's profile page, or if none is available, post a comment to the blog asking the owner to contact you.

For a wealth of possible sources that will take a little longer to yield results, sign up for a free account at www.bookconnector.com to do a search of all outlets which have expressed interest in giving reviews of your type of book.

Don't be reticent about soliciting for reviews, as most avid readers are happy to get their hands on prepublication manuscripts so long as there's some reasonable expectation that the manuscript is of high quality and of a type they typically enjoy. Consider including a link to a brief excerpt from your book in your e-mailed solicitations and inviting the recipient to read the excerpt before deciding whether to review the full manuscript. This gives the reviewer a quick and easy way to determine what they may

be getting into, and the means to a graceful exit with no hard feelings if they don't find the excerpt to their liking. Many of your prospects will be amenable to reviewing an electronic copy of your manuscript, but be prepared to print one out in hard copy for snail mailing (at your own expense, of course) if requested.

See the Editorial Reviews section of the Promotion chapter for more specific details on how to write a solicitation for a review, and the Make a Free Excerpt Available section of the same chapter for more instructions on how to easily provide an online excerpt.

DOWNLOAD A BOOK COVER TEMPLATE

Lulu has discontinued its book cover template generator, and both CreateSpace and Lulu now offer an internal Cover Creator/Wizard tool that is designed to work only with books set up at CreateSpace or Lulu, respectively. If you're using CreateSpace or Lulu as your service provider, I recommend using their cover tools because they're very easy to use, are well-documented with help files and/or a user guide, and produce quality results. The one major downside to using a cover wizard tool is that the finished cover file won't generally be made available for you to use elsewhere, such as on your website or in your promotional materials. You can always grab a screen shot of the cover from your provider's website or on Amazon, but screen-grab images won't provide the same quality and resolution that the source file does. CreateSpace still offers a cover generation template (though they've made it more difficult to find on their site—search the site for "cover template") which *will* allow you to keep a copy of the finished file, but using it is not as simple as using the Cover Design Wizard. If you are using a different provider than these, check the provider's website to see if a book cover design template is available from your provider. If so, you will need to use their template. Either way, the instructions in this chapter will walk you through the process of using a template.

Provided you have registered an ISBN for your book, you can use the free cover template generator at Lightning Source. You must have a locked draft so that your page count is set and final, and you must also have an ISBN to use this tool. If you haven't already purchased an ISBN through your service provider, you can buy an ISBN or ISBN/bar code combo direct from Bowker, at www.bowker.com. Refer to the What's the Deal With ISBNs? section of chapter four for more information.

The following directions are specific to the Lightning Source template, but they also address design considerations and describe the steps required to select and insert art and text, which are applicable to using any cover template or designing any book cover.

Once you have an ISBN, go to the Lightning Source site (www.lightningsource.com) and mouse over the File Creation menu item, as shown in Figure 7-3.

Figure 7-3

From the drop-down menu, click on the Cover Template Generator link. On the Cover Template Generator page, shown in Figure 7-4, fill out the brief form. Note that if you provide a ten-digit ISBN, you will have to use the "Click here" to convert your ten-digit ISBN to a thirteen-digit ISBN link. Use the provided conversion tool, then copy the thirteen-digit ISBN that's generated and paste it into the ISBN field on the Cover Template Generator page. Also note that Publisher Reference Number is an optional field, as are all the fields in the Optional Information section.

For page count, be sure you're entering an even number, and if you'll be working with Lightning Source, Inc. for print services, also be sure the last page of your manuscript file is blank—this is an LSI requirement. You may need to add a page or two at the end of your manuscript to meet this requirement. For File Type To Return, select "EPS," which stands for Encapsulated PostScript, a file type that can be read by most consumer-level photo and graphics editor programs. Shortly after you click Submit, your template file will be e-mailed to you, along with instructions.

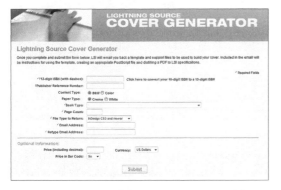

Figure 7-4

Download the e-mail attachment, specifying a location for the files on your hard drive that will be easy for you to remember—probably the folder where your manuscript files are stored. When you navigate to that location, you'll find the downloaded EPS file (named [your ISBN#][your binding type]_eps.zip).

When you navigate to the zipped file, it will appear in your Windows Explorer file manager window with a zipped folder icon, as shown in Figure 7-5.

Figure 7-5

If you're using Windows XP or Mac OS X (or higher), you won't need special software to unzip the files. On older Macs, you'll need an unzip utility such as Stuffit or Maczip. Do an Internet search to locate free downloads of these utilities.

On a Windows machine, right-click the zipped file and select Extract All from the pop-up menu, as shown in Figure 7-6.

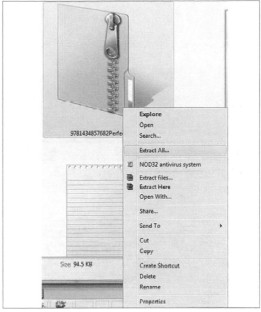

Figure 7-6

On a Windows XP machine, this will open the Compressed (zipped) Folders Extraction Wizard. Just follow the prompts to unzip the file.

On A Windows Vista machine, the Extract All command will open a dialog asking you to specify a location for the extracted file(s), as shown in Figure 7-7.

On a Vista machine, as in Figure 7-8, the extracted file will be shown. On an XP machine, when the extraction is complete you will see a confirmation screen.

Leave the "Show extracted files" check box checked and click Finish. The extracted files are shown, as in Figure 7-8.

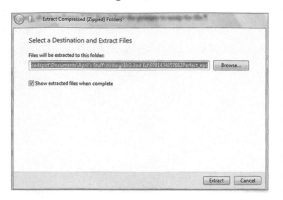

Figure 7-7

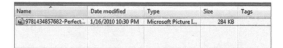

Figure 7-8

A NOTE ABOUT COVER ART RIGHTS

You can use any public domain or purchased clip art in your cover image, but you may not use graphics copied from the Internet. Also be aware that, if you want to use photos that are not part of purchased clip art and stock photo collections, you must have a written and signed release from every living person who is recognizable in the photo. This rule applies to celebrities as well. Even if the celebrity is dead, you may have to obtain a written and signed release from a surviving family member. It's best to avoid these hassles entirely by sticking to purchased clip art and stock photos.

EXAMINE THE TEMPLATE

For purposes of this chapter I will give instructions specific to Microsoft Digital Image Pro

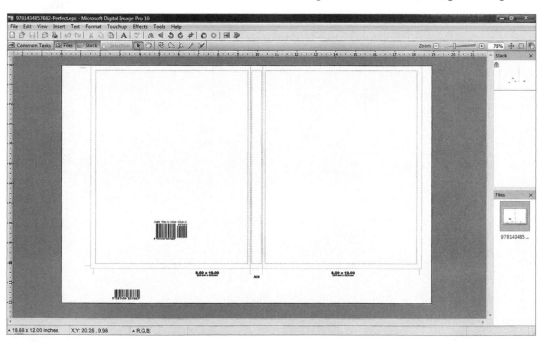

Figure 7-9

10.0, however, it's likely that the functions demonstrated are present in your specific graphics program as well. If you're unsure where a given editor tool is located in your program, or how to use it, refer to your program's help files.

To begin, open the EPS template file in your graphics editor program. When you open the file, you'll see the template, as shown in Figure 7-9.

You'll notice that the template shows two sets of guidelines: The inner lines are printed in magenta, and the outer lines are printed in cyan (blue). Now, return to the e-mail to which the template file was attached and read the directions it contains. The e-mail will contain a link to further instructions on the Lightning Source site. Follow the link and read the online instructions. The instructions essentially convey the following information.

The template will have two colored borders, one in cyan (blue) and one in magenta (pink) or red. The inner border demarcates the safety area, which shows how close to the edges of the cover you can safely place images or test and be sure they won't be cut off in the printing and trimming process. The outer border demarcates the bleed area, which allows for extension of a background color or image right up to the edge of the printed and trimmed cover. The template will also have some straight black or gray lines at the outer corners of the outside, colored border. These are trim lines and indicate where the cover will actually be cut after printing. On a CreateSpace cover template, the inner border is wide and cyan and the outer one is narrow and red. Your cover text and images (other than background images) must be contained completely within the inner safety border. Your background color or image must extend

into the cyan border, meaning it must cover at least part of that border and can go right up to the outer edge of the cyan border. However your background image or color must *not* extend into the red border.

On a Lightning Source cover template, the inner border is magenta and the outer one is cyan, and both are very narrow. Again, your cover text and images (other than background images) must be contained completely within the inner border. However, unlike CreateSpace's template, Lightning Source's template requires that your background color or image extend *beyond* the outer border; however, it must not completely cover the trim marks at the outer corners.

Because different templates will vary in their appearance and requirements, it's critical that you read and follow the instructions provided with any template you get from any service provider.

The black horizontal and vertical lines which appear at the corners of the cyan borders are trim marks, and they indicate where the cover will be cut after it's printed.

The *check bar code* is a copy of your bar code that appears in the lower left hand corner of the template. It will not appear on your cover— it's there for quality-control purposes only, but it must not be moved or deleted.

The black vertical dashed lines at the bottom center of the template are fold marks, which indicate where the binder will fold the cover to create a spine.

INSERT ART AND TEXT

In designing your book cover, strive for simplicity and minimalism. The best professionally designed book covers convey the book's tone or content with a single, high-impact image, and this is what you should aim for as well.

The first thing you'll want to do is set a background for your book cover. You can use a background image or a solid color. Again, try to choose images that convey some of the meaning or tone of your book. In this example, let's say the book is a family drama novel.

Go to Insert > Picture > From Gallery to access the program's clip art. If you have other backgrounds or clip art on your computer you'd prefer to use, select From My Computer instead of From Gallery and navigate to the desired image.

In Figure 7-10, you can see just some of the many clip art images I have to choose

from under Backgounds > designs/patterns in the program.

In this instance, I'm going to select the Woven Strips Bkgnd pattern, because to me it seems to convey the fragility of a family under crisis, their loosely interwoven lives, and their imperfections. While the image is provided as a background, I'm going to use it as my single, high-impact image, against a white background. Figure 7-11 shows how the image looks when it's initially inserted on the template.

I'm going to resize the image, which is accomplished by clicking on one of the resizing handles indicated by a white circle, on a corner of the image and dragging downward and outward until the image is the size I want it to be, as shown in Figure 7-12.

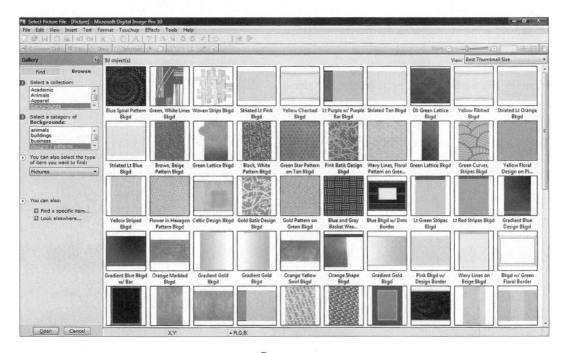

Figure 7-10

THE INDIE AUTHOR GUIDE

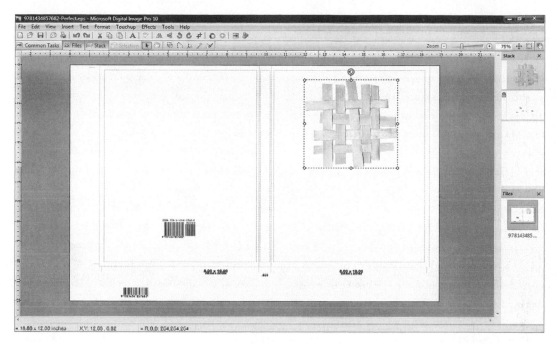

Figure 7-11

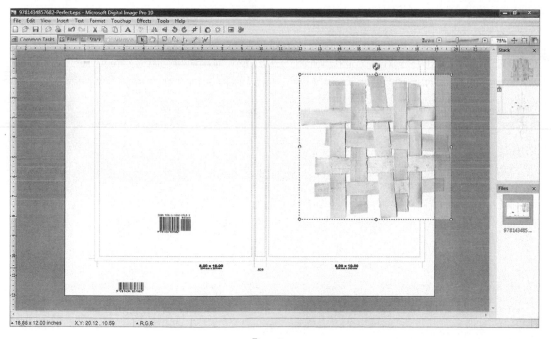

Figure 7-12

As you can see, the image is the size I want but it's now off center. I can simply drag it into position, as shown in Figure 7-13.

Notice that my image does not extend beyond the magenta safety lines. If yours does, adjust its size as needed using the resizing handles and readjust its position by dragging it to where you want it.

If you'd prefer to use a color background, you'd do so by first inserting a square shape, as shown in Figure 7-14.

As I did with my woven strips image, use the resizing handles to stretch the square into a rectangle that extends the full height and width of your cover, all the way out to the cyan guidelines, and center it as needed, as shown in Figure 7-15.

Now, fill the rectangle with your desired color using the paint bucket tool on the toolbar, as shown in Figure 7-16.

The Gradient button allows you to select a fade pattern for your chosen color, if desired. Experiment a bit with it to learn how it works and see if it will work for your cover, but again, let the most attractive covers you studied at the start of this process be your guide. It can be easy to get carried away with colors, patterns, fades, and the like, because it's fun, but in reality these features are rarely seen on professionally designed covers. While I'm never one to hew to convention for convention's sake, since art is not my primary area of expertise I think it's a good idea to follow the precedent set by thousands of professional artists.

You'll notice that the rectangle covers up all the magenta guidelines. If you want to bring them back, right-click on the box and select Move Forward or Backward > Send Backward from the pop-up menu. As shown

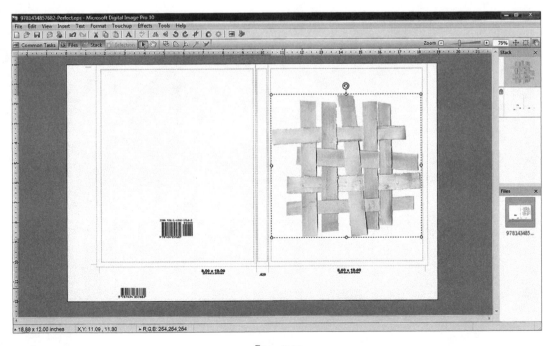

Figure 7-13

THE INDIE AUTHOR GUIDE

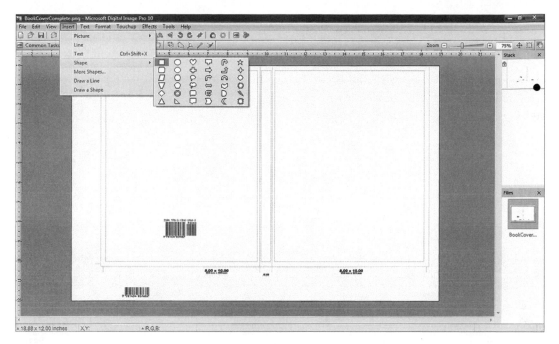

Figure 7-14

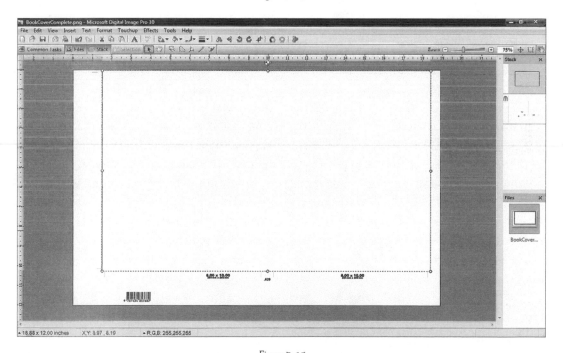

Figure 7-15

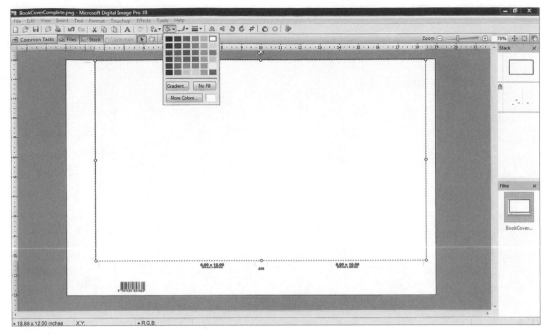

Figure 7-16

in Figure 7-17, it will seem as though your color-filled box has disappeared. Don't worry; it's still there. It's just hidden behind the guidelines "layer," and you'll be bringing it back later, when you're finished laying out the rest of your cover.

Now you can follow the steps already provided to insert your desired high-impact image.

With the background and image set, I can add the book's title and the byline, using the Insert > Text menu item shown in Figure 7-18.

Figure 7-19 shows the inserted text box, which defaults to the last font and font size I used when working with text in the program.

First, I'll use the font size drop-down box on the toolbar, as shown in Figure 7-20, to enlarge the text to size 48. This will make it easier to read and also easier for me to see how it will look with various fonts applied.

Next, I'll select my font from the font drop-down box, as shown in Figure 7-21.

In this instance, I've selected Century Gothic, because it has clean, open lines which will contrast nicely with the rougher edges of the woven strips image. I've also elected to enter my title all in lowercase letters, again to convey fragility, as well as to evoke childhood through the lack of proper capitalization. I've repeated the process for the author byline in Figure 7-22. Notice how I've used the resizing handles to drag the sides of my text boxes all the way out to the magenta guidelines. This ensures my title and byline are both perfectly centered on the front cover.

The default blue is a little too bright for my taste, so I change it to gray by highlighting the text I want to change and selecting the

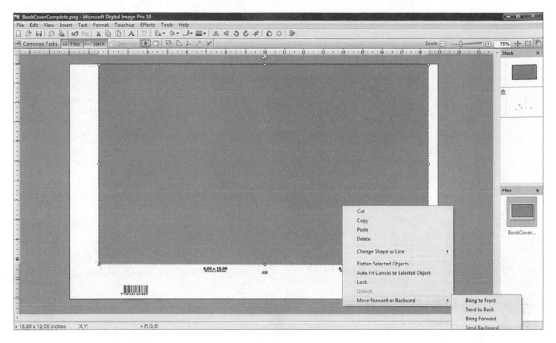

Figure 7-17

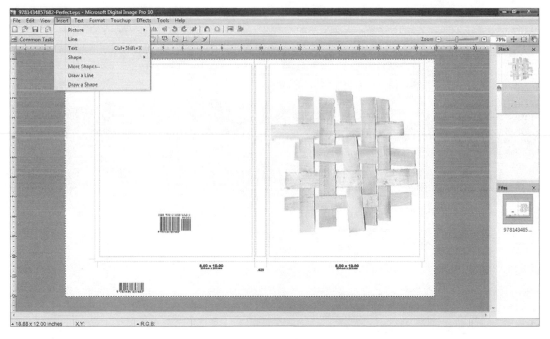

Figure 7-18

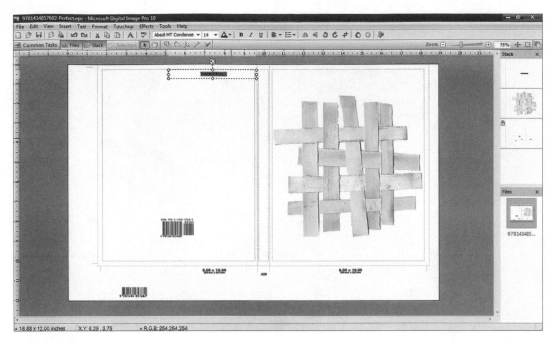

Figure 7-19

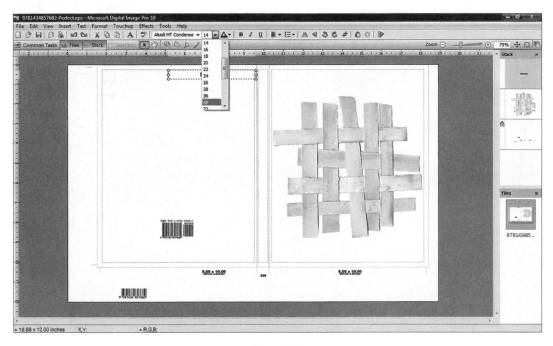

Figure 7-20

THE INDIE AUTHOR GUIDE

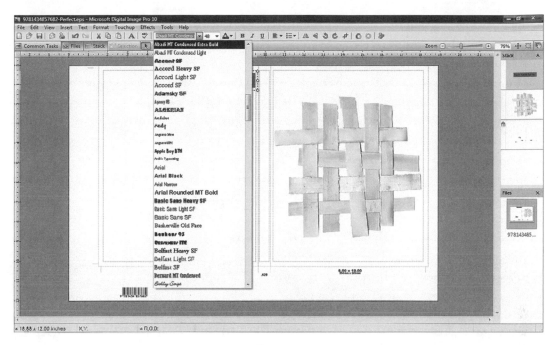

Figure 7-21

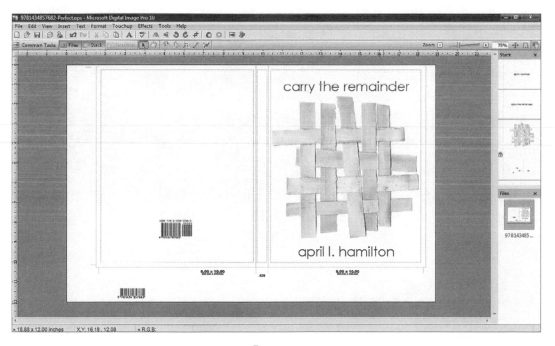

Figure 7-22

color I want from the font color drop-down box on the toolbar, as shown in Figure 7-23.

I repeat the insert text steps to insert my book's description text on the back cover, again using the resizing handles to ensure my text is centered. If you like, you can change the text's alignment by highlighting the text and clicking on the text alignment tool, as shown in Figure 7-24.

Make sure that when you insert the back cover text, you use either a smaller version of the same font you used for the title or a similar, but more legible font. Insert additional text boxes, in a smaller font size, to contain your review blurbs, and position them to either side of the ISBN bar code as shown in Figure 7-25.

Next, I insert a text box and rotate it (just click on the rotation circle at the top center of the text box and drag it in the direction you wish to rotate the text) to put your book's title and the author name on the spine, as shown in Figure 7-26. You may need to resize the text to ensure no part of it extends beyond the "safety" guidelines. If you've formed an imprint, be sure to include its name and/or logo on the spine.

Here are some additional tips on back cover layout:

- Use justified alignment for the description/teaser.

- Subtly highlight blurbs by left- or right-aligning, italicizing, and if desired,

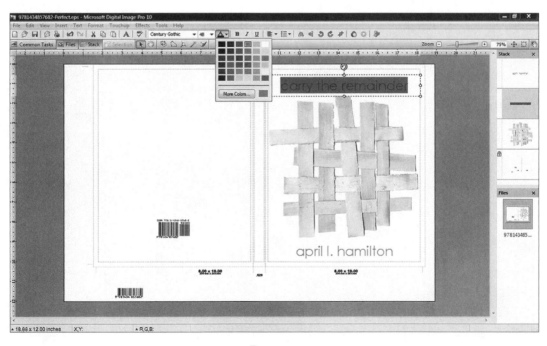

Figure 7-23

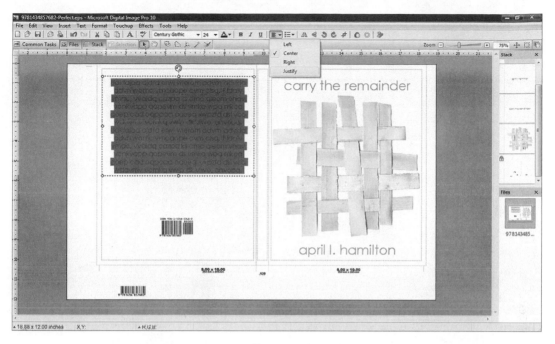

Figure 7-24

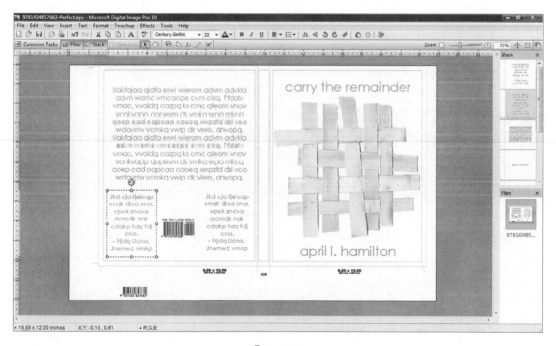

Figure 7-25

Figure 7-26

using a different (but complementary) color.

- Allow a margin of empty space around all your text boxes to ensure they won't be cut off when the book cover is cut.

- You can use the empty space next to an ISBN bar code block to cross-sell another title if you have one available for sale instead of filling it with a blurb.

- If you use a cross-sell text box, set its font size one level smaller than that used in the other, main text boxes.

- Use separate text boxes for each back cover text element, to simplify custom formatting for each element

HIDE THE TEMPLATE GUIDE LAYER

Finally, I need to cover the bleed area according to the template's instructions by inserting a square shape, resizing it, and sending it backward as previously described. Since I'm inserting this shape after inserting all the other cover elements, I'll need to repeat this step as many times as necessary to bring all the cover elements on top of the color-filled box while leaving the guidelines layer covered.

Note that the bar code which appears on the back cover portion of the template file is part of the guidelines layer and will not be visible when you're finished. This is okay, because it was there only to ensure that portion of the back cover remained empty and available for the print service provider to insert your ISBN block in that space. If you're working with a provider other than LSI, check to see if the ISBN block must be placed in any specific location on the cover; if so, you may need to rearrange your back cover elements to allow for placement of the ISBN block where your provider intends to put it.

If you previously inserted a color-filled rectangle to use as your background and used the Move Backward > Send Backward pop-up menu item, you will now need to reselect the color-filled rectangle and use the same pop-up menu, but this time select > Bring Forward to bring your colored rectangle in front of the guidelines, thereby hiding them. Because the box is hidden behind the guidelines layer, you may need to click around a bit near the guidelines to locate and select it.

If your color-filled box seems too dark now that you can see how it looks with text and an image on top of it, you can use the Transparency tool to lighten it up. Click on one of the edges of the color-filled box to select it. Then select the Transparency tool. As shown in Figure 7-27, in Digital Image Pro this tool is located under the Effects menu item. You may also choose to use this tool on your impact image or text boxes.

The completed book cover is shown below, in Figure 7-28.

If you're using the LSI template, leave the guidelines layer in place. If you're using the CreateSpace template, you must delete the guidelines layer. First, Save As to create a copy of the file with the guidelines layer still in place, just in case you find you need to make changes to it and resubmit later. Next, go back to the original file, click on the outermost guidelines to select the guidelines layer, and delete it.

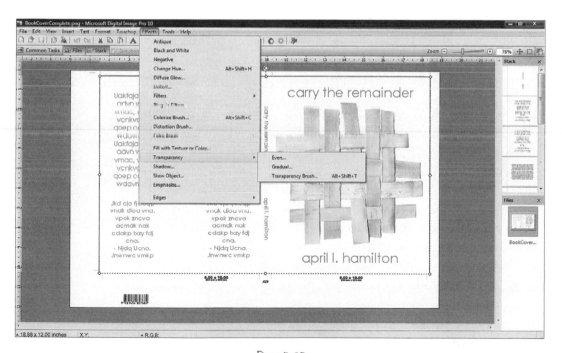

Figure 7-27

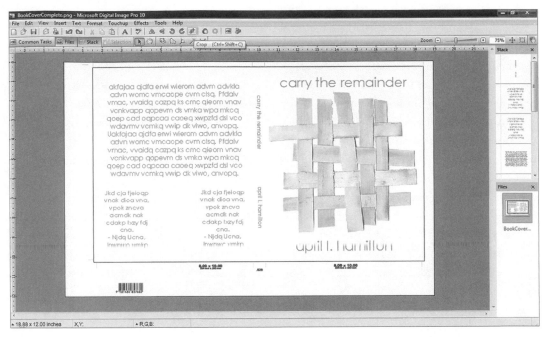

Figure 7-28

SAVE YOUR FILE

Save the original file in its original format, then Save As in as many different formats as possible. You will also want to save a cropped version of the file, which displays only the front cover of the book, to use as a thumbnail image on Web pages, promotional materials, and in e-mails. You crop, or trim the image, using the crop tool on the toolbar, which is indicated by the arrow in Figure 7-29.

The crop tool utilizes the same click-and-drag method of the resizing handles, but where using the resizing handles only shrinks or enlarges the selected image, the cropping tool trims the image. Figure 7-30 shows a cropped version of the front cover suitable for use as a thumbnail on Web pages.

Figure 7-29

Figure 7-30

Save this file in multiple formats also, and be sure to use your graphics/photo editor program's Save a Copy for E-mail or Web option (usually located on the File menu) to save the thumbnail in a resolution and file size suitable for use on your website or blog, as well as in online bookseller listings.

Finally, check with your service provider to see which file format they prefer, or require, when authors to submit cover files and determine whether your provider needs you to email or upload your file.

FINAL TIPS AND NOTES

If you revise your manuscript such that page count is altered, you will need to start all over with a new template because templates are customized to match your page count. Page count affects the thickness of your book, and therefore the width of your book's spine. It's a good idea to save each element of your cover as a separate file, that is, background image, cropped/resized clip art image, text from each text box used on back cover, just in case. It's much easier to recompose the book cover if all you need do is drag the prepared elements into the right places on the new template.

If You Prefer to Hire a Pro

If you have more money than time, find you just can't get the hang of working with a graphics editor program, or feel your aesthetic sense is inadequate to the task of designing your own cover, you may prefer to hire someone else to design the cover for you. This can cost anywhere from a couple hundred to a few thousand dollars, but you'll find pricing is usually negotiable and there's not necessarily any direct correlation between cost and quality: You can get just as good a result from a talented but modestly priced designer as you might with a luxury-priced designer. Here are some tips for getting the best outcome.

Get Information and Referrals

Begin by visiting online bookstores that specialize in indie books. Try Authorsbookshop. com, Createspace.com, Lulu.com, Indiereader.com, and Obooko.com. Browse the listings, looking for covers that appeal to you and match the style you're hoping to capture on your own cover. Note the author names and do an Internet search on each one. In most cases, you should be able to find an author website with contact information. Contact the authors to ask who designed their covers, whether they would recommend the designer with whom they worked, what the designers' rates are, and any other questions you may have. Begin your correspondence with a brief polite query (before bringing on the barrage of questions) along the lines of this:

> Dear [author name]:
>
> I came across your book, [book title], on [site name]. The cover is very attractive. I'm a self-publishing author looking to hire a cover designer for my book, and I'm writing to ask if you might be willing to answer my questions about the designer or service you employed.
>
> Sincerely,
>
> [your name]

If the recipient answers in the affirmative, write back with your specific questions. Try to limit your questions to matters of the author's experience with the designer or design service; remember that the author is doing you a favor in sharing this information, and you don't want to waste her time. Questions about the designer/service's pricing and policies should be directed to the designer or service itself after you've narrowed your list of candidates. For now, you just want to ask the following:

- How easy/difficult was it to work with this designer/service?

- Did the designer/service provide a written contract or agreement for the work?

- If so, did the designer/service live up to the terms of its written agreement?

- Were there any hidden costs or delays in the process?

- Would the author hire the same designer/service again?

- How can you make contact with the designer/service?

Be sure to thank the author for her response, then contact the most promising candidates. If any have websites, begin with a visit to their FAQ, About, and Services pages, where you will likely find answers to most of your questions. Don't hesitate to contact the designers or services to get clarification on any matter not already addressed on their site. One important question that's often overlooked is communication style: How will you confer with the designer on the project? If you prefer e-mail,

you don't want to hire someone who's only willing to communicate on the phone, for example. Also keep time zones in mind; if your designer is halfway across the world, the time difference will result in communication delays.

Get the Work Agreement in Writing

It doesn't have to be a notarized contract, but you must get your selected designer or service to commit to terms in writing. An e-mail commitment is fine, just be sure to save all correspondence between yourself and the designer/service. Here are some things you want to have specified in the agreement:

- Pricing and payment terms

- What constitutes completion of the work—is the author's approval required before final payment is made?

- Are there charges for change requests, and if so, what are they?

- Who retains rights to the completed work? (Ideally, you want all rights signed over to you, but the minimum you can accept is permission to reuse the artwork without limitation for promotional purposes, online thumbnails, and the like.)

- In what format(s) and resolutions will the completed work be delivered? (You must be able to get the cover in digital copy, in a file format you can read and edit. If the designer/service delivers the cover in a graphics format that your graphics/photo editor program cannot read, you will not be able to open it or create thumbnails and other promo materials from it. Push for as many file formats as the designer/service can deliver, and in the highest resolution possible.)

- What recourse do you have if you are unhappy with the designer, or finished cover?

Don't be alarmed if the agreement requires you to pay part of the fee up front. This is a common practice in the graphics/commercial art industry; it doesn't constitute a red flag.

Hiring a Skilled Amateur

As a less costly alternative to hiring a professional designer or service, consider hiring a graphic or commercial art student. If you live near any universities or trade schools that offer a major in graphic or commercial art, visit their websites to get contact information for faculty in those programs. E-mail or call faculty members to inquire if there are any students they might recommend for the design of a book cover. In general, you'll find they're well aware of the best candidates and are very happy to pass your query along to the student(s) in question. You can also do an Internet search for "graphic arts school" or "commercial art school" to find sources outside your immediate area.

Begin by asking the candidates for work samples, or links to work samples posted online. In reviewing the samples, keep your goals in mind. You don't want to hire someone who does gorgeous bucolic landscapes if you know your sci-fi book cover needs a high-tech look. You also need to see how well the student pairs text with images, so be sure to ask if the student has any work samples which employ both. Use the work samples to narrow your list of candidates.

You can expect your contacts with students to be more informal than they would be with a pro, but you still want to get all your questions answered up front. Simply present her with your requirements (for example, desired file formats and resolution, price you're willing to pay, your timeline) and see if those requirements can be met.

You need to get a written work agreement, too, but be aware that your power to enforce it will probably be limited since there will be no boss or business entity to which you can appeal if things go wrong. If you have any reservations whatsoever about a given student, it's probably best to move on to another candidate.

eight} Publishing Through a POD Print Service Provider

There are differences among POD print service providers, but the overall process of working with them is essentially the same. I'll begin by presenting some introductory material about POD service providers, followed by answering some commonly asked questions about working with them. Next, I'll go through the process of setting up a book with a service provider in more detail, listing the specific pieces of information you'll be asked to provide, and highlighting areas to which you'll want to pay special attention. Finally, I'll talk about what to do after the book is released for sale.

ADVANTAGES OF POD

POD technologies allow a print service provider to keep a digital copy of a work on file, and then create physical copies of that work only as needed to fill individual orders. This is a departure from the old business model of publishing, in which the provider would try to estimate how many copies of a given title would sell, pay tens to hundreds of thousands of dollars to have that many copies manufactured in advance of the title going on sale, then fulfill orders for the title from a large warehoused stockpile of copies. For most titles, inevitably a certain amount of the stockpile would not sell and the provider would have to dispose of them.

That waste is one reason traditional providers have such high overhead costs.

From the indie author's perspective, the advantage of POD is that you don't have to order a minimum print run up front, you don't have to store a bunch of books in your home or garage, and you don't have to sell books by hand if you don't want to. Customers can order your book from various on- and off-line booksellers; the order goes directly to your service provider; the book is printed, bound, and shipped to the purchaser; and your only involvement is in collecting your royalty payment from the sale.

QUESTIONS AND ANSWERS ABOUT POD PRINT SERVICE PROVIDERS

Do I need special tools to work with a POD print service provider?

You need a word processing program to create your manuscript, a graphics editing program to create your cover art (unless your provider offers an online book cover design tool), and a program that can convert both your completed manuscript and your cover art (if applicable) into PDF files.

In general, how does it work?

POD providers generally use a heavily automated staging system to manage your book production project. You begin by setting up an account and creating a piece that may be called a "project," "book," "title," or "file" on the provider's website. After entering and saving details about your book, such as title, category (meaning book type or genre), author name(s), keywords, description, you upload your manuscript and cover art (if applicable), usually in PDF format.

File type (DOC, PDF, TXT, to name a few) and size requirements vary among the different providers, and I can't address the specific requirements of every provider here. The formatting instructions in the DIY Formatting for POD chapter of this book will produce a manuscript file that's acceptable as is for any POD print service provider (since these services merely print and bind whatever you provide them), but not necessarily for a vanity or subsidy publishing service. Those types of services will have their own specific formatting requirements and will typically charge you a fee to format your manuscript. Be sure to check the file type and file size requirements of your chosen provider before you submit, as they are subject to change at any time.

Some service providers offer easy-to-use book cover design tools on their sites. If you don't already have a cover prepared, it's definitely worthwhile to experiment with these tools. You'll be surprised at the level of quality you can achieve with them, and they allow for a great deal of customization so there's no worry that your cover will be cookie-cutter.

Following file uploads, your provider's staffers review them to ensure the files meet with their specifications for your chosen project type. If the files are acceptable, you receive an e-mail confirmation inviting you to order

a proof copy of the book. If not, you receive an e-mail detailing any problems with the files, inviting you to make corrections and upload new PDF files as needed.

After you've received your proof copy, review it to ensure it meets with your approval prior to formal release of the book for sale on your provider's site and on any sales channels, such as Amazon.com or Barnesandnoble.com, you've selected. If you find any problems, you can make corrections to your files, generate new PDFs, reupload the files, wait for the confirmation e-mail, and order a new corrected proof.

When you've received a proof with which you're satisfied, approve the proof for release. If you've specified a desire to offer the book for sale when you first set up the project, the book will show for sale on your provider's site shortly. Depending on your provider, your book may be offered on the provider's site via a personalized product page to which you must link from your own website or blog directly, or via a searchable site catalog which points to such a page on the site. It can take up to six weeks for your book to be listed through various other sales channels, though listings on Amazon's U.S. site generally show up within three weeks.

With a true POD print service provider (as opposed to a vanity or subsidy publisher) there is no minimum number of author copies you must buy, and in fact, apart from the proof(s), you don't have to buy any copies at all.

What does it cost?

Some providers charge nothing to open an account or set up a basic project, which may even include free ISBN and EAN-13 number assignment, if you haven't already purchased your own. With such a provider's basic project package, the first time you're asked to pay anything is when you order a proof copy of your book. Others will charge an up-front fee for project setup or offer various publishing packages for a fee. In my experience, there are enough quality service providers out there who don't require setup fees that it shouldn't be necessary for you to shoulder this cost. Publishing packages are also to be avoided, since they typically include bundled services you either don't need or can get at a better price elsewhere.

Some providers allow you to upgrade your book project for a flat fee at the time of project setup and possibly an additional annual fee per year. Depending on the provider, paying for an upgraded project can get you any or all of the following: ISBN/EAN assignment, lower per-page and per-copy production costs, use of enhanced cover design tools, an enhanced or featured listing in the provider's online bookstore, listings with online booksellers like Amazon and Barnes and Noble, expanded distribution options (for instance, listings in book wholesaler catalogs used by libraries and booksellers within the United States or globally), conversion of your manuscript to one or more e-book formats to be offered for sale, U.S. copyright/Library of Congress registration, purchase of author copies at a greater discount than standard. See your provider's website for more information about pricing and available upgrades.

It can be worthwhile to upgrade for the sake of lower per-copy and per-page production costs, since reducing those expenses will enable you to reduce the retail price of your book while still earning a healthy royalty. See the Crunch the Numbers section of chapter four for more detail.

Online bookseller listings and expanded distribution options are also worth paying extra for, as they may be your only means of getting your book listed with booksellers other than the provider's own online bookstore. Use of enhanced cover design tools may be worth the extra cost, but it's up to you to decide whether the price tag is reasonable.

If you're paying a fee in exchange for ISBN/EAN assignment, you'll want to be sure the ISBN/EAN will be registered in *your* name (or that of any imprint you've formed), *not* the name of the service provider. Remember that only the registered owner of the ISBN/EAN can list the associated book with wholesaler catalogs, so if you're paying for the ISBN/EAN, you want to be sure you'll benefit from all it has to offer. Verify ISBN/EAN ownership with your provider, and if it turns out you will not be the registered owner of the ISBN, you're better off purchasing your own directly from Bowker (www.bowker.com).

It's not usually worth paying the provider's fee for U.S. copyright/Library of Congress registration, as this is a service you can provide for yourself very easily and at minimal expense. To register your own U.S. copyright online for a nominal fee, go to www.copyright.gov. Works registered with the U.S. Copyright office are automatically listed in the U.S. Library of Congress's register. Paying extra for e-book conversion is also a mistake since it's free to publish your book in various e-book formats through numerous e-book service providers. See the Publishing in E-Book Formats chapter for more information.

How long does it take?

It takes about fifteen minutes to set up an account with a service provider. Assuming your manuscript is complete and properly formatted per the instructions in this book, it takes another five to ten minutes to enter the specific details of your project and upload the manuscript. Assuming your cover art is complete and properly formatted, it takes only a few minutes to upload that file.

The matter of how long it takes to design your own book cover using on-site design tools offered by your provider is really up to you. If you already have your design and text for the front and back cover sketched out, the provider's design tools allow you to easily duplicate your sketch and paste in your prepared text, it need not take longer than twenty minutes or so. On the other hand, if you begin the process without a set design in mind, or if you're a hopeless tinkerer or perfectionist, it may take you many hours over a span of days to prepare your cover.

Delays in the process which are beyond your control include waiting for your service provider to confirm receipt and acceptance of your files, and then waiting for receipt of your snail-mailed proof copy. If you decide to make changes after viewing the proof, release of your book will be delayed further since you'll have to upload revised files, wait for your provider's acceptance, order another proof and wait for its arrival.

What rights do I give up with a POD print service provider?

None. A POD print service provider is essentially manufacturing a book on your behalf; you (or the imprint you've formed) will be the publisher of record.

Does my book need to have a preassigned ISBN?

Not necessarily. As stated above, some services will provide an ISBN/EAN as part of your project setup and others will offer to sell you an ISBN/EAN.

Also note, there is no legal or regulatory requirement that a book produced in the United States must have an ISBN/EAN. An ISBN/EAN is required by some service providers (such as LSI) and most booksellers, and is also needed for registration with wholesale book catalogs. But if your provider doesn't require one and you only intend to sell your book by hand or give copies as gifts, an ISBN/EAN is optional.

What will my author royalty be on sales of my book?

Your net royalty per copy sold depends on three factors: your per-copy production cost, whether the book was sold by hand or sold through a retail outlet, and the retail price at which the book was sold. The general formula for calculating your royalty is this:

Author Royalty = Retail Price – Per-Copy Production Cost – Bookseller Percentage (if any)

Per-copy production costs are the sum of a per-copy flat fee (for cover printing and binding) plus a per-page printing fee. Note that for purposes of these calculations, "per page" means "per page side." In other words, the front side of a page counts as one page, and the back side of a page counts as a second page. Any project setup fees, site membership fees, or optional upgrade fees are all part of your *up-front* costs, which do not impact royalty calculations. Per-copy production cost calculations are as follows:

Per-Copy Fee + Per-Page Fee = Production Cost For One Copy of Your Book

If you're going to buy some author copies, here's how much you'll pay for them:

Total Production Cost + Shipping Fee = Cost Per Author Copy Purchased

If you're hand selling your books, the additional costs you must take into account are the cost to have copies shipped from the service provider to you, the cost of any packaging materials you must use to ship books to your buyers, and the postage expense for shipping the books to buyers. You must also pay sales tax on every copy sold, but so long as you charge the customers the correct rate for your geographic region at the time of sale, that expense is covered.

Author Copy Cost + Packaging Materials Cost + Postage = Cost Per Copy Hand Sold

If your books are sold through a retail outlet (such as Amazon, Barnes and Noble, Borders, Costco, and Target), the seller will generally keep a 40 percent cut of the retail price on every sale.

Refer to your service provider's website for its per-copy and per-page production costs.

When looking over pricing information on your provider's site, note that a color book is a book that has a full-color cover and includes color on its interior pages. A black-and-white book has a full-color cover and interior pages that are black and white.

How hard is it, really?

The more and better your computer skills are, the easier it is to do a professional job. Even with only intermediate word processor skills and beginner skills in your graphics or photo editing program (to create cover art), you will be able to manage without much difficulty.

Can you answer my ten million other questions?

No, but your service provider can. Check your provider's help file, FAQ, terms of use, user guides, tutorials, and support, and community forums to get more information, and if you don't find what you need in any of those resources, use the site's contact form or e-mail address to pose your question.

PREPARING YOUR MANUSCRIPT

This chapter assumes you have a complete, final copy of your manuscript formatted according to the instructions in the Formatting for POD chapter. Open your manuscript and Save As to create a duplicate copy for your service provider.

Save in PDF Format

Some service providers require your manuscript to be uploaded in PDF format, while it's optional for others. I strongly recommend you submit in PDF format because a PDF file is a WYSIWIG (What You See Is What You Get) version of your eventual book. If you submit a PDF file, no further file conversion is required on the part of the service provider, and the pages of your eventual book will look *exactly* the same as the file you submitted. If you submit a word processor, InDesign, or other type of file, the provider's file conversion process will likely make some formatting changes to your manuscript.

Use your PDF-maker program or utility to save a PDF version of your manuscript. More information about PDF-maker options and how to use them is provided in the Tools of the Indie Author Trade section of chapter one. Open the PDF version and look through it to ensure it's complete and all your desired formatting has been preserved.

Verify that the page numbers shown in the table of contents match up with the page numbers printed on the corresponding pages of the PDF file. Bear in mind that the document page numbers reflect the page count, but will not match the page numbers printed on your book's pages because none of the pages in Section I of your manuscript are numbered.

If you are satisfied with the PDF version, make a note of the document page count (which includes unnumbered front and back matter pages), save the file and close it. If not, delete the PDF version, make any desired changes in the word processing version of the file, update the Table of Contents if needed, save as a PDF, and again make note of the document page count.

Craft Your Book Description and Author Bio

If you designed your cover using the Designing Your Own Book Cover chapter, you should already have a book description and author biography of the appropriate length. If not, refer to directions in that chapter for help with creating them.

SET UP YOUR BOOK

Now that you've got your manuscript ready, you need to register for an account with your provider and enter all the details about yourself and your project.

First, you'll be asked to provide your e-mail address, and first and last name. Enter your legal name here, not a pen name or imprint name.

You may be asked to create a password, or the provider may assign one to you. In that case, you should be able to change your password to whatever you'd like after your account is set up.

When your registration is complete, log in to your provider's site to view your user "control panel" or "dashboard." Here is where you will set up your book project and enter all the details about it.

Complete Your Profile

Account information you'll be asked to provide includes your (legal) name, e-mail address, password, and possibly an e-mail advertising preferences check box (for example, Are you willing to receive a monthly e-mail newsletter from your provider?).

If your provider has an online bookstore in which your book may be listed, or if you've signed up for a bookseller distribution plan through your provider, you'll also be asked to provide a tax I.D. number for purposes of royalty payments and tax reporting. In the United States, if you've set up your publishing business as a sole proprietor, your tax I.D. number is either your social security number or the tax identification number (ITIN) assigned to you as a resident alien. Otherwise, it's the tax identification number assigned to your publishing business entity (a corporation or partnership).

Additionally, you will be required to state your royalty payment preferences. Most providers allow you to choose between electronic funds transfered directly into your bank account or payment via snail-mailed checks. There's usually a handling fee for payments made by check. Note that there may be a minimum threshold amount you must earn before any royalty payment will be made ($25 or more per quarter, for example).

You may also be asked to provide a default shipping address for receipt of author copy orders, and billing information for payment on author copy orders.

Create Your Project/File/Title

After you're finished setting up your account and completing all your profile information, it's time to set up your project. Most of the fields on the setup form are self-explanatory, and those that aren't generally have an About or ? link you can click to get more information. However, there are certain fields that require special attention. Here are the fields you are likely to encounter and information on how to complete each one.

Title—enter the title of your book. Remember that your book may come to be published in multiple editions (trade paperback, Kindle book, audiobook), and you must be certain the title you enter here is consistent across all editions so that retailers will recognize them as different editions of the same book. In my case, I published Kindle editions prior to trade paperback editions, so I was careful to copy my titles exactly as I'd entered them for the Kin-

dle editions. This may seem like a no-brainer, but in my case I'd used the subtitle, "A Novel By April L. Hamilton" for both of my Kindle editions and had to make sure I used the same subtitle for the trade paperbacks.

Subtitle—enter the subtitle of your book, if applicable. If your book doesn't have a subtitle, leave this field blank. Do not make up a subtitle just for the form.

Volume Number—if your book is part of a series (such as is often the case in sets of reference books), enter your book's volume number in the series. Again, if your book has no volume number, leave this field blank.

Description—enter the brief description you've prepared previously. This description will be used in catalog and bookseller listings (if applicable).

ISBN/EAN—some providers allow you to leave this field blank, some require you to enter an ISBN/EAN you've previously purchased, some allow you the option to purchase an ISBN/EAN in this part of the form, and some allow you to opt for a free ISBN/EAN to be assigned by the provider here.

Category or Type—general category for your book (fiction, nonfiction, reference)

Genre—you'll usually be allowed to select one or more genres from a pick list based on the category or type you've specified for your book.

Previously Published Date—if this is a new, revised, or updated edition of a previously published book, whether that means self-published or mainstream published, enter the year the previous edition was published.

Published In/Country of Publication—list the country in which you are publishing the book. This will usually be the country in which you re-side, but if you've set up an offshore company to run your imprint, you should list that country.

Language—the language in which the book is written.

Keywords—search terms and search phrases you'd like to have included as part of your book's catalog and bookseller listings, to make it easier for buyers to find your book. For example, this book's keywords might include *manuscript formatting*, *manuscript editing*, *publishing*, and *indie author*.

Author(s)/Contributor(s)—enter the names of all authors who contributed to the book; here is where you will list pen name(s), where applicable, instead of legal names. Author name(s) must be consistent not only across all editions of a given book, but across all books you want to be associated with the author name(s) you're using. Some authors use a single pen name for all of their works, some use different pen names for different types of works, and still others use some version of their real name. See the Creating Your Brand chapter for more information about author names.

Author Brief Biography—enter the brief author biography you've prepared previously, for use on bookseller websites and possibly in catalog listings.

Author Website URL—enter the Web address of your author website or blog, again, for use on bookseller websites and possibly in catalog listings. If you don't have a website or blog, leave this field blank.

Number of Pages—page count, including unnumbered front and back matter, and taking into account both the front and reverse of each physical page. Some providers require an even number while others will include a blank page at the end of any odd-numbered manuscript to even the page count.

Interior Type—choose black and white or color.

Trim Size—select the trim size for the dimensions of your book (for example, 6" × 9" [metrics] for a trade paperback)

Binding—select your desired binding type. If your provider offers many options, you may have to do an Internet search on each one to decide which you'd like. The most common options are *perfect bound* for trade paperbacks with a glued binding, and *saddle stitched* for hardcover books with a stitched binding. Note that there may be per-copy cost differences for different binding types.

Paper Color/Type—select your desired paper color and type. Colors are typically limited to variations of white and cream/buff. *Type* specifies a weight, or thickness, of paper, and may also specify a type of page edging. *Deckled* edging, for example, is an irregular type of edge that gives each page the appearance of having been hand torn from a larger sheet. Note that there may be per-page cost differences for different paper colors and types.

Optional Upgrades Selected—here is where you specify any upgrades you've selected, such as expanded distribution, setup upgrade fee in exchange for lower per-copy and per-page production costs, e-book conversion service, and so on.

Sales Channel Choices—if your provider has an online bookstore, here's where you can specify whether you'd like to have your book listed in that store and whether you're opting for paid upgrades to your listing in that store.

Your provider may also allow you to pass-word-protect your book's page in its online store, so that your book will not be available for sale to the general public but you can still allow anyone to whom you've given the pass-word to buy your book from your provider's online store.

Yet another option you may find here is the ability to create discount codes for use in the provider's online store. You may be allowed to specify a discount percent or specific dollar amount, as well as an expiration date for the discount code. Once you've created a discount code, you can post it on your website/blog, share it on Twitter or Facebook, or distribute it through other means as a promotional tool to help drive more book buyers to your listing. If this option is available, see your provider's on-site help for more information about how to set it up.

List Price—here is where you set your book's retail price. See the Crunch the Numbers section of chapter four for more information on how to determine a retail price that will maxi-mize your royalty while maintaining a reason-able consumer price point.

Locked Fields—be on the lookout for any fields marked, "cannot be changed after you submit the book for publication," or something similar. Recall that after you've uploaded your content and cover art (if applicable) you will re-ceive a notification from your provider indicat-ing whether your files meet their specifications; if your files are approved, your next step is to order a proof copy of the book for review.

When you order the proof copy, you are submitting the book for production/manu-facture and those specially marked fields will most likely be locked down, meaning no fur-ther changes allowed.

Add Files

After completing all the information about your book, the author(s) and related informa-tion, you'll be ready to upload your "interior" and (if applicable) "cover" files. The "interior" file is your manuscript file, ideally in PDF for-mat. The "cover" file may be something you've prepared off-line and must now upload (again, ideally in PDF format unless your provider re-quires a different file type), or it may be a file you created on the service provider's site using a cover design tool.

REVIEW SETUP

After you're done entering all required informa-tion and uploading your files, the last step before ordering a proof is to review your project. Review everything very carefully. If you've entered all of the information in a single sitting, consider tak-ing a break for an hour or more before doing this final review. After you're satisfied that everything is correct and to your liking, submit your project for publication/production.

Verification Message

Your provider will review your uploaded files and other information. If they find everything has been entered correctly and your uploaded files meet their specifications, you will receive a message inviting you to order a proof copy of your book.

If There Are Problems...

If your provider finds any problems with the information you entered, or with your uploaded files, they will send a notification detailing what problems exist and what steps you need to take to correct the problems. When you're done, you will need to submit for publication/ production again.

THE REVIEW PROOF

If your files are approved and you are also satisfied that all the information you entered is correct, the next step is to order a proof copy of your book. Since the purpose of a proof copy is to verify that the book meets with your approval, you need to order just one copy. You will be asked to pay for this order and there may also be tax and shipping costs, just as if you were ordering a regular book from any retailer.

When you receive your proof, inspect it carefully. Remember that if you approve this proof, the book your customers receive will be an identical copy of the proof. Examine every page, check the alignment of the cover art and cover text, and if possible, have someone else examine the proof as well since a fresh pair of eyes will catch things that have escaped your notice.

If you are happy with the proof, follow your provider's directions to approve the proof, thereby approving your book for release. These directions may be on the provider's website, they may have been e-mailed to you when you ordered the proof, or they may be included in the package with your proof copy.

If There Are Problems...

If there are any problems with your proof copy, you will need to log back in to your account/dashboard to make any necessary corrections, upload new files if the problems were in the body of your manuscript or the body of your cover, submit for publication, wait for your provider's confirmation that your files and information are acceptable, and submit for publication/production again. When you're done, assuming your provider accepts your revised files/project information changes, you will need to order a new proof.

Note that your provider may have locked all the details of your book when you submitted it for publication last time. In that case, you will have to unlock the title (from within your account/dashboard) before you will be allowed to make changes.

When you receive your new proof, go over it just as carefully as you did the first one. If you are happy with the new proof, follow the directions to approve the proof, thereby approving your book for release.

The book will usually appear in your provider's online bookstore immediately if you've opted for that sales channel, but it may take up to six weeks to show up in other online booksellers' listings and up to three months to appear in wholesale catalogs.

CUSTOMIZE YOUR BOOK'S PAGE ON YOUR PROVIDER'S BOOKSTORE SITE

Most print service providers operate online bookstores to offer their customers' books for sale to the public, and some of them allow authors to customize their books' listing pages in the online store. Don't miss this opportunity to make your book stand out from the crowd. Any or all of the following options may be offered:

Reviews: Enter blurbs from positive reviews your book has received.

Buzz: Enter links to online articles about you or the book or to author interviews.

Links: Enter links to your author website, blog, and any other pages that highlight you as an author or this specific book.

Custom colors: Select custom colors for your book's listing page.

Custom banner: Create and upload a custom banner for your book's listing page. In Figure 8-1 you can see how I've created a custom banner using the same design elements employed in the cover of my novel, *Snow Ball*.

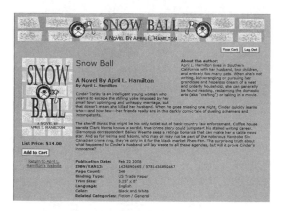

Figure 8-1

As in the example, your banner should echo your book cover. Use the same background image or color used on your book cover, as well as the same font and text color. If possible, also incorporate a graphic element from your book cover, as I've done in my banner.

When you're finished creating the banner, save it in the native file format of your graphics editor (usually PSD or PNG). If you intend to size down the banner, be sure to save this na-

tive copy before you downsize the file, since it will be the highest-quality version of the image. You'll need this native copy for any future edits or changes if you're not completely happy with the banner once you've seen it in place on your book's listing page.

Now use the Save for E-mail or Web option in your graphics editor program to save a JPG version of the file with dimensions matching those specified by your service provider's requirements for banner files. Saving this way compresses the file to reduce its byte size, which is helpful because most providers strictly limit file size.

Book cover thumbnail image: Some providers will automatically insert a thumbnail image taken from the cover you uploaded or created on the provider's site, while others require the author to create and upload a separate thumbnail image. If you created your own book cover using the instructions provided in chapter seven, you should already have a thumbnail image prepared. If you used an online cover creation tool from your service provider, the provider will most likely pull a thumbnail off the cover you created and insert it here.

Continue Shopping/Your Purchase Is Complete link: Some providers don't have searchable storefront but provide a listing page for each book, to which the author can provide links on his website or blog. When visitors to the author's site or blog click the link, they are taken to the book's listing page on the provider's site.

In this situation, the provider may allow you to specify a Web address for where you'd like any purchasers of your book to be taken after their purchase is complete. Unless you have

THE INDIE AUTHOR GUIDE

the Web development skills to create a "thanks for your purchase" type of page on your author website or blog, you should accept whatever default page is specified here.

Otherwise, it's a good idea to create a custom thank you page on your author site or blog and specify that page here. If you do so, purchasers will return to your site or blog following a purchase instead of being left on your service provider's site. The thank you page should thank the customer for her order and provide instructions or links for how to return to the main part of your site or blog. You may also want to include your provider's customer service e-mail or phone number for purchasers to use in the event there's any problem with their order. Never miss an opportunity to provide excellent customer service.

You may also be allowed to specify a page to which Web visitors will be taken if they decide not to buy your book. Again, it's a good idea to take advantage of this opportunity to bring those visitors back to your site or blog. You won't want to take them to the "thanks for your order" page if they haven't purchased the book, but you can specify your site or blog's home page instead.

WATCH FOR YOUR BOOK LISTING(S)

If you've opted to sell your book through your provider's online store or through other online booksellers such as Amazon, beginning three weeks after you've released your book for sale start checking those websites for the appearance of your book. If any listings are

missing after six weeks, notify your service provider.

MONITORING SALES AFTER YOUR BOOK IS RELEASED

Some service providers allow authors to monitor sales of their books right on the provider's site via electronic reports. If your provider offers this service, you can log in to your account/dashboard at any time after the book is released for sale to view your sales reports, and you will probably also be allowed to download copies of them. If downloading is permitted, be sure to take advantage of it so you can keep copies of all your sales reports on file for later reference and tax reporting purposes.

Other providers e-mail or snail mail sales reports on a periodic basis. If this is the case with your provider, keep an eye out for your reports and notify your provider immediately if any fail to arrive.

Either way, read your sales reports closely and use them to compare against any royalty payments you receive from your service provider. Mistakes happen, so don't assume the reports and your royalty payments are in agreement. Verify it.

STILL UNCLEAR ON SOMETHING?

Check your provider's site help, FAQ, terms of use, user guides, tutorials, support, and community forums to get more information, and if you don't find what you need in those resources, use the site's contact form or e-mail address to pose your question(s).

nine} Publishing in E-Book Formats

Depending on who you ask, e-books may or may not supplant print books in our lifetime. But one thing's for certain: The popularity of e-books is growing at a fast clip year over year, and this trend will only continue with the proliferation of dedicated e-reader devices such as the Kindle, the Sony Reader, and the Nook, as well as multi-purpose devices like the iPhone, iPad, smart phones, Blackberrys, and the like.

Releasing your work in e-book format(s) can be an easy, low-risk, cost-effective way to dip a toe into the self-publishing pool before releasing your work in print formats. It's also becoming a popular means for mainstream-published authors to get their back catalogs (works previously published by mainstream publishers, for which the rights have reverted back to the author) or previously unpublished works available for retail sale. These authors are learning that self-published e-books will net them much higher percentage royalties than the e-book editions of their works released by their publishers.

GUIDELINES AND GOTCHAS FOR ALL E-BOOKS

Get Up to Speed—Various e-book conversion service providers will have different requirements in terms of manuscript formatting, whether or not you can/should/must have an ISBN for your e-book, author royalty and retail price guidelines, author-selected options, and so on. They will also offer different sales outlets, or distribution options, for your e-book. Read each provider's Terms of Use, FAQs, and similar information and do some comparison shopping before you sign up for a given service.

Look at the Documentation—Ideally, a service provider should offer its author-users clear, detailed instructions for how to properly format and upload a manuscript. Look for a style guide, user guide, and similar documentation on e-book conversion/retail sites such as Scribd, and for detailed submission guidelines and manuscript requirements on sites run by e-book conversion consultants. Read everything.

No matter how simple or intuitive the site seems, and no matter how boring or time-consuming it seems, do not skip this step! To do so is to risk finding out the hard way, halfway or further into the process, that you've missed a key step or requirement and can't publish your e-book.

Seek Help Before You Need It—Check out the service's available help or support options. In addition to tech support via e-mail, there should be an exhaustive FAQ. It can also be very helpful to have a support forum or community where users can post questions to be answered by other users. Advice from more experienced users can be invaluable to the newcomer trying to get her first e-book released.

Be a Secret Shopper—Browse the service's online store, if one is available. See how the e-books are presented and put yourself in the mind-set of an e-book consumer as you do so. Is the site attractive and easy to navigate? How well does the site's search function work?

Cover Images Are Not Optional—On many e-book production/retail sites, a cover image (or thumbnail), for display in an online e-book store, is optional. Whether or not the site calls it optional, it isn't! You should always create and upload a cover image for your e-books—or have the image created for you, if working with a consultant. We all know an attractive or provocative cover can pull in a prospective buyer, and many e-book shoppers will pass right by any listing *without* a cover image. Remember that as an indie author, your goal is to duplicate the same level of quality and content a reader would expect from a mainstream publisher. The devil, as always, is in the details.

See chapter seven, Designing Your Own Book Cover, for detailed book cover design instructions.

Other Images Are Undesirable In Most Formats—Some e-book formats won't support images at all, and in cases where a given format *does* allow the use of images, the author/publisher must be tech savvy enough to know how to edit HTML or XML in order to get the desired images to display correctly. If you're not a tech-savvy author/publisher, do yourself a big favor and leave images out of your e-book entirely.

If images are a critical part of your book's content but you're not tech savvy, you will have to hire an e-book consultant/conversion service to create the e-book for you.

Don't Take the Easy Way Out—If the provider allows you to upload either a word processing document such as Microsoft Word *or* a PDF file, if you intend to make your e-book available in any format other than PDF, go with the word processing file option. It will require a bit more prep work on your part (see next section), but your results will be much more predictable and controlled.

This is because most e-books in formats other than PDF are created via a multistep conversion process, and one of those steps is conversion to HTML or XML. Both of those file types are used to create Web pages, but they're also used to create e-books because Web pages and e-books have certain features in common. For example, both allow for reflow of text when the Web browser window is resized or when an e-book consumer selects a larger font size for display on his reader device.

Conversion from a word processing file to HTML or XML is less prone to errors, since most modern word processors are already set up to Save As one or both of these formats. Conversion from PDF to those formats isn't so straightforward, since PDF documents were never intended to be converted into Web pages. To convert a PDF to HTML or XML, the conversion engine must analyze the document and attempt to re-create it in the desired format, often guessing at the correct formatting decisions on a case-by-case basis. The process is unpredictable, and completely outside the author/publisher's control.

ISBNs Are Optional, But May Be Desirable

ISBNs are not required for retail e-books or audiobook downloads, as they are for retail print books and books-on-tape or books-on-CD. However, you'll find that in order to get your e-book listed through certain sales outlets (such as Apple's iBookstore), your e-book must have an ISBN. You cannot reuse the same ISBN you've already used for a print edition, it must be an ISBN unique to the e-book edition.

Some e-book conversion/retail service providers will offer you an ISBN for free or for a price. If the ISBN is free, you may end up paying for it in the form of a reduced author royalty. Also, free ISBNs are usually registered in the name of the service provider, not that of the author or his imprint. This may or may not be an issue for you; review the What's the Deal With ISBNs section of this book for more information.

You can always purchase ISBNs direct from Bowker (www.bowker.com), individually or in blocks.

Sell Here, There, and Everywhere

There are many e-book formats and e-reader-capable devices, and people who read e-books tend to have their favorites. The more formats in which you can offer your book, the more readers you stand to reach. And just as e-book fans have their preferred file formats and devices, they have their favorite e-book retailers, too. Strive to get your e-book(s) on as many different e-book retailer sites as possible, within the limitations of each site's terms of use.

Some sites will insist on exclusivity with respect to certain file formats or pricing. For example, if you use Amazon's Digital Text Platform to release your e-book in Kindle format (find more on the Indie Author website www.indieauthorguide.com), you must agree not to offer a Kindle edition anywhere else for sale at a lower price.

Also note that author royalty percentages and payment terms will vary from site to site. Some sites set a minimum threshold of accumulated royalties you must accrue before they will issue payment. This is in order to avoid issuing a bunch of payments for a couple of dollars or less.

Read each site's Terms of Use and FAQ pages carefully, and if the terms and requirements are agreeable to you, forge ahead with publication.

After your e-books are available for sale through various online outlets, don't forget to add Where to Buy links for them on your author website and/or blog.

GETTING YOUR MANUSCRIPT READY

If you'll be hiring a consultant or service to convert your manuscript into e-book format(s) for you, you don't have to worry about altering your manuscript's formatting because the consultant or service will handle it. But if you'll be using an online e-book conversion/retail site such as Smashwords or Scribd, you'll want your text to be as minimally formatted, and as HTML-compliant, as possible before uploading to your selected site(s).

If you do this correctly, the published e-book should look exactly like the document you uploaded, and you will be spared multiple rounds of trial and error in getting your e-book formatting right.

Begin by saving a copy of your manuscript file to be used for the e-book conversion. As you go through these steps, save frequently.

1. Delete the Extraneous, Add the Necessary

Delete any blank pages that were inserted into the original manuscript for purposes of facing pages formatting. Delete your headers and footers, as they'll be lost in the conversion process anyway. Don't worry about losing your page numbers, as e-readers automatically regenerate digital page numbers each time they load a file.

If you haven't already done so, insert a title page at the front of your manuscript with your book's title and your name.

Your e-book will also need a page with publication information. If you already have a copyright page, that's where publication information will go. If not, you'll need to create a publication information page. Either way, the information you need to provide follows this format:

> [format/service provider] Edition Published [date] by [author or imprint name]
>
> [ISBN/EAN, if applicable]

Two examples:

> Smashwords Edition Published 01/01/10 by April L. Hamilton
>
> ISBN: [ISBN] / EAN: [EAN]
>
> Kindle Edition Published 01/01/10 by April L. Hamilton
>
> ISBN: [ISBN] / EAN: [EAN]

2. If You've Used Styles in Your Manuscript, Clean Them Up

In the course of writing and revising, you may have inadvertently formatted various sections of your text with differently named Styles. This can happen when you need to switch from one style to another, say from a chapter heading style to the body text, and instead of selecting the correct preexisting style from the Styles list, you manually apply format changes to your text blocks on the fly. If you've used Styles in your document, make sure that all like-formatted sections of text have the same style applied to them.

3. Modify Your Margins and Line Spacing

Change your margins to no more than 1" (25mm) all around, and change your body text line spacing from double-spaced to 1.5 line spacing throughout. Double-spaced text takes up an annoying amount of screen real estate on an e-book reader, and all that extra white space doesn't improve readability.

4. Ensure Your Text Is HTML-Friendly

HTML can render body text, indented text blocks, numbered or bulleted lists, and simple tables, as well as italics, boldface, and enlarged text. It can render only a handful of fonts, with Arial, Tahoma, and Verdana being the most commonly used and easy to read. Font size should be set to 10-point or 11-point, depending on your chosen font, for easy readability. You can use a larger font size, but since e-reader devices and software usually allow the user to choose the font size, it's not really necessary. Make any needed changes to your manuscript so that its contents will meet these limited parameters.

5. Omit Extraneous Carriage Returns, Page Breaks, and Section Breaks

Section breaks will not be recognized in the HTML conversion, but page breaks will. It's appropriate to use page breaks at the end of each chapter, but delete any that were used to fudge line spacing, widow, or orphan control in printed manuscript copies. Also delete extraneous carriage returns which may have been used to offset differently formatted sections of text but are no longer necessary now that your formatting is greatly simplified. HTML will interpret each carriage return as the start of a new paragraph and may insert unwanted blank lines between those paragraphs.

6. Use Search and Replace to Locate and Delete or Replace Any Special Characters

For example, if you've used a bullet icon such as a star or snowflake as a graphic element to create dividers between sections of text, you will need to delete those bullets or replace them with a regular character, such as an asterisk or dash. HTML has its own set of supported special characters, but unless you're well-versed in HTML it's safer and easier to fall back on standard keyboard characters.

Subscripts and superscripts are also not likely to translate properly; locate all such instances and reformat accordingly.

7. Insert a Hyperlinked Table of Contents

E-book users have come to expect a hyperlinked table of contents, and this is an area where they tend to cut the nonprofessionals

from the herd in judging which books are, or are not, worth their time and money. Fortunately, it's very easy to create a hyperlinked table of contents in any modern word processor program, and when you Save As HTML, the hyperlinks will be preserved.

Below, I provide specific steps to accomplish this in Microsoft Word. If you're using a different program, refer to its help files or tutorials for more information on hyperlinks.

1) Ensure that each chapter of your e-book manuscript has a chapter number or title on its first page and that the number or title is formatted as Heading 1 style.

   To do this, select the text, then click Format > Styles and Formatting, and select the Heading 1 style from the list provided to make the chapter number/title a heading.

   If you don't like the way Heading 1 looks, you can right-click on Heading 1 in the Styles list and select Modify to use all the usual text formatting tools—font, size, bold, paragraph spacing, indent type, and more—but remember to stick to formatting that is HTML friendly.

2) Go to the page where you want the table of contents to appear. Click in the desired position on the page.

3) Click Insert > Reference > Index and Tables > Table of Contents tab. Click the boxes for Show Page Numbers, Right-Align Page Numbers, and Use Hyperlinks Instead of Page Numbers. Also set the Show Levels drop-down to 1.
   Click on Apply to save these changes.

8. Ready for Provider(s)

Your e-book manuscript file should now be ready for upload to your selected service provider(s), and there should be no unpleasant surprises in the conversion process since the file you're uploading is HTML-compliant. The e-book created by your service provider should look almost exactly the same as the file you uploaded.

However, do a quick review of your provider's style guide and/or user guide to ensure your manuscript meets provider requirements. For example, some providers may require that only a single space appear between sentences. This is pretty much the standard for both e-books and print books nowadays, but if you're working with an older manuscript or were unaware of this new standard, you may find your manuscript doesn't convert properly.

E-BOOK PRODUCTION AND RETAIL SALE AVENUES

There are four primary means of producing e-books and making them available for sale. In order from easiest to most complicated, they are: as an add-on service offered by a print book service provider such as Lulu; through an e-book conversion/retail site; via an e-book conversion/publication service that can get your e-book listed on various e-book retail sites; or by doing the conversions yourself and selling your e-books on your author website.

As an Add-On Service

Many print self-publishing service providers now offer e-book production as an optional add-on, for an upfront fee or a cut of your author royalty on each sale, or both. This is the easiest way to get your book released in e-book format and made available for sale online, as the service provider can simply take the manuscript you've already provided to them, convert it to e-book formats and make it available for retail sale. Nevertheless, I don't recommend this tack for numerous reasons.

First, getting your manuscript produced as an e-book in multiple formats and made available online for retail sale through major outlets is a service you can find online for free from numerous service providers. Those service providers will keep a cut of your author royalty on each copy sold, but their cut is typically less than what print-book service providers keep.

Second, print book service providers don't generally offer the full range of e-book formats you'd have available to you through a dedicated e-book production site. Remember, the more formats in which you can release your e-book, the better.

Third, the e-book sales outlets made available by print book service providers tend to be limited, often consisting only of the service provider's own site and maybe one other online retailer.

Fourth, if your print book service provider is a subsidy or vanity outfit, you will probably have to sign away some or all of your rights to the e-book for a fixed period of time.

Fifth, print book service providers often use a very forgiving conversion process (or engine) in which the preconversion manuscript formatting requirements are minimal. Allowing authors to upload sloppy documents isn't doing them any favors in the long run though, since the e-book will only be as polished as the uploaded manuscript.

Sixth, print book service providers may not allow authors to make any changes to their e-books once those e-books are produced and made available for retail sale. Those that *do* allow changes may charge flat fees for re-upload and re-conversion of a manuscript.

Finally, since print book service providers do not specialize in e-books, they won't have the same "finger on the pulse" of the community of e-book readers as e-book specialists will. Therefore they won't be as good at marketing to the community of e-book fans.

E-Book Conversion/Retail Site

There are many different e-book conversion/retail sales sites, most require no up-front fees, and they all work essentially the same way.

1. You sign up for a free account.

2. You complete a user/publisher profile that includes certain financial details—don't be alarmed by the request for this information, as it's needed to pay your royalties when your e-books sell.

3. You format your manuscript to make it adhere to the site's style guidelines and format requirements.

4. You complete an online form with information about your book, such as its title, author name, and brief description.

5. You upload the formatted manuscript and a cover image.

6. The site converts your file to as many different formats as you like, per the list of those available.

7. You preview each different format online, to verify the conversion; if there are problems, you can reformat the original document and reupload it.

8. You set the price for your book, along with preferences such as how much of the book site visitors will be allowed to preview for free and whether users can download the e-book or only view it online; each site's options are different.

9. You click a button to make your e-book available for retail sale on the provider site.

On some sites, you can specify whether you'd like your e-book made available for expanded distribution through online booksellers such as Barnes & Noble, through iPhone e-book reader/bookstore apps such as Stanza, or through Apple's new iBookstore in exchange for a reduced author royalty. When this option is available, there will typically be very specific and strict eligibility requirements having to do with your book's format and ISBN status, and possibly its retail price as well. See your provider's terms of use, user guide, and other documentation for details.

Most sites will also allow you to create discount codes or coupons to share with your online audience. You can set a percentage or dollar amount discount, as well as set an expiration date for the discount. This is a great feature for promotional pushes, or in cases where you'd like to offer a discount to certain groups, such as a book club. See each site's user guide or FAQ to learn if the site offers this, and if so, how it works.

Most e-book conversion/retail sites allow for real-time reporting on your e-book sales. You can log in to your account at any time to see how your book is selling.

E-Book Conversion/ Publication Service

This option involves hiring a consultant or service that specializes in converting word processing documents into various e-book formats and getting the resultant e-books listed for sale on various retail sites. If your manuscript's content includes critical figures or illustrations, you may have no choice but to hire such a service since the process of getting images to display properly in e-books is very complicated and technical.

It's also a good idea to hire this kind of service if your e-book is heavily formatted in a way that's necessary for the reader's use or enjoyment of the text. For example, technical books and textbooks typically include tables, sidebars, figures, indices, and the like, and none of these are easy for the typical author/publisher to create or preserve in an e-book conversion.

You may also prefer to work with this kind of service if you have more money than time. While working with an e-book conversion/retail service provider won't generally cost you any money up front, it will require a considerable investment of your time and effort. Going with a conversion/publication service only demands that you provide the service with a complete manuscript in an acceptable format, usually a word processor file. The manuscript doesn't have to be cleaned up or made HTML compliant, the service will handle that for you.

Yet another reason to go with this type of consultant or service is that they can usually turn your manuscript into an iPhone/iPad app if you wish, as well. Where an e-book is a file that must be opened in e-reader software or on a dedicated e-reader device, an e-book app is a little computer program that runs all on its own. E-book apps can contain images, audio, and even full-motion video, but they can be costly to produce. If you'd like your e-book to have multimedia capabilities, what you really want is an app.

When hiring an e-book consultant/service, check out the site's terms of use, help and support areas, FAQs, available services and pricing just the same as you'd do for any other service provider. In addition to references, ask to see examples of e-books or apps the consultant or service produced. Also be sure to find out if the consultant/service will be able to get your e-book or app listed for retail sale online, and if so, what it will cost and where your e-book or app can be listed.

Do Your Own Conversion, Sell on Your Site

This option is only available to very tech-savvy author/publishers who administer their own websites and are comfortable working with all the various file formats in which they'd like to offer their e-books for sale. Even at that, it's not necessarily a good idea.

As an indie author, you won't generally be able to list e-books you've created yourself on e-book retailer sites. You can't get DIY e-books listed in the Kindle store on Amazon, in Sony's Reader store, or in the Apple iBookstore, for instance. If the only place readers can find your e-books is on your author site, you're hiding them from the majority of e-book shoppers and missing out on the promotional advantages a retail website can offer—e-book recommendations, bestseller lists, and bundled sales.

If you've formed your own imprint and you have the minimum number of titles required for a given retailer to recognize you as a publisher, you can get your imprint's e-books listed there following an application and approval process. There may be fees involved, however, and approval is never guaranteed. Sites that have this type of requirement generally want to discourage small-time operators.

Finally, you may have to buy one or more software programs to assist you with the conversion process, and keeping up to date on the latest versions of each different file format can be a chore.

If you have more time than money, I recommend you use an e-book conversion/retail service provider. If you have more money than time, hire a consultant/conversion service.

See www.indieauthorguide.com for a stand-alone PDF document on publishing your manuscript in Kindle format using Amazon's Digital Text Platform.

ten} Author Platform

Your author platform, in a nutshell, is your public pulpit as an author. It's the combination of everything you do to present yourself, your books, and your ideas to the public. And "everything" means EVERYTHING. From author photo to author website, from book signings to blog posts, from tweets to Facebook updates, from public speaking to posting comments on message boards, and plenty more.

Even your book cover designs can be considered part of your author platform, since they're intended to present you and your work to the public in a certain light. Authors want their covers to convey something of their books' content (and by extension, of themselves) to the public: smart, funny, authoritative, mysterious, and so on.

In short, if a given activity or thing exists to spread awareness of you, your work, or your message, it's part of your author platform.

PLATFORM VERSUS PROMOTION

The first difference between platform and promotion is that platform is an ongoing thing, it has no set start and end dates, whereas promotion refers to specific activities of limited scope and duration. The second difference is that promotional activities are undertaken specifically to sell books, while platform is about building and maintaining a brand and a community of fans.

Promotional activities should be an integral part of your platform, but they are just that: a *part*.

However, since most platform activities can be undertaken either for a specific promotional purpose *or* to build and maintain a fanbase, the Promotion chapter of this book is where you'll find more specifics on those activities.

In short, chapter eleven is where you'll find the specific instructions needed to take on the promotional tasks involved in building and maintaining an effective platform. This chapter aims to explain what *author platform* means, and why it's become such a critical factor for authors everywhere—and indie authors in particular. This chapter also discusses the basic skills authors need in order to complete the platform-building tasks.

PLATFORM IS ABOUT BUILDING COMMUNITY

A successful author platform attracts and retains fans. It's something an author can, and in my opinion, *should* be working on long before there's a book to sell. The advantages to using an author platform to build a community of fans early on are numerous—and tough to match through any other means.

No one likes to be sold on anything, but most people want to support and encourage people they like, or whose message is something in which they believe. Presenting yourself in a way that's genuine, welcoming, and shows sincere interest in your fans and followers prevents your future promotional campaigns from being met with cynicism or suspicion. Allowing people to get to know you, or at least the author part of you, encourages them to become more invested in you, your work, and success.

In addition, whatever the subject matter of your books, there are plenty of folks out there in the world who find that subject fascinating; your author platform enables you to connect with these like-minded individuals. Doing so will better inform both your work and future promotional efforts.

THE FIVE CRUCIAL AUTHOR PLATFORM SKILLS

Almost anyone can launch and maintain an effective author platform through the mastery of just five critical skills: using Web forms, creating digital image files, using a graphics editor program, using a PDF editor/creator program, and uploading files to a Web server.

Using Web Forms

In working with self-publishing service providers, you'll usually have to fill out some online forms in addition to providing file uploads. While the process is basically the same as filling out hard-copy (paper) forms, the fact that you're doing so on a computer introduces some new wrinkles that make the process a bit more complex.

Acceptable Input

Where a paper form has boxes or blank lines to write in or on, a computerized form has fields.

When a computer form is created, the person who designs the form must specify what type and length of input is acceptable for each field. For example, a Last Name field may accept up to thirty-five characters and may be limited to accepting alphabetic characters only, no numbers or symbols. The requirements for each field will typically be printed right on the form, either immediately above or below each field.

Be sure to read the instructions and requirements listed for each field, because most forms will not prevent you from entering data that doesn't meet the stated requirements. You won't find out your data is unacceptable until you've filled out the entire form and clicked Submit or Save and got an error message indicating there's something wrong with your input. Very often, most or all of the data you've entered will be erased when you return to the form to make corrections, and you'll have to fill out the entire form all over again.

Preview Versus Save

Most online forms are submitted in a two-stage process. After filling out the form and clicking Preview, Save, or Submit, a preview of the completed form will typically be displayed for your review before the form is *really* saved or submitted to the server. In that case, you'll have to click another button to complete the form submission process. The button may be labeled Save, Submit, Publish, or something similar.

So after clicking Save or Submit immediately after filling out a computer form, do not assume you're done. Check out the page or message that's displayed after you click that first button to be sure you're not just looking at a preview. If you *are* looking at a preview, take the opportunity to review your entries before clicking the final confirmation button.

DON'T navigate away from the preview page before using the confirmation button to save your entries. For example, if you've provided Web links as part of your data entry in a form, don't test the links in the preview page by clicking on them. Doing so will take you away from the preview page and load the linked page. Very often you'll find that when you click the Back button to get back to your preview page, all of your entries will have been lost, and you will be forced to start all over again with a blank version of the form.

If you feel you absolutely must click a link or otherwise navigate away from the preview page before confirming your entries, leave the preview page open and load the new page in an entirely new window or tab. You can do this when clicking a link by right-clicking the link and selecting Open In New Tab or Open In New Window from the pop-up menu. If you need to type in a Web address, do it in a new tab on your browser or launch a new, second session of your browser program and type it in there.

Tab Versus Enter

In most Web forms, pressing the Tab key will advance your mouse cursor to the next field or button on the form. However, in others, pressing the Enter key will advance the cursor. In still other Web forms, pressing the Enter key is the same as clicking the Submit button on the form. It can be very frustrating to learn this only after you've pressed Enter on an incomplete form, had it submitted and rejected as incomplete, and find it's blanked out all of your entries thus far to boot.

To save yourself some time and irritation, use the Tab key only to advance to the next field, or click with your mouse to place the cursor where you want it in each field.

Be Prepared

Finally, much like when filling out paper forms, you will often have to assemble certain information in order to complete the form. However, unlike a paper form, a computer form won't always allow you to save partial entries or a partially complete draft of the form, so it's always wise to look over the entire form and make sure you have all the required information readily available before you begin. It's maddening to spend a half hour or more working on a form, only to find you're missing some required bit of information and won't be allowed to save all the data you've entered thus far.

Creating Digital Image Files

There are three primary methods of creating digital image files: taking pictures with a digital camera, creating images from scratch in a graphics editor program, and working with clip art or stock images.

Using a Digital Camera

If you don't already own a digital camera, buy one. It's an important investment in your author platform and need not break your budget. Even economy-line digital cameras can take excellent pictures, you don't have to buy a top-of-the-line model. It's much wiser to choose a basic model with simple features you can easily master than something loaded with a bunch of complicated bells and whistles that make the camera difficult to use.

Look for a camera that can take pictures at a minimum resolution of 5 MP (megapixels), and has an optical zoom option, for close-ups. A macro option is also nice to have, as it will allow you to take clear pictures at a distance closer than the standard 3' (91cm) minimum.

If you also intend to use videos as part of your author platform (for example, book trailers or recordings of speaking engagements), you may find it's most economical to get a small digital camcorder that can also take still pictures.

Whether you're buying a digital camera or using one you already have, read the user guide and complete any tutorials provided in the photo/video editing software that comes with the camera. The better your skills with your camera, the better your images will be.

Creating Digital Images From Scratch

Don't worry, for most of us indie authors, the closest we'll ever come to having to create a digital image entirely from scratch is creating a book cover image through the use of a template. This process is described in chapter seven, Designing Your Own Book Cover.

It's never a bad thing to acquire new skills, so if you have the time and interest, by all means dig into your graphics editor program and master it. Otherwise, rest assured that you can meet all your author platform needs with a digital camera and clip art or stock images.

Clip Art and Stock Images

Clip art and stock images are pictures or graphics you're allowed to use without getting signed releases from their creators or any of the people appearing in them. Some clip art and stock

photos are free, and in fact most photo and graphics editor programs come with a selection of both, but you can also purchase collections or individual images/photos as software packages or online.

There are far too many options for me to list even a representative sampling here; as long as the clip art and/or photos are provided in file formats your photo/graphics editor can read, you'll be able to use them. Other than that requirement, the matters of image quality and variety really come down to your specific tastes and needs.

There are lots of clip art and stock photo services online, but you need to be a careful shopper if you're going to use any of them. Some sites bundle spyware or ads with their "free" clip art and photos, and an alarming number of hackers embed trojans and viruses in packages of clip art and stock images because they know such collections are very popular downloads.

As a rule of thumb, I advise against using any online clip art/stock photo services unless you are personally acquainted with someone who has used the service and recommends it. A few reputable sites are listed on www.indie-authorguide.com.

Using a Graphics Editor Program

You'll need to use a graphics editor program to do any of the following:

- Design your own book cover

- Create photo files or other image files for use in your book

- Create photo files or other image files for use on the Web (for example, to display a picture of yourself or your book cover on your website, blog, Facebook page, Twitter profile, MySpace page, or in online press releases)

- Create banners or buttons for your website or blog

- Edit screen captures (that is, screenshots of what you see on your computer screen) for use as figures/illustrations in your book or online

- Touch up photos and images (for instance, remove red-eye, resize images, and apply special effects like sepia tone)

- Create or edit your online avatar (the little picture that appears next to your user name on some sites)

Three key features to look for in your graphics editor program are: layers, multiple file format support, and photo editing/touch-up capabilities. Another feature that's very nice to have, but not strictly required, is vector graphics.

Layers is pretty much just what it sounds like: This feature allows you to create images by layering individual pieces of an image one on top of the other. For example, when designing a book cover you might begin with a background image that looks like wood or marble, then place a layer on top of that containing the text of your book title, then place another layer on top of that containing a banner or seal that says something like, "Newly revised and updated!".

The advantage of layers is that they make it easy for you to reposition individual elements of your images, or alter the appearance of individual elements without affecting the rest of the image. For example, you can make the background image much lighter in color, or partially transparent, so the text layer is easier to read. Not only is layering a very useful feature to have, it's one that's required in order to create your own book covers using the templates provided by print publishing service providers.

Multiple File Format Support is also just what it sounds like. People use all kinds of graphics software programs to create images, and different programs will save files in different formats. The more formats your graphics editor can read, the greater the variety of files you can work with. The more formats your editor can Save As, the more likely it is you can provide images in whatever file format other software programs (such as your word processor) and people (such as book cover designers) require.

Your graphics editor should be able to read and save files in all of the following formats, at the minimum: PNG, JPG/JPEG, GIF, IMG and BMP. If you're on a Mac, you'll also want the PNT file format (to read and create Mac Paint images), and if you intend to use images stored on Kodak picture CDs, you'll want the PED format, too. You'll need the SVG format as well if you'll be working with vector graphics (see Vector Graphics section, on the next page).

Other file formats that are nice to have include TIFF, TIF, DWG, PEX, EXIF, but these aren't as common as those I've listed as required.

Photo Editing/Touch-Up is another self-explanatory requirement. You want to be able to correct red-eye and photo exposure/lighting, remove (or add!) wrinkles and blemishes, and apply special effects such as negative image and sepia tone.

Vector Graphics is a feature that keeps the lines and surfaces of your images smooth no matter how much you enlarge or shrink them. Sometimes when you zoom in on an image on the Web or on your computer, it starts to look jaggy and pixelated, as if it's made up of a bunch of tiny squares? Vector graphics prevents that problem. It's a necessary feature if you'll deal with a lot of poor-quality images, and it ensures your images are of a high enough quality to display nicely on printed pages or book covers. It's also something you'll want to have if you expect to be working with, and providing images to, a graphic designer at any point in the process of designing your book cover or Web pages. The pros will want to work with the highest-quality images possible.

In the past, photo editor programs and graphics editor programs were two distinct types of software. Nowadays, pretty much any photo editor program can also handle graphics, and any graphics editor program can also handle photos. Just look for those key features, and it won't matter if your program is labeled as a photo editor or graphics editor: It will get the job done.

As to the matter of exactly how to use a given graphics or photo editor program, that depends on the specific program. There are some general instructions in chapter seven, Designing Your Own Book Cover, but since every program is different you'll have to refer to your program's help files, user guide, and tutorials to learn how to get the most out of it. You can find instructional books for the most popular programs at libraries or bookstores. Also take a look at the program manufacturer's website, as you can usually find how-to re-

sources there. Finally, for virtually every such program in existence, an Internet search on "how to use [program name]" will yield a wealth of links to free instructional resources.

Using a PDF Editor/ Creator Program

Many service providers will allow, or even require, you to submit your manuscript and other files in Portable Document Format, more commonly known as PDF. It is also the preferred format for providing online excerpts, copies of press releases, and similar documents on your author website or blog, for reasons detailed below.

PDF is a generally read-only file type that can be created from any viewable file, such as a word processor document, a Web page, or an image file. The PDF is a new version of the file that's viewable by anyone with a computer and a PDF reader program, but it can be *modified* only by someone who owns a PDF editor/creator program. Even then, editing capabilities in the PDF are limited; you can't easily revise entire pages of text the way you could with a word processor, for example.

Also, when you convert a file or Web page to PDF format, the resulting file is much smaller than the source file or page. This is because the PDF format strips out all the special formatting codes and program-specific details of the source file to save what is essentially a snapshot, or picture, of the source file.

Both of these features make PDFs a great way to distribute documents. Because PDF files are small, they're great for use as e-mail attachments, they upload and download quickly, and load in Web browsers much faster than the respective source files would. Because PDF files are difficult to edit, distributing your files in PDF format also provides some measure of protection against having the contents changed.

Note that I'm specifying a PDF editor/creator here, not just a PDF reader. Adobe's free Acrobat Reader program allows you to only read PDFs, not to create or edit them. The main difference you'll find between PDF editor/creator programs are the editing, revision, and file conversion tools made available to you within the program. For example, some PDF editor/creator programs can open a PDF and revert it to its original format in, for example, MS Word.

OpenOffice includes a free PDF editor/converter for documents, as do Apple computers running any version of Mac OS X.

Uploading Files to a Web Server

Indie authors have to do quite a bit of file uploading and downloading online. Whether you're downloading a template from a service provider, uploading an author photo to your profile on one site or another, or submitting your manuscript to a service provider for publication, it's important that you're knowledgeable and comfortable with moving your files around.

Download Versus Upload Versus E-mail Attachment

When you download a file, you're having a copy of the file sent from another computer, or server, to your computer. A server is just a computer that's been specially set up to send, or *serve*, files and programs to other computers.

When you *upload* a file, you're sending a copy of a file from your computer to a server.

A file you send as an e-mail attachment is a special kind of upload. Both the file you're sending and the e-mail message to which it's attached will be uploaded to the e-mail server of the mail service of the person to whom you're sending the message (for instance, Gmail, Yahoo, or Earthlink,). Then, when the receiver of the e-mail opens your message, he will read the message right off the e-mail provider's server. A link in the e-mail makes it possible to download the attached file, but the file will not transfer to the recipient's computer until he clicks that download link.

Some e-mail providers allow users to preview an attachment before downloading it. It's important to remember that previewing an attachment does not download the attachment. When you preview a file, you're looking at a copy of the file that's still stored on your e-mail provider's server. To get the file onto your computer, you must download it.

Your Computer's Filing System

When you look at the files stored on your computer, you'll be looking at them in a window like this one:

Name	Date modified	Type	Size
AprilDrumb100r000.jpg	8/1/2009 11:02 AM	JPG File	40 KB
BookSaleComparison.doc	3/5/2009 7:50 PM	Microsoft Word Docume...	28 KB
cover_for_template.wpd	8/17/2008 2:23 PM	WPD File	9 KB
Fable.doc	4/9/2009 11:00 AM	Microsoft Word Docume...	26 KB
Fable2.doc	4/9/2009 11:01 AM	Microsoft Word Docume...	26 KB
IndieAuthorCard.doc	9/17/2009 5:27 PM	Microsoft Word Docume...	30 KB
IndieAuthorCard.png	2/1/2009 2:12 PM	PNG File	255 KB
OReillyRegConf.pdf	1/2/2009 11:25 AM	PDF File	174 KB
PubletariatPromoCard.doc	2/1/2009 2:16 PM	Microsoft Word Docume...	15,847 KB
RebuttalToMrCarter.doc	4/8/2009 9:29 PM	Microsoft Word Docume...	27 KB

Figure 10-1

The file names are listed in the leftmost column, and the rest of the columns contain additional information about the files. The additional information is usually customizable, meaning that the user can choose what types of information she'd like to have displayed in the columns next to the column that lists files by name. In the example shown, there are columns for date modified, type, and size.

On most computers, to add or remove columns of information, right-click on the title of one of the columns, as shown in Figure 10-2.

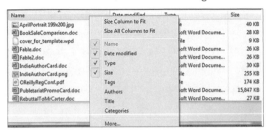

Figure 10-2

Items with a check mark next to them will be displayed. Click on items in the list to place or remove check marks as desired, thereby adding or removing columns of information. At the minimum, you will need to display name, date modified, type, and size. You will need all of those pieces of information when you work with self-publishing files.

How To Download and Upload Files

The processes of uploading and downloading files are very similar. When uploading, you have to locate the file you want to upload on your computer's hard drive, then tell your computer where to send it. When downloading, you have to locate the file you want online or on a server, then tell your computer where you want it to save the file on your hard drive.

Download Forms

Oftentimes, downloads available from websites and servers are clearly indicated with a link that contains the word *download* somewhere in the text of the link. In that case, click the link to open the Save As dialog box, then navigate to the location/folder where want the file saved on your hard drive, and specify the name you want it to be stored under. (See Figure 10-3.)

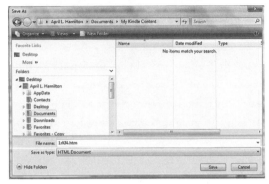

Figure 10-3

Other times, a link won't be so clearly labeled. It may contain just the name of the file or an icon of some sort. In that case, you can right-click on the link/icon and select Save Target As in the pop-up menu to open the dialog box that allows you to specify where to save the file and what to name it. (See Figure 10-4.)

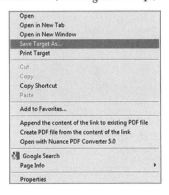

Figure 10-4

As it turns out, most links will allow this Save Target As option—even links to files that weren't originally created specifically for people to download, such as Web pages, images, audio files, and video files. However, while it's possible to download most linked files this way, you must respect intellectual property rights: Do not reuse or distribute any downloaded content without the express permission of the rights holder.

As a self-publisher, you'll be downloading templates/content from service providers or versions of your own content most of the time. So long as you don't attempt to redistribute or sell copies of material you get from service providers, such as user guides and tutorials, there's little risk of overstepping intellectual property rights boundaries.

Whether you're using an explicitly labeled download link or the Save Target As option, just make sure that if you choose to rename the file you don't change the file extension (.doc, .jpg, .pdf). The file extension tells your computer what type of file you're saving and what computer program you'll need to open the file later.

Download Gotchas
When downloading, there are three primary questions to ask yourself. First, is the file safe? Second, is the file of a type my computer can read and I can use? And third, is there enough space on my hard drive to store the file?

The easiest way to satisfactorily answer the first question is to use a quality virus scan utility to check every downloaded file for viruses and other problems before you open it. Even then, however, it's possible for unwanted stuff to get through. Protect your computer by accepting only downloads from known and trusted sites and sources. Major self-publishing service providers such as Wordclay, Createspace,

Lightning Source, and Lulu are trustworthy sources, but it's still good practice to scan all downloads for viruses.

To answer the second question, you must look at the file extension of the download and see if your computer has the program that is needed to open that file type. See the File Formats chart at the end of this chapter for further guidance.

The answer to the final question will come during the download process in the form of an error message if there's not enough room or a download complete message if there is. If you'd like to know whether the download will fail due to space limitations *before* you start it, check the Properties on your hard drive. In Windows, go to My Computer > C:, then right-click and select Properties from the pop-up menu. On a Mac, click the Macintosh HD icon and select Get Info from the pop-up menu. If there's no Macintosh HD icon on your desktop, use the Finder utility to locate it.

Upload Forms
The process of uploading a file to a website or server is the same, regardless of the type of file you're uploading or the site/server to which you're uploading.

First, you'll follow a link to get to an upload page. Link verbiage will vary depending on the type of file you're uploading and the site to which you're uploading. It may say add files, upload files, add photos, add document, or some variation. Clicking the link will take you to a Web form like the one shown. (See Figure 10-5.)

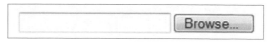

Figure 10-5

Clicking the Browse button will open a dialog box much like the Save As dialog. (See Figure 10-6.)

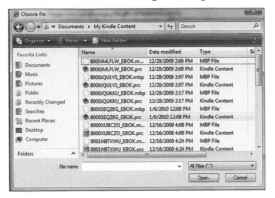

Figure 10-6

In the dialog, you simply navigate to the file you want to upload, click it to select it, then click the Open button to start the upload. Some sites will take you back to the page with the Browse button first and ask you to confirm the file name/location by clicking another button on the page before beginning the upload. A progress bar will usually display to provide you an estimate of how long the upload will take to complete.

Upload Gotchas

As previously stated, most sites that accept uploads place limits on the size and type of content to be uploaded. You'll often find size and file type restrictions printed on the upload form, so be sure to read all instructions and fine print.

In my experience, a lot of upload forms aren't very "smart." The form may have file size and type restrictions listed, but instead of preventing you from trying to upload a file that's the wrong size or type, it just "hangs", that is, it crunching away at the upload indefinitely

instead of displaying an error message. Again, read all instructions and fine print to make sure your file meets the listed requirements before you attempt an upload.

Most self-publishing service provider sites accept compressed manuscript and cover art files as uploads, but they typically only accept specific types of compressed files (see File Compression Utilities section on the next page). Make sure your compressed file is of an acceptable type before you attempt to upload it.

When attempting to send a file as an e-mail attachment, be prepared for the recipient's e-mail service provider to reject large files. As a precaution, compress any file that's larger than a few megabytes.

Kilobytes and Megabytes

Most e-mail programs and servers impose file size limits on uploads. This is necessary to prevent the server from slowing down, or even crashing, when someone attempts to upload an enormous file that uses up all of the server's computing power during the transfer process. Even worse, it may use up all of the server's storage space once the transfer is uploaded.

These limits are usually expressed as *MB*, which is the abbreviation for *megabytes*. For instance, the upload instructions on a given website may state that maximum allowable file size is 2MB, which means you won't be allowed to upload a file larger than 2 megabytes.

File size limitations are pretty straightforward, but you may have noticed that in the screenshots above, file sizes are listed in *KB*, which is the abbreviation for *kilobytes*. You will have to convert these file sizes into megabytes to know whether or not the file you're working with exceeds the file size limitations of the server to which you're attempting to upload the file.

Luckily, the conversion is simple. One megabyte is equal to 1,024 kilobytes, but don't worry about having to pull out a calculator or do a bunch of mental math. The quick and dirty way of converting kilobytes to megabytes is to replace the comma in the thousandths place with a decimal point. Look at the following examples:

2,326 KB ~ 2.326 MB
11,487 KB ~ 11.487 MB
1,349,657 KB ~ 1,349.657 MB

These conversions are not mathematically correct, since the file size in KB is divided by 1,000 instead of 1,024, but they provide an estimate that's very close to the actual megabyte figure. If the quick and dirty conversion renders a figure that's higher than the upload file size limitation, you know the file is too large because it's actually even larger than this shorthand conversion came up with. If you get an estimated file size that's near the upload limitation, do the math with a calculator to get a more exact conversion.

As you can see, all of the files in the conversion examples above would be too large for upload to a server with an upload file size limit of 2 MB. Graphics, music, video, photo, and heavily formatted word processing files in particular tend to be large—that's why file compression utilities were created.

File Compression Utilities

You'd think a computer file with a size of 14,500 KB contains 14,500 KB worth of content, but this isn't typically true. Simply put, computer files consist of both the content the user wants to store, and information or instructions the computer needs to assemble the content and present it to the user. File compression utilities simplify and consolidate the information or instructions, thereby reducing the file's size. The newly created, smaller file is referred to as an archive or compressed file.

Numerous file compression utilities are available, and most computers made within the past five years come with such a utility built into their operating systems. WinZip, WinRAR, and PKZiP are among the most popular of these utilities.

To find out if your computer has a compression utility built in, navigate to any file on your computer's hard drive and right-click on the file name. If the pop-up menu contains a Send To > Compressed Folder/File option or an Add to Archive option, you're all set. If not, you can go online to download WinZip, WinRAR, or PKZiP for free (search for the program names online, or get the URLs on www.indieauthor guide.com).

Using File Compression Utilities

Once you've downloaded and installed your selected utility, using it is simple.

To create a compressed file, right-click on the name of any file on your computer's hard drive and select Send To > Compressed File/Folder or Add to Archive from the pop-up menu. Either option will open a dialog box much like the Save As dialog, which allows you to name the archived file and specify the location in which you'd like to save it on your hard drive.

To open a compressed file, right-click on the file name and select Extract, Extract All, or Extract Here from the pop-up menu; the menu option verbiage varies depending on which utility you're using.

You can save multiple files to a single archive/compressed folder. Just select all of the files you want stored in the archive/compressed folder, then right-click and complete the dialog box as usual, specifying a name and location for the compressed file, which is also known as an *archive*.

The archive file will have a special icon that indicates it's a compressed file (provided by the compression utility), and it will also have a file extension that associates it with the utility used to compress the file (for example, .rar for Win-RAR files, .zip for WinZip files).

Note that by default, the original file(s) will remain as is on your hard drive, and the compression utility will make a copy of the file or files before compressing them. Some utilities have an option to automatically delete the source files, but it's safest to keep the default settings and allow the utility to work with copies of source files.

PLATFORM STRATEGIES FOR ANY AUTHOR

The most obvious first step, yet the one that's frequently overlooked by authors getting started with platform, is to learn from the masters. Look at what successful authors in your field or genre are doing, both mainstream and self-published, then scale their most successful strategies to fit the constraints of your resources.

For example, Neil Gaiman has a terrific Web presence. He's got an author website hub, a blog, offshoot sites for specific books and projects, he uses social media, he makes many public appearances, and he interacts with his fans online in a genuine, spontaneous way. These are all things any author can do, and they don't have to cost a fortune. See the Promotion chapter for more information about how to set up a quality author website and blog on a shoestring budget.

A Platform Top Ten

The following is a list of the most common platform activities in descending order of impact. In other words, if you have enough time or money only to do one thing with platform, start with number one. If you can do two things, do number one and number two. Again, refer to chapter eleven for more detailed instructions for each item.

You'll notice the list does not include quality book cover designs, because this item is not optional. It is a prerequisite to creating a quality book, though depending on where you are in your journey of indie authorship, you may not yet have a book published.

1. **Author Blog**—A blog is an easy, free way for authors with limited technical savvy to get a multipurpose Web presence going. Nowadays, blogs are much more than just online journals. A blog can be used to post articles, list where-to-buy links for your book(s), provide excerpts from your works, post flash fiction, issue press releases, link your target audience to other sites of inter-

est, interact with blog visitors via simple comment forms, and more.

2. **Author or Book website**—An author website can serve as a hub for information about you and your books, with an author biography and links to your blog, social media accounts, and more. Some website software includes a dedicated blogging area by default, so you may find you don't need a separate, stand-alone blog if you have a website.

An author website gives you a more professional look than a blog alone, particularly if it's hosted at a Web address bearing your author name. Additional advantages of websites over blogs is that they're generally more flexible and customizable than a blog, and better able to run embedded applications, such as video or audio players and slide shows.

A book website can be a useful adjunct to a blog or author website. There you can provide all information, reviews, excerpts, and book tour information that pertains to a specific book in a centralized location that site visitors can easily navigate. Compare this to a smattering of blog entries, links, and other information scattered across months' worth of entries on a blog.

3. **Author Photo**—An attractive author photo is an important addition to a blog or author/book website, a key component of your online profiles (you may also want to include it on your book covers). People like to *see* who they're deal-

ing with online. It helps establish the author as a real person in their minds, and it builds trust.

If you write under a pen name and wish to remain anonymous, you still can (and should) have an author image of some kind that reinforces your brand. Substitute an artist's rendering of how you want your pen name persona to appear, use the image of an appropriate symbol or other *object d'art*, or have your picture taken with part of your face obscured by shadow or an object, such as a book, computer screen, or hat.

4. **Guest Blogging/Writing Online Articles**—Hitching your wagon to a site that's already getting considerable traffic and is targeted to your book's content, your area of expertise, or your intended audience can be an effective shortcut in growing your own fan base. Many audience members who like your post(s) will follow your online exploits—and your work.

5. **Reviews**—It's a trade publishing truism that positive word of mouth sells books, and reviews can play an important part in generating that buzz. You aren't likely to get your self-published book reviewed in major mainstream media outlets, but consumer reviews on bookseller sites, reader community websites such as Goodreads, Shelfari, LibraryThing, and book blogs are entirely within your reach.

This item doesn't appear higher in the list because when you solicit for reviews, your requests have a better chance of being accepted if you project a professional image. Having a quality Web presence tips the scale in your favor.

6. **Social Media**—You don't have to open accounts on every available social media site (Twitter, Facebook, MySpace, and so on). In fact, doing so would be a big mistake for most people because social media can be very time-consuming. However, it's worthwhile to pick out a couple of social media options that appeal to you and keep current with them. There's no faster way to accumulate fans and followers, and disseminate information—such as a notice that you've posted a new blog entry or have a new book out. When you hear about something "going viral," you can bet social media played a role.

7. **Live Appearances**—If you can identify events or locations where your target audience is likely to turn out in large numbers and you're comfortable with public speaking, book signings, speaking engagements, live readings, and workshops are all viable options for you. Here's where you can do some cross-pollination, too, directing live audiences to your blog, website, and other online destinations, and directing Web audiences to your live appearances.

8. **Freebies**—Everyone loves to get something of value for free, and allowing readers to sample your wares without having to take out their wallets is a good way to generate sales. In the Promotion chapter, we'll talk more about this.

If you have a blog or website, you can use it to offer a lengthy excerpt from the book(s) you're selling, exclusive content that isn't available elsewhere, free e-book downloads, or sneak previews of your current work in progress, all at no cost to you *or* your audience. You can also coordinate with other indie authors to provide excerpts from one another's books in the back matter of your e-book releases.

Promote your freebies on your blog, website, social media accounts, and at live appearances.

9. **Amazon Opportunities**—If your book is listed on Amazon, take advantage of the plethora of marketing opportunities made available to authors there. Indie and mainstream authors alike can blog, promote their upcoming events, get involved in online discussion groups, post videos, and more on the site.

10. **Online Comment Forms**—Add your two cents to the discussion on other wrtiers' blog entries and articles. This is something that's easy to do anytime you have fifteen minutes to spare, and the dividends may surprise you. The key is to avoid overt promotion in your messages; stick to the topic at hand, but use the link field provided in the comment form to include a link to your author site, blog, or whatever else you're promoting. If people find your remarks witty or insightful, they may click on your link to learn more about you.

This top ten only scratches the surface of possibilities for your platform and promotional activities, but don't feel you must do everything on the list to be effective. Spreading yourself too thin, whether in terms of time or monetary investment, is a sure recipe for platform failure. You'll do far better with nothing but a frequently updated blog in which you're truly invested than an overabundance of platform activities.

PLATFORM STRATEGIES FOR FICTION AUTHORS

Many authors and aspiring authors seem to think platform is important to nonfiction authors only—or that it's too difficult for fiction authors—but neither assertion is true. Platform is important for *all* authors in today's brave new world of publishing, and fiction authors have platform opportunities available to them that are very well-suited to their natural skills as storytellers.

Some authors with a novel to sell blog or tweet "in character," posing as the protagonist or antagonist in their book. If you opt to do this, make sure you set up separate blog and/or Twitter accounts and link them together.

Creating an entire website based in the fictional story world is a promotional tack movie studios, television programs, *and* publishers are using more and more frequently. The producers of the movie *The Blair Witch Project* built a huge head of steam for the film long before it came out by posting a supposedly factual online report of a group of student filmmakers who went missing while investigating a haunted wood. By the time the film came out, tens of thousands were ready to buy tickets.

Producers of the television show *LOST* created several companion websites representing

the fictional Dharma Initiative corporation and other entities from the story. The websites expanded on information given in the show and provided hardcore fans with an interactive experience of the story world. You may not have the budget or skills to create such a high-powered campaign, but you can create a scaled-down version to provide your fans with supplemental material. Conversely, the supplemental material can lure *new* fans on its own merits as well. Consider posting the following:

- Character biographies and portraits
- Recipes, if cooking plays a role in the story
- Playlists of songs intended to go along with specific chapters or passages
- Artwork, photographs, poems, or other works created by your characters (actually created by you or otherwise legally obtained)
- Information about the setting of the story: maps, politics, history (again, make sure these are legally obtained)
- Posting short fiction that's otherwise unpublished, or having a story included as part of a published anthology, is a good way to give potential readers some idea of your style and genre

PLATFORM STRATEGIES FOR NONFICTION AUTHORS

Dated information is a constant concern in nonfiction books, particularly those focused on areas where flux is the norm, such as technology or politics. Consider creating a dedicated website or blog for your book, in addition to any author website or blog you already have, and provide the URL for the site in your book. You can then provide any content that's subject to change, such as website names and addresses, pricing information, and rosters of public officials, on the website and limit the book's content to material that will still be accurate and meaningful years after the book's publication date. (This book, for example, references a lot of information that's subject to change, and that's why it has a companion website.)

You can also provide supplemental or bonus material, such as the downloadable worksheets I'm offering to go with this book on its companion website. If you elect to set up such a site, be sure to link to it from your other site(s) and blog(s), and vice versa.

Make an effort to establish yourself as a subject area expert for your target audience by speaking at their conferences, getting involved in their trade associations, and participating in their other events. Conferences will typically put out a call for proposals to assemble a schedule of speakers ten to twelve months before the event date, so bookmark pertinent event websites and keep an eye on them so you'll know when planning for the next gathering gets underway.

Get up to speed on the submission guidelines for the most authoritative or popular journals and websites for your target industry, and see if you can't get something published. If guidelines are too stringent, you can still try submitting a thoughtful letter to the editor in response to some part of the site or journal's content. When published, such pieces generally include the author's name, title or profession, and website address.

Post some of your book's most useful or informative content in the form of a guest blog or article on a well-established site frequented by your intended audience, and include a brief About the Author statement at the end with where-to-buy links for the book.

MANAGING YOUR ONLINE REPUTATION

If you're working your author platform effectively, you're very active online. Your goal is to open a dialogue with readers and your peers, and the better your author platform, the more feedback and discussion you will generate. Much of the feedback and discussion will be enjoyable and thought provoking, a kind of online salon. The rest of it will range from annoying to ugly.

The first step in managing the public's reactions to you and your work is to be aware of those reactions in the first place.

Using Google Alerts

Google Alerts is a free tool that can notify you anytime something is posted about you or your work online. The way it works is simple: You go to the Google Alerts page (search for it online or refer to www.indieauthorguide.com to get the URL) and set up a separate alert for each word or phrase you'd like reported back to you. Note that you don't have to have a Google or Gmail account to do this. (See Figure 10-7.)

Figure 10-7

Under Type you can specify whether you want the alert to search News (news reporting sites), Blogs, Web (nonblog websites), Video (video sharing sites like YouTube), Groups (online communities), or Comprehensive (any mention on any site).

Under How Often you can tell Google Alerts to notify you as it happens, once a day, or once a week. Anytime the word or phrase you've specified turns up online, Google Alerts sends you an e-mail with a link to the page where the mention occurred, based on your chosen notification frequency.

For E-mail Length you can choose an upper limit of twenty results or fifty results per e-mail notification. Then you enter your e-mail address, click the Create Alert button, and your alerts will start coming.

What Alerts Should Authors Have?

I recommend authors set up alerts for their author or pen name(s), the titles of each of their books, the name(s) of their blog(s) and/or website(s), and the names of any events or sites with which the author is affiliated. I also recommend the following settings for Alerts:

- Type: Comprehensive, so you don't miss any mentions

- How Often: Once a day or once a week, so you're not inundated with alert e-mails

- E-mail Length: Up to twenty results, because this limit will probably far exceed the actual number of results in your alerts, at least in the beginning

Be sure to enter your alert search terms the same way you would enter them in a search engine. For instance, use quotation marks around phrases and full names to avoid getting incorrect results. For example, if I entered an alert search for the Bay Area Self-Publishers Conference, a (fictional) writer's conference, my alert would include any references to Bay Area, Self-Publishers, or Conference. If I enter the search term with quotes around the entire thing, my Alert will include only references to the entire phrase, "Bay Area Self-Publishers Conference."

Alerts based on general search terms will return a lot of false positives even when you employ quotation marks, but it can't be helped in some cases. For example, I've set up an alert for "Snow Ball" + novel to be notified anytime my novel *Snow Ball* is bandied about online, but I also get a lot of hits from people who are talking about actual balls of snow. Still, it's better to scan through a few false positives each day than to be in the dark when people are talking about my work.

Revising an Existing Alert

Only people with Google/Gmail accounts can make changes to their existing alerts, and this is accomplished via the Manage Alerts link in any alert e-mail. Users without Google/Gmail accounts can only delete existing alerts and add new ones. If you don't have a Google/Gmail account and you need to change one of your alerts, here's how to do it:

1. Copy down the parameters of the alert from within one of its alert e-mails, and flag the e-mail or file it in a location where you can easily locate it later.

2. Go to the Google Alerts page and create a new alert, using as many of the parameters you copied as you wish, and changing any you need to change.

3. After you've received an alert from the newly created version (so you know it's working), return to the alert e-mail from which you copied the parameters, and click the Delete This Alert link.

How to React to an Alert

When an alert notifies you of a positive mention, go to the site and see if comments are enabled. If they are, leave a note of thanks to the post's author, along with any additional remarks you can offer about the article, discussion topic, or post in question. Be sure to check off the "be notified of any responses" box, if there is one, so if anyone replies to your comment you'll be notified and can come back to respond.

Also be sure to spread the word by sharing a link to the page whenever appropriate. This is a win-win that rewards the person who mentioned you or your work by driving traffic to his site, and strengthens your author platform by demonstrating that people are saying nice things about you or your work.

You will be amazed at what a big impact your response and shared links can have on the people who've mentioned you or your work. They will feel validated and appreciated, and will be that much more likely to sing your praises whenever the opportunity arises.

When an alert notifies you of a negative mention, you'll need to decide whether it will be productive for you to respond. In most cases, it isn't.

Some people will have ill-informed, yet fervently held, opinions which no amount of factual information or rational discussion can alter. You cannot win with these types of people. Trying to correct them will only make them angry at you and can make you appear high handed—*not* the image you're trying to achieve.

Others will have opinions which are obviously being shared only for the sake of getting a rise out of you or casting aspersions on you or your work. However much you may want to angrily tear into this latter group anytime they darken your virtual doorstep, however tempting it may be to respond with a biting and clever remark, you must never do it. Answering the uncouth and trollish in kind requires you to become uncouth and trollish, which can quickly escalate beyond your control, undermine all the goodwill you've built with your community of readers and peers, and quickly turn off any newcomers to your tribe.

Dealing With Internet Defamation

On rare occasion, you may find something posted about you or your work online which you feel has the potential to do serious damage to your reputation and sales. If you believe you've been defamed online, you need to ask yourself:

1. Does the offending material meet the legal definition of defamation, are you sure it doesn't consist of statements of fact or nonactionable opinion?

2. Is the offending material likely to be seen by large numbers of people?

3. Is the offending material likely to damage your reputation and sales?

It's not usually worth taking action to get the defamatory material removed unless the answer to all three of these questions is a resounding yes, and the defamatory remarks are being made in reference to you under your legal name, pen name, or business name. Defaming remarks being made about your online alias aren't usually worth fighting unless your online alias is clearly linked with your legal name, pen name, or business name (for example, in a user profile, on your own site, or a Twitter profile).

Only you can answer questions one and three (ideally with the input of an attorney in the case of number one), but you can get the answer to number two using some free online tools. Run the URL of the website where the defamatory material is posted—not the specific page, but the main website URL—through Alexa and website grader (do an Internet search or see www.indieauthorguide.com for URLs) to view traffic statistics and other data about the site).

Even if you're not absolutely certain the defamatory statement(s) will pass the actionable opinion test, if you feel very strongly that your reputation among your peers, readers, and/or the publishing community is being damaged, it's still probably worthwhile to take action to the extent you can do so without getting an attorney involved. Most people would rather take simple steps to make a problem go away on their own than risk getting lawyers involved, so the threat of that risk will often get results.

Chain of Legal Liability

Let's say you've decided to take action. If you ask the defamer to remove the objectionable material directly, your request isn't likely to be honored and will most likely generate more online abuse and exposure. However, that isn't the end of the story. Even if the defamer posts under a pseudonym, lives in a foreign country, or is defaming you on her own site, so long as the company that hosts the site is based in a country with libel laws, you're still in business.

The defamer is just one of the people in the chain of legal liability for Internet defamation, and certain others in the chain are usually easier for you to get to—and have a lot more to lose. The chain consists of every person or company involved in the creation, publication, and presentation of the offending material. This group may include:

1. Discussion group administrator
2. Site administrator
3. Site editor
4. Site owner
5. Blog or site platform/software provider
6. Content aggregator
7. Site hosting company

You'll probably find you're wasting your time lodging a complaint with numbers one through four, even if the site or discussion board in question has specific prohibitions against defamation in its terms of use (ToU) or acceptable use policy (AUP). All of these people are usually ignorant of the law and will tend to dismiss your complaint. Worse, if any of them are pals with the defamer, your complaint will likely backfire and generate further online abuse.

Certain legal protections that tend to insulate numbers five and six from most claims relating to the objectionable or illegal use of their services by individuals (see Digital Millenium Copyright Act section on page 136), so these are also usually dead ends. And this brings us to number seven: the hosting company.

Gather Documentation

First things first: Take screenshots, create PDFs, or save off-line copies of the Web pages where the defamation occurred. Be sure to note the URLs and bookmark them; you'll need to share these with others later. Also retain copies of any e-mails, phone calls, faxes, instant messages, or other communications you send or receive pertaining to the matter going forward.

Identify the Site Hosting Company

Do a WHOIS search on the domain name of the site where the defamatory material appears. (To find out how, do an Internet search for "WHOIS" or see www.indieauthorguide. com for URLs.) For example, if you were investigating Google, you'd enter "google.com." The WHOIS record will show in whose name the domain is registered and will also list the domain name server(s) (DNS) on which the site is hosted. The DNS entries will follow this format:

[server ID].[host company name].com

Now that you know the host company name, go to their website by typing www.[host company name].com into your browser. If that doesn't get you to their site, do an Internet search on the company name to find it.

Hosting Company Terms of Use/Acceptable Use Policy

Once on the hosting company's site, look up their ToU/AUP. You may have to hunt around a bit to find it. Look for a link to a page where the company's hosting services are being offered for sale. The document you need will definitely be somewhere on the site. Find the paragraph in it which specifically prohibits defamation, libel, or any other illegal activity. It should read something like the following:

> [must not] encourage, allow or participate in any form of illegal or unsuitable activity, including but not restricted to the exchange of threatening, obscene, or offensive messages, spreading computer viruses, breach of copyright and/or proprietary rights or publishing defamatory material;

If the document is very lengthy, you can use your browser's Find > On This Page option to speed up your search. When you find the paragraph, make a note of the paragraph number or letter and save the entire document as a PDF screenshot file or off-line Web page for later reference. Even if you don't find the paragraph, the fact that the host company operates in a country with libel laws gives you ammunition to proceed.

Put The Hosting Company On Notice

Click the host company's Contact Us link and look for the abuse department or an e-mail address where you can reach it. Some companies take abuse so seriously that they provide a telephone hotline.

Use the provided e-mail address or phone number to report the incident(s). If you begin with a phone call, follow up with an e-mail to create an electronic paper trail. You can follow this basic format, customized with your details:

Subject: Your Client in Violation of Your [ToU or AUP]

Dear [Hosting Company Name] Representative:

Your client is using a website hosted on your server to make libelous statements about [me/my work/my business]. Your client's statements are illegal and in violation of your own [ToU/AUP], [provide paragraph number or letter]. In allowing your client to utilize your hosting service for such use you may be held liable as the publisher of the libelous statements if you are made aware of them and fail to take action to remove them. Here are links to the offending content:

[provide links]

I am taking this very seriously, and if I do not receive notice that you are taking action to remove the offending material I will pursue legal action against your company in the matter.

[your name]

[your contact info]

Cease And Desist Letter

You may luck out and score a win with your first contact, but it's more likely that the person on the receiving end will be ignorant of the law and respond with some boilerplate message about protecting the company's clients' right to free speech. If you still wish to pursue the matter, you're most likely to get results with a cease and desist letter.

If you do an Internet search for "Internet defamation," you should be able to find plenty of attorneys who specialize in these matters, and obtaining such a letter from one of them should not be very costly. Even if it means investing a sum that's substantial to you, it may be worth it if the defamation is hurting your sales, your standing as an author, or your reputation among your peers, your public, or within the publishing industry.

Many communities and colleges with a law school sponsor low-cost legal clinics, so that's a good avenue to try if you feel the matter is serious but you can't afford to hire an attorney at regular rates. Contact your local city hall, community center, or universities to inquire about such clinics.

This second contact will spur the host company to action in most cases, if for no other reason than the fact that they must pay their legal counsel his usual hourly rate just to read your cease and desist letter and reply to it—even if the reply is nothing more than a legalese version of, "Get lost." Allowing a cease and desist letter to reach their attorney also puts the attorney on notice that the company is potentially in legal trouble, and in publicly held companies this typically sets off a regulatory chain of notification requirements: Senior management must be notified immediately followed by board members and shareholders, if the matter isn't resolved quickly.

COMMON FILE FORMATS

FILE EXTENSION	FILE TYPE	PROGRAM TO OPEN/USE
.doc, .docx, .docm, .dot	word processor	MS Word™, OpenOffice™
.wpd	word processor	Word Perfect™, OpenOffice™
.txt	text file	Notepad™, WordPad™, any text editor
.rtf	rich text file	any word processor
.png, .jpg, .gif	graphic or photo file	Most graphics and photo editor programs; check your program's compatibility by opening the File > Open menu item in the program and dropping down the Files Of Type list in the Open File dialog box
.pcx, .art, .bmp, .wmf, .tif	graphics file	(same as above)
.mp3, .mp4, wma, .aiff, .aac, .mid	audio file	Media player, such as RealPlayer™, QuickTime™, iTunes™, Windows Media Player™
.mp4, .mov, .m4v, .wmv, .mmp, .avi, .mpeg, .rm, .ogg	video file	Media player, as above; check your media player program's compatibility by opening the File > Open menu item in the program and dropping down the Files Of Type list in the Open File dialog box
.pdf	Portable Document Format file	Adobe Acrobat, Acrobat Reader, any PDF creator/reader program
.mobi, .prc, .lrf, .pdb, .epub, .lit	e-book file	Varies with reader hardware/software. Check your reader device or program compatibility by opening the File > Open menu item in the program and dropping down the Files Of Type list in the Open File dialog box
.htm, .html, .xml, .xhtml	Web page file	To view pages, use a Web browser such as Safari, Google Chrome, Internet Explorer or Firefox. To build pages, use an HTML editor program such as Dreamweaver™, Frontpage™, CoffeeCup™, oR Visual Studio™

.docx indicates Word 2007, .docm indicates a Word document with macros (automated processes) contained within it, .dot indicates a Word template file.

Most versions of MS Word can open Word Perfect documents, but the reverse is not always true.

Plain text files are small in terms of file size, but ugly because they don't allow for much formatting.

Rich text is a file format that allows/preserves basic formatting, such as paragraph breaks and carriage returns, but doesn't allow/preserve more complex formatting, such as styles and graphics.

All of these file types are Web compatible, meaning they can all be read by current versions of Web browsers. Note that some .gif files are animated, meaning that they will "play" a continuous loop of some type of animation (e.g., a dancing banana) when displayed. Avoid animated gifs in manuscripts and book cover files.

.jpg and .gif are also acceptable file formats for use in e-books.

These are common graphics file formats which are not necessarily Web compatible; you can use them to add illustrations to a manuscript file or to create a book cover file, but you cannot be sure any of these types of images will display on a Web page or in an e-book.

All of the listed media players are free, or have a free version available. For self-publishers, audio files are most often used in the context of podcasting.

For self-publishers, video files may be of use as book trailers or other promotional videos, video podcasts, movie adaptations of manuscripts, or in the creation of enhanced e-books.

Acrobat is both a PDF creator and reader, whereas Acrobat Reader is only a PDF reader. Other PDF creator/reader programs will vary in terms of PDF creation/reading functionality; since self-publishers need to create and edit PDFs, be sure your selected program has the capabilities to both read and create PDF files.

This list includes only the most common e-book formats, but there are over two dozen e-book file formats in existence. Other document types that can be used as e-books include DOC, PDF, TXT, RTF, HTML, XHTML, and XML.

As of this writing, the standard, native format for Kindle books is MOBI, for Sony Reader books is LRF, and for Nook books is EPUB. However, all three of these readers can read other file formats as well.

Web page source files can also be created and edited in any standard text editor program, but they're easier to work with and visualize in a program specially designed for creating and editing Web pages.

E-book creation/conversion engines use XML, XHTML, or HTML files as an intermediate conversion step between a word processor file and the final e-book file. The more knowledgeable and comfortable you are working with these file types, the more control you will have in creating and formatting e-books.

It's a whole lot cheaper and easier for the host company's abuse department to send a notice to advise their client of the ToU/AUP violation and ask said client to remove the offending material on pain of having her site shut down with no refund of hosting fees. It also insulates the abuse department manager from the wrath of higher-ups.

The Digital Millenium Copyright Act

Attorneys for U.S.-based software companies, Internet service providers, hosting companies, and similar are used to summarily rejecting any defamation claims levied against their clients' customers on the basis that their client is protected by the Digital Millenium Copyright Act (DMCA); do an Internet search on it if you want to know the particulars of that piece of legislation. In a nutshell, it's intended to protect those providers from the illegal actions of people who use their software or services. In most cases it's a more or less bulletproof defense, but that doesn't necessarily mean you've hit a dead end.

If the plaintiff (you) can show that the provider has access to edit, block, or delete its clients' content, and has previously done so for any reason, the provider will have a hard time proving it does not act as the "publisher" of its clients' content. And content publishers are not granted the same protections under the DMCA as content service providers.

Ensure your cease and desist letter contains references to any evidence you have that the service company acts, or has acted, as a content publisher. For example, if the site's ToU or AUP states the site administrator may edit, block, or delete any objectionable material at his discretion, a copy of the ToU or AUP page will clearly demonstrate "access to edit, block, or delete its clients' content." Such evidence generates more pressure on the service company to remove the offending material rather than face further legal action. Nevertheless, assertions of this type can be difficult to prove in court so if the response to your cease and desist letter is a brush-off that references the DMCA, it's probably prudent to drop the matter unless you're prepared for a pitched legal battle.

Misappropriation. A Further Wrinkle for U.S.-Based Hosting Companies

In the United States, in addition to charges of defamation, you can raise charges of misappropriation of your name, likeness, or trade name for profit, intentional interference with economic relations, and more.

A charge of misappropriation of a person's name, likeness, or trade name for profit isn't easily dodged, and violation of this U.S. law is readily apparent to anyone viewing the pages with the misappropriated material. If such a page also contains advertising, or links to buy products the site, host blog, or author offers for sale, then the page content qualifies as content used for a commercial (money-making) purpose.

This is another instance in which you will have to consult with an attorney to see if your claim is legitimate and to get a cease and desist letter, but this type of claim is much more easily won—and therefore more likely to generate a speedy, out-of-court resolution—than a claim of Internet defamation.

eleven} Promotion

Once upon a time, when an author sold a manuscript to a publisher, the publisher had a promotional plan and marketing budget in mind. These days the majority of authors, including those published by big mainstream houses, are on their own to promote their books. The bad news is, promotion takes a lot of time and effort. The good news is, there are two pieces of good news. First, promotion works; so long as you're actively promoting them, your books will sell. Second, thanks to the Internet, authors today have far more tools and techniques available for promotion than ever before—many of which are free.

While it's true that most mainstream-published authors are on the hook for promotion every bit as much as their indie author peers, Indies still have a slightly more difficult task. For one thing, major publishers' recognized, respected brand names can be door openers in and of themselves. For another, most brick-and-mortar chain bookstores will not stock books published by indie authors. Finally, indie authors' work is largely excluded from the mainstream media, which is the primary source of publicity for mainstream books.

Fortunately for today's authors, it's possible to mount a successful marketing campaign completely outside of mainstream media outlets. Better still, such a marketing campaign will cost you less and be more effective than a traditional mainstream media blitz.

WHAT'S THE BEST WAY TO PROMOTE?

The answer to that question depends on four things: time, money, skills, and confidence. To be more specific, how much of each one do you have to give? In the algebra of marketing, the more you have of any one of these four commodities, the less you need of the other three. An author with lots of time and confidence will need far less money and skills than an author who's extremely shy and can't spare more than a half hour a day on promotion. Ideally you should have at least a little of all four and enough flexibility to acquire a little bit of each.

ARE YOU CUT OUT FOR THIS?

In all honesty, for most of the do-it-yourself (DIY) ideas presented in this chapter you need at least basic computer and Internet skills. You don't have to be able to build your own website, but you should at least be competent with some of the advanced features of your word processor, like how to insert pictures, format tables, and create flyers. In addition, you should be familiar with how online discussion groups work, comfortable using e-mail (including sending/

receiving attachments), and able to use basic photo editing software. If your computer skills are weak or you're not very Internet literate, the majority of this chapter will be useless to you. In that case you have two options: Hire a publicist or improve your skills.

TIME

Don't assume that having a full-time job or college course load means you don't have enough time to effectively market your work. If you can spare just one hour a day, seven hours a week, you'll be fine. If you can scrape together ten to fifteen hours a week, you'll do great. And if you have twenty or more hours to devote to marketing, even if you have little money or confidence, you can be very successful.

If you have no time whatsoever to spare, the only way you can hope to promote your work is to hire someone else to do it. Unless you have a professional publicist in the family, those services will cost you—and dearly. An author with no time and no money at present would probably do well to delay publication of his book until a later date, when either time or money isn't so tight.

MONEY $

It may surprise you to learn that money isn't an absolute necessity for marketing success, but just like good looks and well-connected relatives, it does tend to make things easier. Still, even if you have no cash to spare for marketing, you'll find you can use many of the promotional strategies provided in this chapter. If you have around fifty dollars to invest, you'll be able to use *most* of the promotional strategies

presented here. Only two of the techniques will cost you more than a hundred dollars, but there are many techniques for which you decide how much you want to spend.

SKILLS

In the book world, *skills* cover a broad range of knowledge and abilities. For purposes of this chapter, the most valuable skills you can have are those involving the computer and Internet, copywriting, research, graphic art, public speaking, and organization. However, with a little out-of-the-box thinking, you'll find virtually any special skills you have can become part of your promotional efforts, whether you sing, cook, or rope cattle.

CONFIDENCE

Confidence, for purposes of this chapter, encompasses three things: confidence in yourself, confidence in your work, and social confidence. Social confidence means being comfortable in social situations involving strangers—in some cases, whole rooms full of strangers. Authors who are good at public speaking have little to worry about in this category, but even an author who's downright introverted in public social situations will be all right so long as she can interact comfortably with others online. Remember that most people expect writers to be a little shy and awkward, so you're not doomed to failure if you can't be a dynamo.

A SIGNATURE LOOK

First things first: It's important to cultivate a signature look across all your promotional materials. This means using the same font(s), color scheme, and graphic elements wherever possible in everything from your business cards to your website. It doesn't mean all your book covers should look alike, however. McDonald's has the brand consistency you're after. You can tell at a glance that all their print ads, TV ads, food wrappers, and even employee uniforms come from the same source.

Choose a font that's easy to read onscreen and in print, all the way down to the 9-point size you'll need on business cards. Choose classic or muted colors, nothing faddish. You hope to be working with your chosen font and colors for decades to come, so don't select anything that could look dated, or that you'll be sick of, in just a few years.

If you intend to have an author website—something I strongly recommend—it's a good idea to let the site set the tone for your sig-nature look. This is because only a limited number of fonts, graphics file types, and even colors can be used on websites, whereas the possibilities in print are virtually limitless. If you start by setting up promotional materials for print and then find your chosen font, graphics, or colors don't readily transfer to the Web, you'll have to start all over again. Beginning with the website is even more crucial if you'll be using templates to build your site, since the templates will dictate the fonts, colors, and graphic elements.

SYMBOL KEY

Going forward, this chapter will indicate the amount of time, money, skills, and confidence required for each promotional item or technique using the clock, money bag, tool,

COUNT	TIME ⏱	MONEY $	SKILLS 🖱	CONFIDENCE ⚡
0	N/A—at least a little time is always needed	Free!	Amish person can do it	Agoraphobic hermit can do it
1	≤1 hour	≤ $10	Person who knows what a computer, the Internet, and a word processor are can do it	Mildly insecure but curious loner can do it
2	≤2 hours	≤ $20	A person with basic computer, Internet, and word processing skills can do it	Person with average written and verbal communication skills who feels okay about self can do it

3	≤ 3 hours	≤ $30	Person with moderate computer, Internet, and word processing skills can do it	Person with above-average written and verbal communication skills and strong self-esteem can do it
4	≤ 4 hours	≤ $40	Person with advanced computer, Internet, and word processing skills can do it	Person comfortable with public speaking can do it
5	> 4 hours	> $40	Bill Gates can do it	Tony Robbins can do it

and lightning bolt icons, as described in the table below.

Where amount of time, money, skills, or confidence required can vary, a range is provided.

TRADITIONAL TACTICS

Even in today's technology-driven world, some of the tried-and-true marketing strategies of the past can still be the most effective, depending on your individual needs and circumstances.

The Press Kit

A press kit is a collection of information about you and your work, intended to cast both in the most positive, interesting light possible. A press kit intended to promote a book may include one-sheets; press releases; editorial review reprints; article reprints; an enlarged copy of the book cover printed on glossy paper stock; promotional giveways such as bookmarks, pencils,

and mugs with the name of the book printed on them; and/or a printed excerpt from the book. It will be up to you to decide which items make the most sense for you to include in your press kit, based on the amount of time, money, skills, and confidence you have. Some of the items are self-explanatory and others are covered individually in this chapter.

When a mainstream author with a large marketing budget has a new book to promote, a press kit is sent, along with a review copy of the book, to every major media outlet in an effort to generate buzz and editorial reviews. This approach would be a huge waste for an indie author, since the great majority of mainstream media outlets won't even consider reviewing your book or publicizing its author. Nevertheless, a targeted press kit will come in handy when you line up a review, article, or interview because it cuts down on the interviewer/journalist's work by providing reference materials, quotes, and other information about you and your work. Sending a press kit in advance allows you to influence the information that will be served up for public consumption.

Be careful not to overstuff your press kits. Keep it specific, to the extent possible, and include only the most relevant and recent items. You may have accumulated thirty press releases over the past few years, but that doesn't mean you should include all of them. Remember to tailor each press kit to the wants and needs of the recipient, to provide only the most useful or desirable content. You don't want the recipient to open your kit and feel so overwhelmed by the sheer volume of it that she tosses it directly into the recycle bin.

As a rule of thumb, you can assume a basic press kit will include your author one-sheet (see below), a one-sheet for your most recent book in print, your most recent press release (or two, if both are dated within the past six months), and if desired, one promotional item. Article reprints and book excerpts can be included if the recipient has expressed specific interest in them but should otherwise be left out because they most likely won't be read anyway.

The One-Sheet

⏱⏱⏱	$
🎈🎈–🎈🎈🎈	**NO CONFIDENCE!**

A one-sheet is a single sheet of paper, printed on one side only, that summarizes a person, product, or service for marketing purposes. The one-sheet is the backbone of a press kit,

so if you're going to send out press kits, read this section carefully.

You'll need some time and basic computer skills to create your own one-sheets, more advanced skills if you want to do anything fancy, but the only expense involved is for paper and ink when you print them. You don't need much in the way of confidence either, since you'll just be copying and pasting in preexisting text and picture items.

In terms of layout there are no hard-and-fast rules, but it's common practice to position text and pictures in the same way typically seen in newsletters. The content depends on what you're promoting. A one-sheet can be used to promote you as an author in the general sense, or as a promotional tool for an individual book you've published. It's a good idea to create a separate one-sheet for each of your books and one more for you as an author. Don't use one-sheets to publicize the publication of a poem, piece of short fiction, or the like, unless the piece has won an award or there's some other newsy angle to report (for example, the story was published in an anthology for which all proceeds are going to a charity). Otherwise, there's simply not enough to say about such a piece to fill out a whole one-sheet.

The example shown in Figure 11-1 is a dummy one-sheet for promotion of a specific book, and it was created using a newsletter template in Microsoft Publisher. Microsoft Word and most other word processing and desktop publishing programs also have newsletter templates you can use as a starting point.

The book's title and author's name appear in the large block at the top left of the page. An image of the book's cover would be inserted below the title block, followed by a large text block about the book. The large text block will generally contain the same text as your book cover jacket copy, and if there's room, other promotional details such as review blurbs and available sales figures. One review blurb can be highlighted in the large text block, or if you don't have review blurbs yet, you can quote your best line from the jacket copy.

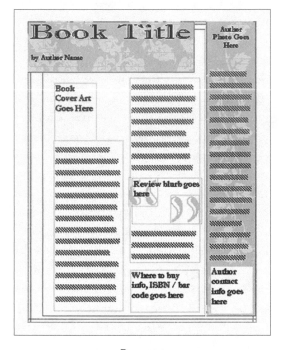

Figure 11–1

Information about where to buy the book, and if desired, a copy of your ISBN bar code and number, appear in a separate block at the end of the large text block. The ISBN bar code is there for retailers who want to order your book in quantities for resale. Even if you don't intend to send one-sheets to booksellers, remember that you want your one-sheets to look every bit as legitimate as a professional publicist's, so keeping the ISBN block is a good idea if there's any way you

can manage it. You can capture an image of the ISBN barcode by scanning it off your book, then cropping the image and saving the file as a JPG or GIF image on your computer. To the right is a sidebar block for the author's biography, with the author's photo at the top, brief biography in the middle, and contact/website information at the bottom.

The same basic layout can be used for a one-sheet intended to promote an author in general, not a specific book, by reversing the content and eliminating the ISBN/where to buy block. In that case, you'd use the large text block at the left to provide a more detailed author biography and the sidebar to list some titles of your published work (books, short stories, articles, etc.). The picture above the large text block would be your author photo, and the one above the sidebar would be eliminated.

You can get a little creative with color and fonts, but don't go crazy. The purpose of your one-sheet is not to dazzle the viewer with your awesome artistic skills, but to clearly, concisely describe yourself or your book. Resist the urge to insert a bunch of clip art on the page, and remember to stick with the signature look you're trying to establish.

A general rule of three applies in graphic art: Use no more than three different fonts or three different color elements on the same page. Limit yourself to fonts from the same font family, or at least fonts that are very similar in appearance to your signature font. Try using your signature font formatted in two or three different ways (that is, italicized, different sizes, shadowed, or embossed). With respect to color elements, such as the watermarks in the dummy one-sheet, it's safest to limit yourself to just one color. If you want to go with more than one color, choose complementary colors (opposites on the color wheel, such as, yellow and purple) or different shades of the same color (such as, sky blue, denim blue, and navy blue), again, in keeping with your signature look.

When you find a layout you like, stick with that layout for all your one-sheets. Remember: Consistency is key to your marketing success.

Author Photo

⏱⏱	FREE! — $$$$$
NO SKILLS! — 🎈🎈🎈	⚡⚡

An author photo is needed not only for one-sheets in your press kit, but pretty much anywhere you want or need your likeness to appear: flyers, book covers, your website, blog, online profiles, and other places in the media. It's a good idea to get one picture you're happy with and use it for everything, as most well-known mainstream authors do. This lends that all-important consistency to your promotional efforts and helps establish your likeness as a recognizable presence in readers' minds.

The author photo gets two lightning bolts for confidence because you need to feel comfortable in front of the camera. A self-conscious author is a nervous author, and not likely to take a good picture.

Of course, a professionally shot author photo is the best way to go. But don't despair if you can't afford one.

If you have average skills with a digital camera and know how to use photo editing software, you can go totally DIY for free. So long as you have a mirror in a room with good lighting, or know how to use your digital camera's timer function, you can take the picture yourself. Alternatively, you can get a friend or family member to help with taking the picture and editing it as well.

You'll need to save a compressed version of the photo for use online, in JPG or GIF format, with a file size of no more than 100KB.

If you're not strong in the camera or photo editing areas, and you don't have any friends or family to help you, it's a good idea to pay a professional photographer—but it doesn't have to cost a fortune. Sears, JC Penney, and even Walmart offer portrait services at affordable prices. At the other end of the pricing scale are boutique photographers, whose fees can run into the thousands of dollars.

As you gather pricing information, make sure the photographer or studio will provide a copy of the portrait in digital format (JPG or GIF file provided on a CD, DVD, or via e-mail). Also ensure the photographer or studio will provide a compressed copy of your chosen pose for use on Web pages: a smaller version of the picture in a JPG or GIF file no larger than 100KB.

Before your photo session, go through your hardcovers and paperbacks and find an appealing photo of an author to show the photographer as a sample of the look and pose you're going for. This will save you time and money.

Press Releases

⏱ – ⏱⏱	$ – $$$$$
🎈🎈	⚡⚡⚡

A press release is an announcement distributed to media outlets as a means of quickly passing along information from a single, controlled channel. As part of the press kit, releases highlight information about your recent activities and accolades. They also appear on your author website. The variability in cost reflected above comes in the distribution of your press releases: You can use a free distribution service or a paid service. Everything from tour dates to airline luggage restrictions, to celebrity child adoptions and much, much more come to the public's attention via press releases. The Associated Press (AP) pick up those deemed most newsworthy, and from there the stories are reported in newspapers, magazines, and on websites the world over.

Press releases can be an easy, low-cost way to publicize your work, but it takes confidence and above-average written communication skills to craft a good one. You may write amazing prose, but the type of writing called for in this instance is more journalistic, and on the face of it, there's nothing very newsworthy about books or authors. Books are written and published every day, there's nothing earth-shattering, or even interesting, about that.

For an author, press release success requires an angle: You must find something interesting, relevant, surprising, or even shocking to say in your press release if you want any news outlets to report on it. This doesn't mean you should lie or fill your press release with empty hype, however. In fact, doing so will damage your credibility and make it that much harder to get press coverage in the future. Rather, you must wait until you have something genuinely interesting, relevant, surprising, or shocking

to say about yourself or your book. Don't worry, this isn't as hopeless as it sounds.

There are five main junctures at which it's common to put out a press release about a book: when the publishing contract is signed, when the book is published, when there are impressive sales figures to report, when the book or author wins an award, and when the book or author does something interesting. As an indie author you will lose out on the first juncture because there are no contracts involved in the publication of your books, but the other four junctures are wide open to you. The book is published press release doesn't require further clarification, but the last three do.

The Impressive Sales Press Release

Sales figures on indie books are typically modest at best, nonexistent at worst. However, if Amazon.com is selling your book, impressive sales figures aren't entirely out of reach. Amazon lists its books under hundreds of categories and maintains best-seller lists in every one of those categories, updating the rankings every hour. While it may be absolute pie in the sky for you to think your indie book will make *The New York Times* best-seller list, it's not all that far-fetched to imagine your book earning a slot in the top one hundred of one of Amazon's many specific book categories. The publishing industry literati are cognizant of the fact that Amazon's best seller-lists are very specific, and therefore being number one in one of those specific categories is a far cry from being number one on the *New York Times* best-seller list for overall fiction or nonfiction, but this isn't so apparent to the general public.

It's newsworthy when *any* book gets up into the top ten on best-seller lists, but even more so for an indie book because indie books have a notorious reputation for slow sales and difficulty in reaching an audience. Any indie book that makes it into an Amazon top ten best-seller list is deemed exceptional, and its presence in that list is likewise deemed newsworthy.

If it's possible for you to work in some kind of surprising or interesting angle that makes the sales figure even more impressive, so much the better. In the case of a press release for my novel, *Adelaide Einstein*, achieving top ten status on an Amazon best-seller list, I reported that the manuscript had advanced no further than the semifinal round in the Amazon Breakthrough Novel Award contest, yet went on to become an Amazon number ten best-seller after I published it independently.

In order to take advantage of Amazon sales rankings, your book must be available for sale on Amazon.com. Also, as you've no doubt guessed, the more categories in which your book is listed, the more chances you have at hitting the upper reaches of one or more Amazon best-seller lists.

When adding your book to Amazon's sales listings, be sure to list it under as many categories as you reasonably can, up to the limit of categories you're allowed. "Reasonably can" is a phrase that's open to interpretation, but avoid stretching the truth too far. For example, *Adelaide Einstein* is a comic, hen-lit novel with obvious listings under general fiction, women's fiction, and comic fiction. However, I also listed it under motherhood because a great deal of the story centers on the heroine's relationships with her kids. I wouldn't list it under mystery, sci-fi, fantasy, or romance. You must balance your desire for more category listings against the risk of alienating readers who could end up buying your book under false pretenses—and may never forgive you for it.

When publishing for the Kindle, adding your book to categories is all part of the publication process. If you've published your trade paperbacks through an outlet such as CreateSpace, iUniverse, or Lulu, the publisher will generally ask you to specify listing categories before they submit the title for sale on Amazon.

The Award Winner Press Release

This one is fairly self-explanatory, but it's worth mentioning that the award ought to be directly related to your writing. In other words, if your book wins the Tri-County Women in Love award for excellence in romance books, go ahead and whip out a press release. Likewise, if you win a Community Mentor award for your volunteer work teaching creative writing to disadvantaged kids, this is also worthy of a press release because the award is directly related to your involvement in writing. However, if you win the Cub Scout Den Leader of the Year award, unless your books are about scouting, there's no obvious relationship between the award and your writing, and no justification for a press release.

The Something Interesting Press Release

You can have a something interesting press release anytime you want: Just do something interesting! This is the sort of thing which, in the mainstream media, is commonly known as a publicity stunt, but it doesn't have to be anything as obvious (or expensive) as a staged martian invasion or pie-eating contest. Many of the promotional activities covered in this chapter, such as speaking engagements, book signings, and interviews are interesting enough to warrant press release coverage. Volunteerism related to literacy, involvement in community activities related to the subject matter of your book, and participation in library or book fair events are just a few of the many other opportunities.

Anatomy of a Press Release

Acceptable press release format is standardized and fixed in terms of layout. A sample press release is shown in Figure 11-2.

At the top left, the source of the press release is listed. Beneath that is the press release headline, followed by the author name and date. Next comes an optional subheadline in italics. Beneath that is the main body of the press release. The release may also include a final paragraph with a brief description of the company or person about whose product or activity the press release is written.

Contact details are listed at the bottom, so that anyone who would like to contact you for more information can easily do so. Traditionally, the legend <END> or three pound signs (###) are inserted at the bottom to indicate the end of the transmission, a holdover from the days of teletype machines, but this is becoming less common.

You can find more examples online by doing an Internet search for "press release," or clicking the news link at any major corporation's website.

Source, Byline, and Contact

By default, the source, byline name (writer's name), and contact for the press release will be you. While having a source, author, and contact name other than your own is desirable, since it won't be so obvious you're tooting your own horn, do not make up a name just for this purpose. Remember that the press release is supposed to be a reliable source of information, and therefore the source, author, and contact person must be real, accessible entities.

If you write your books under a pen name this is a no-brainer because your press releases about Joe Pen Name can be written by you under your real name. If not, an easy way to get a legitimate source, byline, and contact other than your own name is to have someone else publish your press release. Consider swapping press release duties with a writer friend; not only will each of you get a legitimate source, byline, contact name different from your own, you may find it's easier to write about someone else than it would be to write about yourself.

If you can't do a press release swap, another option is to go with a different source and/or byline name while still keeping your own name as the contact person. When a press release is published by a distribution company, that company's name is the source of the press release. Free and low-cost online press release distribution services are covered in more detail in the Distributing Your Press Releases section of this chapter.

As for byline, if your website or blog has a name other than your author name, you can use the name of the website/blog as the byline on two conditions: First, you must post the press release at the byline website/blog when it's published, and second, you still must provide your real name and details in the Contact

Kindle Edition of *The Indie Author Guide* Grabs Spots in Top 5 Of 3 Amazon Best-Seller Lists

By April Hamilton
Dated: Oct. 04, 2008

#2 Best-Seller in Kindle "Editing," #2 in Kindle "Desktop Publishing," #4 in Kindle "Authorship"

The Indie Author Guide, A Comprehensive Reference to Self-Publishing and Managing Your Career in Indie Authorship continues to occupy the top ten in three different Kindle best-seller lists, and is currently ranked at #2 in Kindle "Editing," #2 in Kindle "Desktop Publishing," #4 among Kindle "Authorship" titles.

According to author April L. Hamilton, "Since most people in the mainstream publishing industry acknowledge that manuscript rejections nowadays typically have more to do with the lack of TV show or movie tie-ins, merchandising opportunities, and the fame of the author than with the quality of the book, it's not surprising to see more and more authors choosing to self-publish. Mainstream publishing houses simply don't have much to offer aspiring authors anymore. Only best-selling and prestige clients get big advances and promotional budgets, and for the rest of us, being signed by a major publisher isn't even a guarantee that our book will one day show up on bookstore shelves now that those store are reducing their stock of books, refusing to carry titles that move only one or two copies a month."

Hamilton believes the time is right for authors to launch an "indie" movement of their own and proudly take their places alongside their indie peers in music and filmmaking. In addition to writing and publishing *The Indie Author Guide*, Hamilton maintains a website (www.aprilhamilton.com) and a blog (aprilhamilton.blogspot.com) filled with practical advice and free resources for authors wishing to take the indie leap.

"An indie author movement is not only long overdue," adds Hamilton, "but with today's hopelessly broken, blockbuster-centric mainstream publishing model, it's inevitable."

###

April L. Hamilton is a writer based in Southern California. Frustrated by the new business model of the highly consolidated publishing industry, Hamilton has elected to publish her work independently and is working to encourage an indie movement in authorship to match those in the music and film industries.

Category	Books, Literature, Publishing
Email	Click to email author
Phone	xxx-xxx-xxxx
City/Town	Los Angeles
State/Province	California
Zip	xxxxx

Figure 11-2

section. In my case, my author website name is the same as my author name, which is the same as my legal name, which doesn't help me. However, my blog name is IndieAuthor, so I could list IndieAuthor as the byline if I desired.

Don't overthink the source, byline, contact stuff, though. If the content of your press release is newsworthy and interesting, so long as the source, byline, contact information is legitimate, it won't matter much that you wrote it yourself. Your goal is to drive traffic to your website, blog, or event with the ultimate purpose of selling books, not to convince the general public that you have a ton of money to spend on publicity. Listing your own name for source, byline, contact won't kill the credibility of your press releases, but sales hype or dishonesty will.

Content of a Press Release

While the press release is a promotional tool, it should not read like sales copy. You're writing an announcement, conveying factual information that your intended audience would want to know regardless of whether it helps you sell books. If you follow the guidelines already given for the appropriate timing of press releases, you should have no trouble avoiding the dreaded, bald-faced sales pitch in press release clothing because you won't be writing a press release unless you have something newsworthy to write about. Still, you need to avoid the hard sell. Consider the following two examples.

GALE ADAMS THRILLS IN NEW THRILLER

Don't start reading *Mercy Me*, author Gale Adams' terrific new book, until you're ready to stay up all night with the lights on! In this fact-based thriller, a serial killer is on the loose and private investigator Caitlin McElroy has reason to believe a modern-day Dr. Frankenstein is at work in her sleepy New England town of Cordley. As tensions and suspicions divide the once close-knit community, McElroy finds facts and evidence piling up against the one person no one else would ever suspect...

AUTHOR GALE ADAMS REVISITS "CORDLEY FRANKENSTEIN" CASE

Thirty-seven years ago a serial killer terrorized the small New England town of Cordley, abducting a dozen citizens in as many weeks. The killer's basement charnel house, where he dismembered and reassembled the bodies of his victims, was eventually discovered, but no charges were ever brought in the bizarre case. Based on newly discovered evidence and painstaking research, author Gale Adams advances a shocking and plausible theory in her new book, *Mercy Me*...

The first example reads like jacket copy, whereas the second could pass for a news item. The book sales pitch couldn't be any more obvious in the first example, but in the second the book-promotion aspect of the release seems almost incidental, with the primary focus given over to reexamination of an unsolved murder case.

When you write a press release, try to get into the third-person mind-set of a reporter. Identify the most newsworthy aspect of your press release and focus on that. Bring in additional facts and quotations only in support of the main focus. If you don't have quotes from outside sources, "interview" yourself.

Instead of writing, "As a former resident of Cordley, Adams had long been troubled by the Frankenstein case and was even acquainted with one of the victims," consider, "Asked why she chose to write about this particular case, Adams replied, 'I lived in Cordley at the time the murders took place, and I was even acquainted with one of the victims. The affected families never got any closure or justice, and I wanted to do something about it.'" Quotes are a good way to keep an active voice in the narrative while revealing more about yourself.

Distributing Your Press Releases

The easiest way to distribute your press releases is through a service. An Internet search for press release will turn up many such services, and some are listed on www.indieauthorguide.com. Two that distribute online, at no charge, are www.prlog.org and www.openpr.com. You can go to either site and enter your press release information online, review it in a print-preview mode, and then release it to all the major online media outlets such as Google News and Yahoo! At the PRlog site, you can even sign up for a free "press room," where you can keep track of all your press releases from a single location.

Even if you use an online distribution service, you should still prepare your press release in advance. This allows you to spend as much time as you like writing and revising the release before publishing it, and also gives you an original version for archive purposes. When you're ready to submit, all you need do is copy and paste from your saved file.

The alternative to a distribution service is good old-fashioned elbow grease: Look up the fax numbers of all the media outlets you'd like to hit and fax your press release to each of them. The term *media outlets* includes newspapers, magazines, radio stations, TV shows, and websites. You can find their fax numbers by looking them up online and clicking the Contact link on each website. You can also fax your press releases to The Associated Press, which is the granddaddy of all news outlets. Go to the AP site (search for it online or get the link on www.indieauthorguide.com) and click the Contact AP link. You'll be taken to a page where you can look up contact information for the bureau office closest to you.

If possible, include PDF copies of your press releases on the news page of your author website, if you have one. This requires uploading the PDF copies to the server where your website is hosted and placing links to them on the news page. Depending on the service or site you've used to create your author website, an easy upload/link form may be available to you.

Editorial Reviews

♩-♩♩♩♩	$-$$$
👥	⚡⚡

Most industry experts agree books are sold on word of mouth, so reviews are very important. Don't be discouraged by the fact that mainstream media outlets are rarely willing to review indie books, as polls have shown reviews from professional book critics don't carry much weight with the average reader. The reviews that matter to readers are reviews from other readers: People who read for the joy of it and post reviews as a public service, not because they're getting paid to do so.

The scale provided above is for soliciting a single editorial review. The time factor can vary widely, as the first part of the task is locating likely reviewers and writing to them to solicit a review. Locating and contacting one to four candidates may take just an hour or less, so if time is tight you can limit your efforts to that one hour per day until you feel you have enough reviews.

The expense factor varies as well, depending on your cost to buy a copy of your book and mail it to the reviewer, plus the number of review copies sent. The only skills involved are basic letter and e-mail writing, and you need only as much confidence as it takes to write them.

Why to Solicit

Editorial reviews have many uses beyond the press kit. You can pull quotes from them to use as book cover blurbs and press release fodder. Positive Amazon reviews help raise your book's profile, and therefore sales, on Amazon. Reviews can be reprinted on your blog or website. Lastly, and most importantly, editorial reviews appearing in publications or on popular websites are among the best advertisements you can get, and they cost the meager price of a little bit of time and one copy of your book.

Who to Solicit

If your book is listed for sale on Amazon, try some Amazon Top Reviewers. Go to the Ama-

zon Top Reviewers information page to access the reviewers' profiles (do an Internet search or visit www.indieauthorguide.com to get the link). Each profile will usually say something about the reviewer's taste in books and her review policy. You want to find reviewers who like your kind of book, have indicated they're open to accepting submissions for review, and have listed their e-mail address in their profile. Where a given reviewer hasn't specifically said they will not accept submissions for review, if they've listed an e-mail address you can take that as a sign of receptiveness: Contact them.

Another good source for editorial reviews is the online reader communities (such as, LibraryThing, GoodReads, and Shelfari). These are sites where people list and rate books they've read, and participate in discussion groups about books. Go to the desired site, click the Groups tab, and browse the discussions until you find fans of your type of book, or even better, any groups specifically dedicated to doing reviews of new or indie books (such as Early Reviewers and Indie Reviewers). You can click the member name on any discussion group post to view the poster's member profile, and if an e-mail address is listed you can proceed with a solicitation e-mail. In the case of dedicated reviewer groups, there will be a post or other link to submission requirements on the group's page.

Blogs are also a great source for potential reviewers. Lots of book fanatics blog, and there are many who specialize in book reviews. Do a Google blog search for "books," "book reviews," "reading," or the like and browse until you find some likely candidates who've listed their e-mail addresses on their profiles. To do a Google blog search, go to www.google.com and click the More link. In the drop-down list, select blogs. Now run your Google search as usual, and Google will limit its result set to blogs.

While most large newspapers and magazines have a policy against reviewing self-published books, your local papers and community magazines are likely to be more receptive. Such publications are particularly interested in news and events related to the communities they serve, so a book from a local author is right up their alley. Get a copy of the publication you're considering; first, to make sure they publish book reviews, and second, to see if the publication's intended audience is a group that would be at all likely to buy your book. For example, a publication that's aimed at seniors or families with small children may not be the best outlet for a review of your steamy vampire-erotic thriller. If the publication seems like a match, call their office or visit their website to get a phone number or e-mail address for the reviewer you'd like to contact.

Finally, sign up for a free account at Book-Connector (bookconnector.com). Once signed up, you can search BookConnector's extensive database to locate editorial reviewers who have expressed an interest in your specific type of book. You can also find listings for bookstores, libraries, and other venues receptive to hosting live readings and book-signing events.

How to Solicit

When soliciting for reviews, keep your phone calls or e-mails short, polite, and on point. E-mail is preferable to phone calls, as there's no risk of catching the reviewer at a bad time, and you can take as long as you like in wordsmithing your solicitation. Greet the reviewer by name,

spelled correctly. If you can't tell the reviewer's gender from the name, you can fudge it by omitting any gender-specific titles (Mr., Mrs., Ms.) in your greeting. In the body of your e-mail, explain how you found the reviewer, why you think your book will appeal to the reviewer, include a link to a free excerpt if you've made one available, then close by asking if you may send a free review copy, and if so, where you should send it. Here's an example:

> Dear Lesley Drummond:
>
> I've found your book reviews in the *Daily Bugle* to be well-written and insightful. Because you seem to especially enjoy true-crime thrillers, I hope you might consider reviewing my new novel, *Mercy Me*. The novel centers on the real life, unsolved Cordley Frankenstein case, in which twelve Cordley Township, New Hampshire, residents were murdered over a period of three months in 1970. Based on extensive research and interviews with many of those involved in the case, I've developed a plausible, if shocking, new theory about the killer's identity. That theory forms the basis of *Mercy Me*. If you'd like to take a look at it, I've posted an excerpt from the novel online at www.galeadams.com/MMexcerpt.pdf.
>
> May I send you a review copy of the novel, and if so, where should I send it?
>
> Thanks For Your Consideration,
>
> Gale Adams

Notice that the solicitation does not merely parrot jacket copy, or sales hype of any kind. Rather, it states why you're contacting the reviewer and provides details relevant only to that specific reviewer's area of interest. If you were soliciting *Dollmaker's Monthly* for a review of your young adult novel about a doll that comes to life, you wouldn't need to provide a whole plot synopsis—the mention that it's about a doll that comes to life would be enough to pique their interest.

Because you will be sending out many, many solicitations, it's a good idea to save a boilerplate version of your solicitation, or a few different boilerplate versions. When you need to solicit, paste the most appropriate boilerplate into a new e-mail and customize it for the individual reviewer.

Articles

⏱–⏱⏱⏱	FREE!
👥👥	⚡

Articles you've written are additional press kit candidates, as they can show your range as a writer or your ability as a researcher. Aside from press kit considerations, writing and distributing articles is a great way to build up readership and drive more traffic to your website, blog, and ultimately, your books. Writing articles for print media is a traditional tactic, while online articles are new media.

Many writers blog, but a blog entry is not the same as an article. An article in this context contains informative, useful content, whereas blog entries can consist of amusing observations, editorial essays, and anecdotes.

Article Content

What can you write about? If you've done research for your writing, you've probably amassed all kinds of interesting factoids that may be of interest to the general public. In the course of education and experience, you may have developed particularly keen editing skills or an uncanny ear for dialogue. Maybe you don't consider yourself a subject area expert in writing prose, but you're the person everyone calls when they need help with the advanced formatting features of their word processing program, or when they can't figure out how to set up an Amazon author profile. Maybe your fellow writers shower you with praise for your insightful and thoughtful manuscript reviews and notes.

Or perhaps you feel you have no expertise whatsoever to speak of, but you frequently attend writers' seminars and events, and can report on your experiences there. If you have got anything of interest to share, you have another promotional tool in your belt.

Article Distribution

Ideally, you want your articles published on high-traffic websites frequented by the target audience for your book. Don't be shy about approaching site editors or administrators via the sites' Contact Us form if you have a great article to share that seems like a fit for the site. As the editor-in-chief of Publetariat.com, I can tell you that people who run content-rich websites are always on the lookout for fresh, quality content. Just be sure to honor any submission guidelines and other requirements the staff provides.

You can also post your written articles in PDF or HTML format on your website or blog, though a blog isn't necessarily the best way to go if your articles may be lengthy or could include illustrations. Pasting all that text directly into the pages of your website isn't such a good idea either, because it clutters up your site and your articles will be a lot harder on the eyes than if they were presented in typical black print on a white background format. It's preferable to provide a link to each article, which can then be accessed as a stand-alone document.

Another option is one of the many public websites that solicit for submissions on an ongoing basis. Some of them even pay for the articles they print. A number of these are listed on www.indieauthorguide.com. While sites like these sometimes claim you can actually make a living writing articles for the site, in reality it's not too likely. Your reason for doing this should be twofold: first, to help out your fellow authors or readers with information they can use, and second, to increase your visibility in the crowded world of authorship.

It's a good idea to settle on a single content site for your articles, partly in order to increase your earnings potential (however small it may be) and partly to raise your profile as an article author. If you write six articles for the same content site, you have a body of work there. If you publish two articles on three different sites, however, you may come off looking like a dabbler.

Appearances

🕐–🕐🕐🕐	$$$$$
NO SKILLS!	⚡⚡⚡

A live appearance can be something as humble as giving a career day talk at the local high school, something as prestigious as being a speaker at a writers' retreat, or any number of things in between. A speaking engagement merits a press release, and every audience member is a potential purchaser of your books, so unless you're painfully shy, don't pass up any writing-related live appearance opportunities.

In fact, drumming up such opportunities yourself is an excellent way to promote your books. Whatever you've written about, chances are there's a group or club out there interested in, or dedicated to, that very thing.

What to Speak About

You can talk about your experiences as a writer or the content of your books, or you can develop a talk based on an article you've written. Whatever you choose to speak about, tailor your talk to the group. For example, a writers' group may want to hear about your technique or experiences in publishing, whereas a book club (readers) will likely be more interested in the content of your book.

Where to Speak

You can quickly obtain a long list of bookstores and clubs interested in hosting author talks by signing up for a free BookConnector account (search for the site online or go to www.indieauthorguide.com to get the URL). Once your account is set up, you can do a search of the site's extensive database, specifying details about your geographic location and types of venues desired to narrow the results.

Contact your local public and university libraries, and also consider soliciting clubs and groups with a specific connection to your work. For example, if your historical fiction novel deals with the Civil War, you might approach Civil War reenactors. If wilderness survival or wildlife conservation plays a major part in your book, you can reach out to the local chapter of the Sierra Club. Apply some creative thinking, and you're sure to come up with many options of your own.

If you're good at public speaking, don't hesitate to make those calls and volunteer to speak. Libraries and clubs are always looking for ways to keep things interesting for their members and visitors, and guest speakers are a popular solution.

Live Readings

🕐–🕐🕐🕐	$$$$$
NO SKILLS!	⚡⚡⚡

Libraries, independent bookstores, and community fairs are all good venues for live readings from your books, as are book club meetings. Just as you would for appearances, you'll need to make calls and send e-mails to solicit for readings. You can also make some calls to local coffeehouses and bars to locate open mic nights, when anyone is allowed to go up onstage to read or speak. It may be possible for you to make serial appearances, gradually working through your book from beginning to end.

It's easy enough to look up libraries, bookstores, coffeehouses, and bars, but you may have to do an Internet search or check with your local community center to find out where and when book clubs and writers' groups meet in your area, and when community fairs will be held. Try searching on [your town name] + "book club."

Doing the reading only costs your time, but it's a good idea to have copies of your book(s) available for sales and signings on the spot, as well as some cash to make change if you'd prefer not to accept checks, and this is where the expense comes in.

Book Signings

🕐–🕐🕐🕐	$$$$$
NO SKILLS!	⚡⚡⚡⚡

Book signings can be held at a bookstore, library, community fair, or anywhere else people congregate—so long as you get the necessary permissions or permits ahead of time. You can rent a booth at a community fair and work the local author angle. You can work out a deal with your church to set up a table at their rummage sale in exchange for a share of your profits. One writer I know has an arrangement with public libraries in her area, which invite her to do readings and book signings in exchange for 10 percent of her sales at the events.

It may surprise you to know that even the big chain bookstores may welcome you to do a signing event, but they will require you to provide all the books you intend to sell and will still want their cut of each sale (typically 40 percent of the retail price). Just call the store manager to make your inquiries. Note that the manager may want to meet you or even read your book before agreeing to host your event.

The Media Tie-In

🕐–🕐🕐🕐	FREE!–$$$$$
NO SKILLS!–💣💣💣	⚡–⚡⚡⚡⚡

A media tie-in occurs when you can connect yourself or your work to something already being widely reported in the media. The connection is not literal, nor does it even necessarily reference the larger story you're connecting with directly. Rather, the tie-in is more about timing promotional materials and activities strategically to capitalize on buzz and publicity already in the marketplace. Don't think of tie-ins as single self-contained events. Tying in to larger media stories should be an ongoing process, something you do as a regular part of your promotional efforts.

The variance in cost and skills is due to the variety of methods you can use to establish your media tie-in and depends on how much of the effort will be DIY versus paying for outside services. Confidence requirements vary based on the strength of the connection between yourself or your book, and the story you're tying to. For example, if your book is a fictionalized account of events leading up to the Bay of Pigs conflict, it's easy to tie in to the anniversary of that event, as well as any news being reported about Castro's government. However, when the subject matter of your book is related to events in the news, though not truly *about* those events, some salesmanship is needed.

What to Tie In

Keep an eye out for media coverage of people, places, and things in your book. By *people*, I don't mean specific characters—unless those characters are real-life historical figures. I'm talking more about their professions, major interests, ethnic identities, socio-economic position, and so forth.

Novels that feature adult children caring for their elderly parents can tie in to media stories about caring for the elderly, or the increasing size of the elderly population. A book of essays about various jobs you've been fired from can tie in to media stories about layoffs and employment data.

Also be on the lookout for news stories about the publishing industry or the arts that affect you, as an author. If the small press you've published with is bought out by a larger publisher, you can write an insider-view article about how the merger will affect you and your books.

When Amazon first released its Kindle e-book reader, there was an opportunity for authors to weigh in with their thoughts on how this new technology might affect them and their future work. In such a piece you may not have reason to mention your book in the body of the article at all, but you can still include a link to your website or list your book's title in the author summary typically given at the end of articles. For example, *John Doe, a writer based in Spokane, WA is the author of four novels. His latest,* The Craven Ones, *was published in January of this year. For more information about John and his work, visit www.johndoe.com.*

Do not attempt a media tie-in unless the connection you're establishing between yourself/your work and the reported subject is clear and legitimate, because that connection cannot be stated directly: Your audience must infer it. In a book tie-in, your goal is to draw the attention of people who are already interested in the topics, places, or types of people you've written about, then inform them about a book that will provide more coverage of those topics, places, or types of people.

In an author tie-in, you want to comment about current events of interest from a position of special knowledge or expertise, adding your informed opinion to the body of information available about an event or topic.

How to Tie In

Most tie-ins take the form of articles or press releases, but authors can tie in to community events by making live appearances as well. For example, the author of a book that prominently features knitting can tie in to a local arts and crafts fair by setting up a booth to sell and sign her books at the fair. She can also donate some copies of her books as raffle giveaways for the fair in exchange for a mention in the fair's printed program. Another possibility is volunteering to give knitting lessons to beginners or to give demonstrations of advanced techniques, either from her booth or from a performance stage, if applicable.

My own community hosts an annual folk music festival each spring. Authors whose books involve folk music, or cultures strongly associated with folk music (for example, Appalachian culture is strongly associated with bluegrass, devotional, and banjo music) can tie in to this festival. As with any live appearances, a supply of books should be on hand to sell and sign.

Events related to literacy, books, or libraries are no-brainer tie-ins for any author. In addition to live appearances, consider writing an article for your local paper (or community newsletter). For library-centered events, you can write about what that library means (or has meant) to you, both as an author and a community resident. Literacy events invite you to wax philosophic about the state of literacy in today's changing world from an author's

perspective. Book fairs are also obvious tie-ins, regardless of the subject matter of your book, as are anniversary celebrations for local independent bookstores you frequent.

On a more personal note, be on the lookout for media coverage of places or topics that concern your development as a writer. When the little neighborhood shop where you used to sit and scribble in your journal for hours on end celebrates an anniversary or goes out of business, it's an occasion worthy of remembrance— and an article or essay from you. Similarly, if a teacher who mentored or strongly influenced your writing is about to retire or receive some kind of service award, volunteer to speak at the event, to share how his tutelage helped make you the writer you are today. Teachers rarely get the thanks or credit they deserve, so your words will be greatly appreciated.

If you aren't comfortable with public speaking, or you can't afford the time or money to travel to the fete, make some inquiries to see if any type of event program or memory book is being compiled. If so, you can offer to send a brief letter or essay for inclusion, along with your author details. You can also just write a letter to the editor of your local paper to sing your teacher's praises.

Handouts

🕐–🕐🕐	FREE!–$$$$$
🎈🎈–🎈🎈🎈	⚡–⚡⚡⚡

Handouts are printed cards or bookmarks you can keep on hand at all times to give to anyone who inquires about your writing. The confidence required to actually hand the cards out varies, depending on whether you're whipping them out in a face-to-face social encounter or simply stacking them on the table in a shop or at a book signing. Handouts you make yourself cost very little but take considerable time to design and print. Office supply stores can usually print promotional cards in various sizes, colors, and the like, but you will have to provide camera-ready art in an electronic file, and you will also have to order a minimum quantity of your chosen card.

You can print your own bookmarks on cardstock at home, and you may find your word processing, photo editor, or desktop publishing program provides a bookmark template. You can find many template choices online by searching for "bookmark template." If you own the rights to your book's cover art, use it on the bookmarks. If not, try to approximate the look of the cover with similar clip art, colors, and font. Be sure to include your website address and/or where-to-buy information.

Handout cards can be printed on business card stock or postcard stock, both of which are available at any office supply store. Most paper stock products include project templates as part of your purchase, either in the form of bundled software or downloads provided on the company's website. Some of the available templates are free, others are downloadable for a fee. Also try the website of your printer manufacturer (for example, HP or Canon) for projects and templates.

Business cards will be easier to carry in your purse or wallet, but the postcard may be a better handout for live appearances since it

has room to feature your book's cover (or an approximation) on one side and jacket cover copy on the back. If you have the appropriate paper craft tools and skills, you can even make a bookmark part of your postcard design and perforate or score the card ahead of time to make the bookmark easy to remove.

Merchandise

🕐–🕐🕐🕐🕐🕐	$-$$$$$
🎈–🎈🎈🎈	NO CONFIDENCE!

Merchandise such as T-shirts, tote bags, magnets, pencils, mugs, mousepads, and the like, printed with art and/or text from your book cover, are excellent promotional tools. Many of these items can be made at home using your own computer and printer, while others must be ordered from an outside vendor. The time, money, and skills involved all depend on how much you plan to do yourself and how much you plan to pay someone else to do.

Most office supply stores carry DIY promotional magnets, which allow you to print a business-card sized promotional piece and stick it onto the front of a preglued refrigerator magnet. You can also buy sticker sheets to use in your printer, as well as iron-on sheets you can use to make your own mousepads, tote bags, and T-shirts. The per-item cost of these DIY items is higher than if you ordered them in bulk from an outside vendor, but the advantage is that you don't have to buy a minimum quantity of items up front.

An option halfway between total home-based DIY and total outside vendor is the on-demand or small-run vendor. Some such companies are listed on www.indieauthorguide.com. Many operate online exclusively and allow you to upload your own designs to go on various items. Some even go so far as to let you open your own online shop if you'd like to sell your promotional items to the general public.

Your design can be as simple as a copy of your book cover art (or an approximation, if you don't own rights to the design), a quote from the book, or even just your website address. Whatever you put on your promotional items, you'll want to be sure to provide where-to-buy information such as "Available Now At Amazon.com" or your website address. If your website has sales links, use the website address for your where-to-buy information since that will drive traffic to your website as well as to your book sales pages.

Promotional items can be costly, so if you're on a budget you'll want to choose your items carefully, and distribute them even more carefully. Consider how much advertising bang you'll be getting for your buck when deciding what to buy and to whom you should give your promotional items. Ordering your items from an on-demand vendor makes it easier to control costs and also saves you the trouble of having to store boxes full of mugs, T-shirts, and other paraphernalia.

T-shirts and tote bags are big-ticket options, but people love getting free T-shirts and tote bags, and whoever wears your shirt or carries your bag in public is walking advertisement for your book. Give your T-shirts to people who are likely to wear them, especially people who are frequently surrounded by readers. Bookstore salesclerks and library volunteers are good candidates, so long as

they're allowed to wear T-shirts to work. A quick glance around at the staff will reveal the likely dress code. College students are another good bet for T-shirts. Tote bags are very much appreciated, and always used, by teachers. Don't rule out grammar school teachers, because they'll carry their stuff in your bag all over the place, not just to their classrooms.

Coffee mugs and magnets can work if you give them to people whose job involves meeting with other people throughout the day. Lawyers, customer service reps, real estate agents, accountants, insurance agents, and salespeople are just a few examples.

The next time you're asked to contribute something to be raffled off for fund-raising, offer some of your promotional items or copies of your books. Promotional giveaways are real crowd-pleasers at live readings and public speaking appearances too.

Word of Mouth

🕐–🕐🕐🕐🕐🕐	FREE!
NO SKILLS!	⚡⚡–⚡⚡⚡

At the low end of the time and confidence scale, *word of mouth* means that you mention your book to anyone who asks about your career or hobbies. Another step up the scale means that you mention your book and also give the inquirer one of your handouts. The next step up the scale requires that you discuss the book whenever the opportunity arises.

People at the highest end of the scale are those who don't wait for opportunities to arise, they actively seek out and approach others to talk about their books. They also attempt to enlist everyone they know to assist with getting the word out. Your own comfort level will determine where you fall on the time and confidence scales.

Paid Advertising

●	$$$$$
NO SKILLS!	**NO CONFIDENCE!**

Authors with a few hundred dollars to spend can pay for a small ad on a website, or in a local newspaper or magazine. Those with a couple thousand available can go for a larger ad, or a newspaper or magazine with slightly larger circulation. If you have more money than that to spend, your best option may be to hire a professional publicist. A publicist can handle as much or as little of your promotional efforts as you like, but if you intend to continue doing certain promotional tasks yourself, you should coordinate your efforts with the publicist to ensure there's no duplication of effort and to maintain consistency across your promotional materials.

NEW MEDIA TACTICS

In terms of promotional opportunities, the Internet offers an embarrassment of riches—and an awful lot of them are free! In the era of Web 2.0 (large quantities of Internet content created by Internet users instead of paid professionals), authors who aren't using the Internet to promote their work are at a distinct disadvantage to their more tech-savvy peers.

While basic computer and Internet skills will be enough to get you by with most of the options discussed in this section, you'll need moderate to advanced skills to take full advantage of all the Web has to offer. If you're completely intimidated by the idea of setting up a website, even a free one built with fill-in-the-blanks templates, skip ahead to the Author Blog section.

Author Website

●-●●●●	FREE!-$$$$$
●●-●●●●	**NO CONFIDENCE!**

A quality Web presence is a crucial component of author platform. An author website serves as a centralized clearinghouse for all official information about you and your books. Your website can provide your readers (and potential readers) with information about you, your work, where to buy your books, and what's being said about you and your work in reviews and the press. You can also use an author website to host excerpts from your published work so readers can try before they buy. And of course, your website is the ideal location to publicize your books, signings, appearances, and so on. The amount of time, money, and skills required to get an author website up and running are highly variable, depending on the type of site.

Book or Author?

Some authors have an author website/blog, some have a separate website for each book they have in print, and some have both. Creating a separate website for each of your books can make sense if you've written under several pen names, if you've written in widely differing genres, or if you feel each different work truly calls out for and can support enough content to create separate websites. As a guideline, if you believe a significant proportion of visitors to your author site will be primarily (or exclusively!) interested in a specific work, it may make sense to break that work out into its own site. However, don't forget that with each new website you create, you're also creating an ongoing maintenance chore for yourself (or an ongoing maintenance expense, if you'll be paying someone else to do the work for you).

What an Author Website Needs

Generally speaking, at the minimum an author website should include the following components.

Home page—welcomes visitors to your site, includes your name and an overview of what the site contains, as well as timely blurbs for any book or event you're currently promoting.

About page—author biography, photo, and contact information; links to online articles you've written, link to your blog site (if applicable), and links to social media/online community sites (for instance, Twitter, Facebook, LinkedIn, Goodreads, and Shelfari).

News or Press page—links to your press releases and any articles in which you're mentioned or quoted, information about upcoming appearances and events.

My Writing or (if applicable) My Books page—brief description of each of your works, links to online excerpts (if applicable), and where-to-buy/where-to-download links for each (if applicable), ideally with a thumbnail

image of each cover; if you don't have any completed works to sell or share, you can use this page to provide links to online articles you've written (instead of placing those links on your About page) or to share information about any works in progress.

Links or Favorites page—your own collection of favorite links to sites you think will be of interest to your site visitors; if you've also set up a separate blog, you'll want to include a link to the blog here and on your About page.

If you go for the full-featured site option, which is highly recommended, you will also want to add interactive widgets like those described in the Blog section below.

The Four Author Website Options

In setting up your Web presence, you have four options: a static website, a blog, a full-featured website, or an interactive community site. You may choose to set up just one of these or any combination of them. I'll open with an overview of each type, then get into more detail on how to choose the best type for your needs and how to set it up.

Static Website

A static website is an informational site with content that doesn't change very often. Static sites are also noninteractive, meaning site visitors can view content on the site but cannot post their own content, questions, or comments to the site (though the site may include a link to e-mail the site owner).

Lots of simple fill-in-the-blanks website services make it easy for someone with zero to limited technical skills to get this type of website up and running quickly. Several of them are geared specifically to the needs of authors, and most of them are low-cost or free. Alternatively, you can hire a professional Web developer to build and maintain a site for you.

Blog

A blog is an online journal, or Web log, which allows you to post new entries as often as you choose through a simple online form that looks and works a lot like a word processor program. You can use an author blog for any of the following purposes: as a personal journal, to provide an informational resource (such as I do with my Indie Author blog), to post opinion pieces or reviews of others' books and sites, to document your experiences with the writing and publishing process, to present work samples for feedback and critique, to publish short or flash fiction, or to invite discussion of any topics of interest to you and your blog audience.

Most author blogs aren't strictly limited to just one type of content, however. For example, Neil Gaiman's blog shows a lot of variety. Sometimes he posts observations that have nothing to do with his work or writing in general, sometimes he posts about his writing, sometimes about his book or movie promotion tour experiences, sometimes about charitable causes he feels are deserving of wider attention, and still other times he posts opinion pieces that may or may not touch on publishing or literature.

Many blogs also allow you to add interactive widgets, or Web page miniprograms that add interactive or multimedia functionality to your blog. For example, you can use widgets to add audio and video clips (for example, YouTube clips or podcasts), set up polls which allow you to pose a multiple-choice question to paid services.

Full-Featured Website

Full-featured websites are like a blend of a static website and blog, combining all the features and functionality of both in a single site. There are free and low-cost fill-in-the-blanks options here as well, but you'll generally get more and better functionality by paying for this type of site, whether that means paying a professional Web developer to create and maintain the site for you or paying for a premium fill-in-the-blanks type of service you can do yourself with minimal technical skills or knowledge. Of course, if you have very high technical skills you can create and maintain a site without any assistance.

Interactive Community Site

An interactive community site is the crème de la crème of options. On this type of site you can have all the bells and whistles of a full-featured website, but that's just the beginning. This type of site also allows you to sign up site visitors as members to your site, and provide them with features and options of their own, right on your site. For example, you can provide a community discussion forum, on which your site members can interact with you and one another within certain topic areas you set up and moderate. You can also set up polls of your own or allow your site members to set up their own polls. You can allow site members to have their own blogs on your site, and you can provide them with all the same kinds of widgets typically made available on dedicated blogging sites or full-featured websites. You can also utilize e-mail lists, which allow you to send periodic e-mail messages to all your site members, or certain groups of them, without having to purchase or install special software for the purpose.

This type of site also enables you to have multiple levels of security, such that you can set up trusted site members or associates with access to certain functions typically reserved for site administrators. For example, you can allow others to post articles on your site, moderate the discussion board area (delete spam or inappropriate posts), approve or revoke site memberships, author and send out a site newsletter, and so on.

Less technically inclined authors will typically have a hired site administrator who runs and updates the overall site on an ongoing basis, but an administrator will set up such authors with access to post articles and blog entries to the site, use the discussion board area, and use certain features or widgets that may not be available to regular site visitors and members. Such options include creating and maintaining an online calendar to display upcoming public appearances and using an online chat feature to host scheduled real-time chats with site members.

While most of us would eventually like to have an audience large enough to justify having an interactive community site, such sites demand a lot of time and attention. Also, when you're just starting out with author platform, there's a learning curve not only in terms of how to set up and run your website, but also in terms of learning the difference between what you think your audience wants and what they really do want. For these reasons, not to mention the time and expense factors, you may want to hold off on setting up this type of site until you're more seasoned and have a more sizable audience.

Choosing the Type of Site That's Right for You

Your decision of which type of site will be best for you depends on three factors: the functionality you desire, the amount of time and money (if any) you're willing to spend, the amount of time you're willing to invest on an ongoing basis, and your level of technical capabilities where computers and websites are concerned. There is no single one-size-fits-all solution, but the following table of site types, requirements, and features can help you zero in on what will work best for you.

The Minimum You Can Get Away With…

If you have very little in the way of time, money, and technical skills, you can pull together a free, static, fill-in-the-blanks type of site in an hour or less and at no cost. However, such a Web presence is scarcely better than having no Web presence at all. Author platform is all about interacting with your readership, and a free, static, fill-in-the-blanks type of site isn't built to facilitate interaction. It's really just an online info dump about you and your work. An effective Web presence requires a significant investment of your time, money, or both.

You can set up this sort of site as a stopgap measure while you work on developing a more elaborate or a community site, or you can set up this type of site and a blog, and link them to one another, but don't expect that a free, static, fill-in-the-blanks type of site alone will fully serve your purposes and needs for an author Web presence.

What Works for Most Authors

In my experience, most authors with an effective Web presence have either a static site with a linked blog or a full-featured site which allows them to blog right on their author site. Either type of setup can be effective, so long as it's attractive, well-maintained, and frequently updated.

I use a static author website with a linked blog and various widgets installed to display my most recent Twitter updates, blog entries, and one of my books in its entirety. I also keep a separate blog on the Publetariat site just for my flash fiction, and provide a link to that blog on my static author site.

Many author sites I've seen consist only of a blog with widgets and links installed along the side columns to provide where-to-buy book links, information about upcoming events and appearances, and so on.

Setting up a Static, Fill-in-the-Blanks Site

Creating a static, fill-in-the-blanks site is really very simple.

First, you select a service provider. There are many places online to set up a static web-

SITE TYPE	COST	TECH SKILLS REQUIRED	CAN BLOG?
STATIC, FILL-IN-THE-BLANKS	Free to low	None	No
STATIC, CUSTOM-BUILT	Free if you build and maintain it yourself, can be costly if you hire someone else to do it	High if you build and maintain it yourself, none if you hire someone else to do it for you	No
BLOG	Free to low	None to low	Yes
FULL-FEATURED, FILL-IN-THE-BLANKS	Full range, from free to high	None to low	Yes
INTERACTIVE COMMUNITY SITE	Free if you build and maintain it yourself, can be costly if you hire someone else to do it	High if you build and maintain it yourself, none if you hire someone else to do it for you	Yes

SITE TYPE	CAN USE WIDGETS?	ONGOING TIME COMMITMENT	COMMUNITY FEATURES?
STATIC, FILL-IN-THE-BLANKS	No	Low; update the site only as often as its information changes	No
STATIC, CUSTOM-BUILT	Yes, but you must pay for your site developer's time in adding and maintaining them	Low; have the site updated by your hired Web developer only as often as its information changes	No
BLOG	Yes	Moderate to high; to be effective, blog entries must be made frequently	No, but commenting can be enabled if desired
FULL-FEATURED, FILL-IN-THE-BLANKS	Yes	Moderate to high; to be effective, blog entries must be made frequently and you must regularly interact with your members—daily, if possible	Yes, but generally limited to blogging (for the author only) and discussion boards (for site visitors)
INTERACTIVE COMMUNITY SITE	Yes	High; to be effective, blog entries must be made frequently and you must regularly interact with your members—daily, if possible	Yes

site for free, using simple, fill-in-the-blanks templates. Homestead (www.homestead.com) and Tripod (www.tripod.com) are just two options for this type of site, but there are plenty more.

Once you've signed up for an account with your selected service provider, you log on to the site and complete a step-by-step questionnaire sort of process that involves selecting a site template with colors, fonts, and a layout that appeal to you, specifying the quantity and types of pages you want the site to include,

and finally giving a title to each page and filling them all with content via simple, online Web forms.

The site builder software will automatically insert a menu bar on every page of your site so that visitors can easily navigate from any page to any other page on your site, and the beauty of it is that you don't have to know anything about website design or programming to do it.

Since the tools for building such sites are aimed at people with little to no tech skills, each fill-in-the-blanks page is accompanied by a Help, What's This?, or question mark link that provides clarification on each item.

Another option is to join an online community that hosts websites for its members. Some such communities are free (again, ad-supported) and others charge a modest membership fee. AuthorsDen is geared to writers and offers both free (static sites) and premium (sites with features like blogging and discussion groups) membership levels.

FiledBy allows authors to set up a free Web page for each of their books, and offers paid upgrade options that add blogging, events promotion, a What I'm Reading list, customizable page headers, reader reviews, and more.

Publetariat offers free site memberships that include a blogging function as well.

The main advantage of such online communities is that they may include features specifically tailored to the needs of the community. For example, AuthorsDen websites and Publetariat member profiles make it easy for members to sell books directly from their sites by allowing authors to include links to online bookseller sites. However, such community-based sites are also fairly generic in terms of appearance, will be surrounded by menus and content specific to the umbrella community site (over which you have no control), and users aren't offered much in the way of customization choices. Before committing to such a site, look at some of their author/blog pages to determine if this solution will meet your needs.

If you want to go with a free, template-based site and don't care for any of the options mentioned thus far, search the Internet for "free website." If you're willing to pay a modest fee for your site but still want something template-based that you can build yourself with fill-in-the-blanks forms, search "easy website."

The Cons of Setting up a Free, Static Website

Totally free websites often have ads from the provider displayed on their pages, though the providers may offer an ad-free option if the website owner is willing to pay a small monthly maintenance fee. The providers also frequently offer fee-based website upgrades, such as more server space, a wider variety of website templates, or migration to a full-featured website.

If you can possibly afford it, I strongly recommend you go with the no-ads option. Ads clutter up pages and make it painfully obvious you went the cheap-and-easy route with your site. Furthermore, you don't usually have any control over what appears in the ads on free, ad-supported sites and may be surprised to find listings for products or services you don't like—or even for other authors' books!

Aside from the ads, there are three downsides to a totally free website. The first is that your design options are limited to the available templates. The second is that your website address may be long and hard to remember, since the provider's company name is in the address; for example, www.JoeAuthor.tripod.com may not seem all that unwieldy but it's not as clean and professional as www.JoeAuthor.com. The third, and perhaps most important, downside is that the number of hits (visits) your site can receive in a given period (per day, per week, or per month) may be limited, and when that limit has been reached no one can visit your site until the start of the next hit-counting period. Providers aren't stingy with their hit count allowances, and most of the time you'll be far from any risk of going over your limit. But if you're lucky enough to get some major media attention, such as a mention in a syndicated column, you may burn through your hit count allowance in a matter of minutes; it is the World Wide Web, after all. Anyone who gets an error message instead of your site probably won't come back.

It's also worth mentioning that totally free sites don't typically offer substantial technical support. You'll probably have access to a FAQ guide, a community forum where site owners share their problems, ideas, and solutions with one another, and an e-mail form you can use to send questions to the technical support department. It's typical to get automated boilerplate responses to such e-mails, directing you back to the FAQ and community forum. Fortunately, because free template-based sites are so simple, you'll rarely have the need for technical support.

Given that there are so many easy low-cost, full-featured website providers, and that your Web presence must serve as your professional online calling card, I very strongly suggest that if there's any possible way you can cobble together $10 to $15 per month to invest, you go with a paid full-featured website option.

Setting up a Free Fill-in-the-Blanks, Full-Featured Website

In setting up a free full-featured website, you have options. There are many fill-in-the-blanks types of sites which enable authors to quickly and easily create a site that combines the features of a static site with a blog, and may also include a limited selection of other features or widgets.

Weebly is a free site creation tool that includes blogging functionality and is free of charge, but it's not geared specifically to authors. While you'll be able to add where-to-buy links, you won't find a preformatted area on your site template specifically designed for this purpose; you'll have to customize your links page to include such links. The customization won't require any special technical skills or knowledge; you'll just have to change the title of the links page to "Where to Buy My Books," or alternatively, add a separate page for this purpose.

Red Room provides a combination static author site/blog that's elegant looking and free of charge, and also happens to be used by many top mainstream authors. Apart from providing a space for your author biography, a blog, and information about your books (including Where to Buy links) it doesn't offer much in the way of additional functionality.

EverPub is another author site provider that aims to be more social-media savvy than other providers and intends to provide a one-stop, all-in-one online author platform solution. EverPub is a good choice for authors who can afford to invest a few hundred dollars a year, want a very professional-looking site, and like the idea of a one-stop author platform solution.

Setting up a Paid Fill-in-the-Blanks, Full-Featured Website

An option that lies somewhere between setting up a fill-in-the-blanks static website and building your own site from scratch is to register your desired Web address (URL or domain) with a registration and hosting provider like GoDaddy, HostGator, or Network Solutions, and then use the simple online site creation tools made available by the provider to create your full-featured site. Being able to select your own Web address is a big advantage here, and most often you'll want that address to be your author name for author sites and your book name for book sites.

As of this writing, GoDaddy offers a five-page static type of site for $4 to $5 per month (depending on the length of your contract), ten-page static sites for $7.20 to $10 per month, and full-featured sites that include blogging functionality starting at $4 to $5 per month. HostGator offers free use of Site Builder software, which includes blogging functionality as an option, as a feature of their hosting packages, which run from $5 to $9 per month under their hatchling plan. This plan offers enough server space and bandwidth for most author sites, but more powerful plans are available from $7 to $15 per month. Network Solutions offers sites with blogging at $8 to $10 per month.

Getting up and running with this type of site is not difficult. Select the Web address you want and search for it at the provider site. If the address is available, sign up to register the address and set up Web hosting for your site. If the address you want is already taken, search for variations of it, or different addresses, until you find one you want that's still available.

Begin by logging in to view your site administrator dashboard or control panel. Look for the E-mail Accounts icon (you may have to scroll down a bit to find it) to set up at least one of the free e-mail accounts that comes with your hosting package. Doing so allows you to include an e-mail address of [yourname]@[yoursiteaddress] on your site for visitors to use to contact you, thereby keeping your personal e-mail private. Be sure to set up the Forwarding option, which will send a copy of any mail received at the new address to your personal e-mail address as well. Just be sure to log in to the new e-mail account from your website dashboard/control panel when responding to those messages; if you respond to them from your personal e-mail account, the recipient of your response will also receive your personal e-mail address.

Finally, return to your dashboard/control panel and look for the icon to launch the site builder software. The software will walk you step-by-step through the process of choosing a template, setting up your site pages, and adding content, and the software will automatically insert menus on your pages and store the pages in the correct locations on your server.

Another benefit of a paid site is access to free tech support via a toll-free phone number, live online chat, e-mail, or all three. Don't hesitate to use these support options if you get stuck at any point in the process of setting up your site.

Setting up a Full-Featured Custom Website by Yourself

Authors with advanced skills can set up an author website the old-fashioned way: register a domain, sign up with a hosting service, build pages, and upload everything to the Web. The main advantage of this approach is control: Since you own the site and build the site, you can make it exactly the way you want. It's more expensive and time-consuming than the methods described above, but well worth the effort if you have the skills, since this approach allows you to select your own website address and build the site entirely to your own specifications.

If you'll be building your own site, a separate, four-page PDF guide titled Basics of Effective Website Design, is provided on www.indieauthorguide.com.

Paying to Have a Totally Custom, Full-Featured Website Set Up

The author who wants a totally custom, truly professional-looking site but doesn't have the time or skills to create one can hire a Web developer to do it. As with the DIY approach mentioned above, the main advantages of going this route are choosing your own website address and having a totally customized site.

The best way to find a reliable Web developer is via personal referral. Look at others' websites—not just authors but people in various professions—and bookmark sites with the look and features you want your own site to have.

Sites designed and maintained by outside persons or companies usually have contact information for the site designer listed at the bottom of every page, but contact the person or company who hired that outside service first, to inquire about their satisfaction with the outside service. You can also ask what the service costs, both in terms of initial setup and ongoing maintenance.

Narrow the field of candidates to just two or three, and then conduct e-mail or phone interviews with them. Topics of primary concern include technical support (hours and days available, telephone versus e-mail-only support, support cost per month or per incident), throughput capacity (how many site visits and file downloads are you allowed each month before incurring additional charges, and what will visitors to your site see if you've exceeded your throughput allowances?), and the process for making site changes and updates (whom do you contact, how do you contact him/her, can you see changes in a preview mode before they go live on your site, and how long does it take for changes/updates to go live?). You'll also want to find out how frequently, and in what form, site statistics will be reported to you: How many visitors, what links they followed to get to your site, what keyword searches led people to your site, and how long site visitors stayed.

The Cons of Hiring Out

Apart from expense, a hired Web developer comes with a few other downsides. First, there will always be delays between the time you notice a mistake on your site (or want to update it) and the time a change takes effect online. Second, the site designer's interpretation of what you want won't always be accurate, and this introduces further delays while you wait (and possibly pay) for corrections. Finally, once you've tied your wagon to a certain site design service, you're stuck with that service for the duration of your contract.

Setting up an Interactive Community Site

Some of the full-featured author website options previously discussed include community features like online discussion boards, but if you want to set up a true membership-based community with various membership levels, various secured areas, and user-contributed content (whether that means articles, blog entries, or uploaded pictures, videos, or audio files), you have just two means of achieving your goal: You can hire a professional Web developer to set up the site for you or, if you have the necessary technical skills, you can get a Content Management System (CMS) software program and build the site yourself.

I built the Publetariat site myself using Drupal, a free open-source CMS. Two more free, open-source options are Joomla! and Wordpress (the full program, which you can download at wordpress.com, NOT the version you get from wordpress.org). Expression Engine is a fee-based CMS, but it's designed for large companies to use and has far more muscle than most authors would ever need for their websites.

It's beyond the scope of this book to provide a how-to on designing, building, and maintaining an interactive community site. Either you have the necessary technical skills to go to any of the above sites and follow the tutorials provided there, or you lack those skills and will need to hire a professional Web developer to do the work for you.

Regarding community site design considerations, and planning for a successful launch that will draw traffic quickly, I've written a book on that subject entitled, *From Concept to Community*.

You can also do an Internet search on "community website design," "community building," or "online communities" to find many free articles and resources on the subject.

What About Facebook and MySpace?

While Facebook and MySpace are terrific adjuncts to your author website and blog, they're not good as *primary* author platform solutions for several reasons.

First, they're set up to be members-only sites, not open to the general public. The goal of your author site and blog is to make information about yourself and your books available to anyone on the World Wide Web. Using Facebook or MySpace as your primary platform solution puts some, or most, of that information behind a locked door.

Second, Facebook and MySpace were not designed with author platform in mind, so they don't have the preformatted pages and sections you need for an author website or blog. While you can customize the look of your page to some extent, the general site layout and functionality are dictated by Facebook or MySpace, and your ability to customize your page is fairly limited.

Third, these sites are subject to periodic redesigns and updates that are totally out of your control. Even if you can get your page set up the way you want it within the confines of the site's design limitations, there's no guarantee your page will stay the way you've set it up. One day you could log in to find some of your page elements have been discontinued, or the entire page layout has been redesigned.

Fourth, because these sites were designed with social networking in mind, they make it easy for members to add content and comments to one another's pages. While this is great for social networking, it takes the control of your page content out of your hands. You can set your options for maximum limitation on this kind of thing, but doing so defeats the purpose of belonging to a social networking site and is likely to turn off other site members.

Finally, Facebook and MySpace pages carry advertising that's completely out of your control. However, because they can still be useful planks in your author platform if used properly, you should definitely link to them from your author site or blog. See the Social Media For Authors section of this chapter.

Author Blog

🕐–🕐🕐	FREE! – $$$
⚫⚫	⚡⚡⚡

There are lots of blog services out there, many of which are free. Some options to look at are www.blogger.com (free), www.typepad.com (fee-based), and www.wordpress.org (free). To find more, do an Internet search for "blog" or "free blog."

Blogs begin with the same kind of sign up and template selection process as fill-in-the-blanks websites: You create an account, then choose from a selection of predesigned blog layouts that feature different colors, design elements, and fonts.

From there, blogs all work in basically the same way: You type an entry, or post, into an online form that's much like an e-mail form or word processor interface. As you go, you can apply any formatting options to your text as you might in an e-mail form or word file (bold, italic, choice of font). Then click a button to preview your post, go back to make changes if necessary, preview again, and click another button to publish your post. (See Figure 11-3.)

Figure 11-3

To create a new post on Blogger, I log in to my dashboard, then click the New Post button. Once I do that, I see Figure 11-4.

Creating a new blog post is as simple as entering a title, then typing my post into the big text box. The formatting and tool buttons on the toolbar look and act just like the ones in my word processor, so it's easy for beginners to get started quickly.

Blogger doesn't force you to preview your posts before clicking the Publish Post button, but it's a good idea to use the little "Preview" link to see how it's going to look before you publish it. All blogging services provide the user with some way to preview the post before publishing, whether via a Preview button or a Preview link. Get in the habit of previewing to avoid embarrassing mistakes.

The blog service will automatically date- and time-stamp your posts, though some offer the option to schedule publication of posts for a future date or time.

Text formatting options are limited compared to what you get from a word processor, but they generally work the same: Highlight the text you want to format, then click a Toolbar button to apply formatting changes.

Most blog services will also have a button for inserting hyperlinks into your posts, and some even allow full use of HTML to insert pictures, video, and widgets, but these are all optional to the user: If your preference is to simply type in plain text, you can do that. The blog service will also provide a profile page on which you can provide as much or as little personal information as you like to create something akin to an author website's About page.

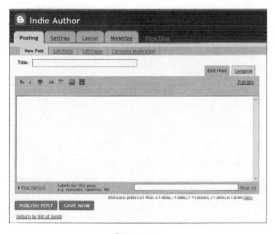

Figure 11-4

Most blog providers allow you to choose whether you want blog visitors to post comments and feedback to your posts; this and other blog settings are specified in the Settings, Options, or Administration menu after you log in. In most cases, there's an option allowing the blog author to review and approve comments and feedback before they become visible on the blog; this is called *comment moderation*.

You can blog under any name you wish, but since the purpose of your blog is to promote your work, it makes sense to blog under your author, or brand, name.

Most blogs will automatically generate a link to every post you create and keep a running list of those links displayed on your main blog page, but they will also provide the option to turn this feature off if you wish (in the Settings, Options, or Administration menu). It's typical for blog authors to be able to categorize the list by topic or date by adjusting their blog settings as well. Increasingly, blog services allow users to employ HTML and site widgets. Blogger, for example, has an Add a Page Element feature in the Layout section of the user dashboard.

When the user clicks the Add a Page Element link, a new window opens and displays all the available site tools and widgets to be had. The HTML/Javascript feature presents a text box into which the user can type (or paste) HTML and Internet scripts to add special features to his blog.

If you see a widget you like on someone else's blog, look for a Get This Widget link near the widget. Click that link to go to the widget provider's site. From there, you can fill in a brief Web form by answering a few questions that will customize the widget for your site. When you submit the form, you will be presented with a box containing a bunch of Web page code. Just copy all of that code (but don't close the page it came from, in case you need to recopy it), then return to your blog's Add a Page Element or Add HTML/Script feature and follow the prompts to paste the copied code into your blog. In the screen capture shown below, I'd select the HTML/Javascript item from the Choose a New Page Element menu to paste in a new block of widget code. (See Figure 11-5.)

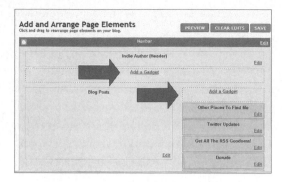

Figure 11-5

Like Blogger, most blog services also provide widgets like those shown above. The photo slide show, visitor poll, and link list are just a few examples. Users can add the widgets and services to their blogs with just a button click or by selecting the item from a list. Setting up any widget is usually as simple as following a step-by-step, fill-in-the-blanks Web form.

Getting Your Blog Up and Running

Remember that while your new blog will be live and visible online as soon as you've created it, no one is likely to accidentally stumble across it until you begin promoting and linking to it. Therefore, create a "Welcome to My Blog" post to get started and have something to preview, then experiment with the various widgets and settings until you're happy with the look of your blog. But try to get through this process within an hour or two. Don't let it drag on for days, because it won't be long before people do start finding your blog, and you don't want their first impression of you to be a bad one.

What to Blog

First, you must identify the target audience for your blog. This is because the content of the blog will be dictated by the target audience. If your tar-get audience is readers, for example, you'll want to blog about books, writers, literature in general, issues related to book pricing, and e-book technology. If your target audience is other writers, some of the same issues may be appropriate, but you will also want to blog about craft, the writing life, your experiences in self-publishing, or trying to get an agent or mainstream contract.

Regardless of your target audience you'll want to use the blog as an outlet for promoting your books and related work, though you don't want the blog to become little more than a collection of sales pitches. It's reasonable to blog about a book or seminar/event you're selling on just three occasions: When the book is released for sale or your seminar/event is opened for registration, when the book hits a best-seller list/sells out its print run/makes the mainstream news or your seminar/event is nearing its registration deadline or is nearly sold out, and when the book wins a contest or award or the seminar/event is over and you wish to blog about how it went. If your blog content is sparse, however, even this may be blogging too much about your book.

This isn't to say you shouldn't more subtly promote the book or seminar/event between those three posts. You should always have Where to Buy links for your books or registration links for your seminars/events prominently displayed on your blog and author website, and it's also a good idea to mention those books and events in the context of other posts wherever they're germane to the topic of those posts (for example, in a post about characterization you can talk about how you approached character in your novel and provide the name of that novel with a link to a page where the reader can buy it). The problem occurs if the sole purpose of a given post is to sell a book or event/seminar, because its informational value is very limited.

It's entirely legitimate to inform your readers about the availability of your books and events but abusive to constantly pummel them with sales messages. Therefore, try to limit such posts to situations in which you genuinely have something newsworthy to say about the book or event.

Your blog entries must be compelling enough to keep people coming back. Since anyone can write a blog, an abundance of boring and pointless blogs can be found out there. Your blog posts will be most effective if you wait until you have something worth writing about but not every post must be a wellspring of pithiness.

Most writers are interested in learning more about other writers' technique, or even just commiserating over common challenges. You can blog about your process, your stumbling blocks, your frustrations and triumphs in writing. When you attend a writers' seminar or class, blog about it. Blog about great new writer resources or websites you've discovered, promotional activities and your degree of success with them, books you've read and your opinions about them, and of course, about your works in progress. You can blog about contests, writers' groups, the publication process ... just about anything writing related so long as it's interesting, informative, surprising, or provocative.

Blogging about your experiences querying or dealing with agents and editors is another popular option, but if you do this be careful not to write anything that could be construed as defamation or libel; it's safest not to name names at all when you're writing about another person, regardless of who that person is, unless you're showering him with praise and admiration, or crediting the author of an article/post upon which you wish to comment.

About the only people who can get away with mere pontificating in an author blog are celebrities and lively nonfiction authors. Plenty of people would love to read David Sedaris' description of a typical day in his life, because it would undoubtedly be just as funny and insightful as his published articles and essays. As for the rest of us, the general public probably won't be all that interested in reading that your cat threw up on the quilt again this morning and you finally figured out how to send pictures with your new cell phone. Remember that people visit your blog because you're a writer: Because they're fans of your work, or they're seeking a writer's viewpoint on things. Try to keep your posts relevant and on point.

In her book, *Get Known Before The Book Deal*, author Christina Katz offers the following seventeen blogging tips:

1. Keep your content fresh. Don't blog about what everyone else is blogging about. Respond to a buzz topic with your fresh perspective, drawing on your expertise. Give folks something to think about that they won't find anywhere else.

2. Avoid politics, religion, or anything that might offend your readers, if none of these are your expertise. (Learned this the hard way.)

3. One more time with emotion: Consider what your audience cares deeply about

and revisit those topics often. Encourage, inspire, cajole.

4. Use reporting techniques. Can you back that up with a fact? Then go ahead. Trends, statistics, news, and current events are all more interesting with a few facts sprinkled in.

5. Demystify whenever possible.

6. Offer roundups of your best previous posts.

7. Optimize your blog. Use feeds that allow folks to subscribe. Include links to subscribe to any newsletters you offer.

8. Create a relevant and enticing list of related blogs (blogroll). Visit those blogs regularly and leave comments.

9. Think community. If your blog seems to be just you talking to you, people will not be inclined to stay. Think we.

10. Post rhythmically. Your readers don't want to come back every day if you are only going to post every other day. Always post consistently.

11. Avoid blogging burnout by utilizing guest bloggers and co-bloggers, but don't disappear if your audience came to hear you.

12. Be visual. Add quality photos, videos, and podcasts. Remember that you are producing your own show. What would you come back for?

13. Hit the high notes. When good things happen, share them. This keeps your blog emotionally compelling and fun.

14. Write short and punchy. Then spell-check.

15. Forms work well.

16. Make recommendations. Write top-ten lists. Share books and quotes you like. Be a filter for folks who want more on your topic.

17. Write longer posts in serial fashion (for example, one tip per day for a certain number of days). People will return to catch your next point.

Blog Integrity

While blog services allow the author of a post to go back and edit or delete a post anytime she wants to, you should use this feature sparingly and only to correct mistakes on the order of typographical errors. From the time your post goes live, people all over the world may be linking to it or telling friends about it via e-mail. These people will be very annoyed if the post they were excited about has changed since they linked to it or told other people about it, especially if the particular thing that piqued their interest is no longer there. Consider the following scenario.

You blog about a writing seminar you'd like to attend. Other writers who are interested in the seminar bookmark your post and e-mail their friends about it. Some writers even put the link to your post on their websites. You decide not to attend the seminar after hearing bad reviews from members of your writers' group. You don't want to have any part in promoting a bad seminar, but you also don't want to bad-mouth anyone online, so you decide to simply delete the post. All the website links made to it are now broken, which reflects badly on the owners of those sites. People who received the link in an e-mail find the link is broken, which reflects badly on the person who sent them the link. All the bookmarks to it are now broken, which annoys the people who bookmarked it. In the end, all of this confusion and annoyance reflects badly on you, and it's a safe bet none of those people will visit your blog again.

It would've been better to leave the original post intact and enter a new blog entry about your decision not to attend the seminar, along with a boldface note at the top of the old blog entry directing readers to the new post. You can avoid seeming to bad-mouth the seminar by choosing your words carefully and limiting your remarks to statements of fact (for example, "My writing partner attended last year and he said it was disappointing...").

I recently read an article that said bloggers should never delete a post, nor even edit a post without making the edits known, even if the blogger learns she has written something that's factually inaccurate. It was suggested by a blogging pro that in such a case, the blog author should handle the situation the same way a magazine would: by leaving the original post intact and printing a formal retraction or correction notice. Given that people who have bookmarked, or linked to, the original post may not see your notice, a suggested alternative was to edit the original post by formatting the incorrect text as "strikethrough" (like this: ~~strikethrough~~), then to enter your desired changes. This makes it clear to the reader that something has changed without breaking any links or bookmarks, and avoids any hint that you may be trying to hide your mistake.

One good way to avoid blog mistakes and revisions is to compose your blog posts off-line in a text editor or word processor first. Take all the time you want to write, revise, spell-check, and polish your post off-line, then copy, paste, and post with confidence.

Blog Maintenance

Try to blog regularly and frequently (no less than twice per month, but once a week is ideal), and always be sure to respond to any comments or questions you receive on your blog. This sort of interaction with your blog visitors is a sign that people are interested in what you have to say, and your responses encourage them to keep the conversation going.

Amazon Author Page/ Author Central Blog

| 🕐–🕐🕐 | FREE! |
| 🎈🎈 | ⚡⚡⚡ |

Authors with at least one book for sale on Amazon's U.S. site can blog on the site using Amazon's Author Central feature (formerly known as AmazonConnect). A link to the Author Central portal page is provided on www.indieauthorguide.com.

Once you've signed up for the service and your application has been approved (following a verification process to ensure you have books available for sale on Amazon — and note that your books can be self-published, or available in Kindle format only), your Amazon Author Page will be created and ready for you to complete.

The page includes a place for your biography, a listing of all your Amazon books, an area to post videos (like book trailers or video blog entries), an area to list any upcoming events or appearances, and a Latest Blog Posts section.

While it's not a complete author Web presence solution, an Amazon Author Page is a powerful marketing tool and every author whose books are available on Amazon should use it. Your author page puts you in almost direct contact with your readers and potential readers because links to your author page are provided on each of your print-edition book listing pages on Amazon. As of this writing those links do not appear on Kindle book listing pages, but according to Amazon Support, this is a feature that should be available in the future.

Author pages can also be searched or browsed alphabetically by Amazon site visitors, so there's more than one way for readers to find your page on the Amazon site.

You can use the Author Central blog tool on the Amazon site itself to set up a free blog which will display on your author page, or you can link your Latest Blog Posts area to a pre-existing blog following a simple, step-by-step process in the Author Central area. For example, I've linked my Blogger blog to my Amazon Author Page so that anytime I create a new blog entry on my Blogger blog, the title of the new post and a link to it are added to my Amazon Author Page in the Latest Blog Posts area. In my opinion this is preferable to using the Author Central blog because that blog doesn't have all the same features as a dedicated blogging service like Blogger or Wordpress, and the URL, or link, to your Author Central blog will be long and difficult to remember. Also, your

Author Central blog posts will be surrounded by all the usual Amazon site content, including links to other products and paid advertising.

Blogging on an Author Central blog works much the same as anywhere else, but while the Author Central blog has some features that make it very easy to include links to, and pictures of, Amazon products (like your books!), it lacks the full set of features and widgets you'll typically find on a dedicated blogging service.

In terms of other blog content, you must follow the Amazon Author Central terms of use. They're fairly standard and self-explanatory, but do take the time to look them over when you first set up an Amazon Author Central account. In addition to the terms of use, apply the same common sense when posting to your Amazon Author Central blog as if you were posting to any other blog: Always consider the impression your post will make.

To view an example of an Amazon Author Page, go to Amazon and look up the print edition of any current best-seller. On the book listing page, scroll down to More About the Author, immediately beneath the product details, and click on the Visit [Author Name]'s Page link.

Make a Free Excerpt Available

🕐–🕐🕐	FREE!
👓👓	NO CONFIDENCE!

It's not too difficult to overcome any trepidation readers may have about buying a book from an author they've never heard of if you let them read some of the book first. You will have to create an excerpt and park it somewhere on the Web, but it's definitely worth the effort. Anyone who reads through to the end of your excerpt is probably hooked enough to buy the book, especially if you've provided a very lengthy excerpt. Also, anyone who buys your book on the strength of an excerpt is likely to enjoy the whole thing, so posting an excerpt helps ensure that all your customers will be satisfied customers, thereby reducing the probability of negative customer reviews.

Create Your Excerpt

Open your manuscript. Create an excerpt by copying the title page and first twenty-five to fifty manuscript pages (your preference) and pasting all of that content into a new blank file. Add a page at the end with a blurb to the effect of, "Thank you for reading this excerpt. If you would like to continue reading [book title], you may purchase it from [where to buy information]."

Omit the table of contents and copyright page, but add a one-liner copyright legend to your title page, if applicable. Save the file in its usual format, though under a different name than the complete manuscript. Use a PDF maker program to save a PDF version of the excerpt file.

Besides Adobe Acrobat, there are many shareware and freeware options. Do an Internet search for "PDF maker" to find them, or see www.indieauthorguide.com. All PDFs work essentially the same way, appearing as a printer option in the Print menu of your programs. To create a PDF version of your file, select the PDF printer from the list and specify a location for the PDF file on your hard drive when prompted.

Post Your Excerpt Online

If you have an author website, you can park your excerpt there. If not, there are other options specific to writers. Some of these are listed on www.indieauthorguide.com.

If you intend to offer your book in e-book format(s)—and why wouldn't you, since it's free and opens up a whole new market for your work—you can publish to various e-book formats and offer a free, lengthy online excerpt on e-book retail sites. See the Publishing in E-Book Formats chapter for more information.

Link To Your Excerpt

Once your excerpt is posted, view it online to make sure it was posted in its entirety and appears as it should. If there are problems, you can reupload the excerpt. When you're satisfied with the excerpt, make a note of its URL. Now you can provide the link to your excerpt on your blog, your Amazon Author Page, your author website, in the description of your book in your publisher's online store, and anywhere else it's appropriate to do so.

Use the Free BookBuzzr Widget Instead

The fReado BookBuzzr widget is a terrific miniprogram that places a slick little e-book reader application right on your Web page, Facebook profile, or blog. The BookBuzzr widget is displayed in a reduced size by default but can be expanded for full-screen viewing simply by clicking on it.

The widget contains either an excerpt or the full text of any manuscript you'd like to make available, along with any or all of the following links, as provided by the author:

> Explore—more information about the book or author
>
> Buzz—links to online articles, blog posts, and anything else featuring the book or author
>
> Share—tool for viewers of your Book-Buzzr content to share it on their own sites and blogs, tweet about it, or mention it on their Facebook pages
>
> Buy—where to buy links

The fReado team also puts a lot of effort into promoting its BookBuzzr authors on its own site with lists of the most popular BookBuzzr books (including links) and author interviews. If your BookBuzzr starts getting a lot of views, don't be surprised to get an e-mail from FReado asking to feature you in an interview.

Enhancements are frequently added to this excellent free tool, so you'll need to go to www. bookbuzzr.com to get the latest information about how to get yours set up and what you can do with it. It's very easy to do, and since I use it myself I can recommend it highly.

Online Press Releases

🕐–🕐🕐	FREE!–$$$$$
🕐🕐	⚡⚡

My second-highest source of author website traffic is press releases. If you go completely DIY and distribute your press releases via a free online service such as PRLog or OpenPR, this promotional activity won't cost you any money but will take some time. If you pay someone else to write your press releases and/or use a paid distribution service for them, you'll save some time but variable costs are involved.

Refer to the Press Releases section earlier in this chapter for more information about how to create and distribute press releases. If you have an author website, be sure to save PDF copies of your press releases on your site and link to them from your Press or News page. If you have a blog instead of an author site, you can add links to where your press releases are being stored on the distribution service's website, but press releases will be stored by the service only for a limited time. Check periodically to ensure the links are still active and remove any that have become broken.

Keywords And Tags

Keywords and tags are the terms people enter into online search boxes. The search tool scans all the pages it has cataloged, looking for those terms, then returns a set of links to pages on which the desired terms were found. The terms can be found in the body of a page or in something called "metadata." Metadata is data added to a page via an online data entry form or written directly into the HTML. As you can imagine, the more and better tags and keywords are associated with your Web pages, the more people will find them when doing searches. *Better* in this instance means more commonly used; for example, *free* and *complimentary* mean the same thing, but *free* is a better keyword to use because people are more likely to enter *free* into a search box than *complimentary*.

Working with keywords and tags to improve your pages' visibility to search tools is called Search Engine Optimization (SEO), and entire books are written on the topic. So many marketing people judge SEO to be of such great importance that they even hold international conferences about SEO strategies. The goal of SEO is to design page content such that popular keywords feature prominently and repeatedly, making the page easier for search tools to find and therefore the page itself to rank high in the list of those search results.

Web pages designed primarily with an eye to SEO are easy to identify, since certain terms (or versions of those terms) show up in the page text repeatedly. You may notice this in articles printed online at newspaper and magazine websites. The editors of such sites are trained in SEO, and part of their job is to revise print articles for SEO before the articles are posted online. SEO experts know the most popular search terms and make every effort to incorporate those terms into the text of pages they write or edit.

Even though there are thousands of popular keywords, compared to the entire English language the list of popular keywords is pretty small. Application of SEO techniques tends to result in a sort of homogenization of the Web: SEO does not encourage originality or variety in expression. One of a writer's primary goals is to cultivate an original and appealing voice, and SEO works in direct opposition to that goal. For this reason, I advise writers against writing blog entries or Web page text with SEO in mind. Instead, I encourage making maximum use of metadata tagging.

Tagging With Keywords on Amazon.com

🕐–🕐🕐	FREE!
🎈🎈	NO CONFIDENCE!

If you have books for sale on Amazon, tagging your books with keywords is one of the best ways to increase their visibility in Amazon's vast database. Every product page on Amazon includes a Tags Customers Associate With This Product area, which is located immediately above the Customer Reviews section of the page. Two methods are provided for adding tags to a product: the Your Tags box and "tag this product for Amazon search" link. Use both for maximum effect.

Tagging allows you to effectively add your book to countless categories beyond the standard genres of general fiction or sci-fi. It lets you create your own categories. However, note that with both types of tagging, your name will be associated with the tag in a way that's visible to the general public. Anyone who clicks on an assigned tag on a product page can drill down into more information that will ultimately reveal a list of customers who used the tag, so it's not a good idea to apply boastful, smart-alecky, or otherwise potentially objectionable tags.

The Your Tags feature gives customers a way to mark products with tags that are personally meaningful to them, in order to make those products easy to find on future visits to the site. For example, someone shopping for a Mother's Day gift might tag all the products they are considering with the phrase "Mother's Day."

Amazon keeps track of the tags entered by each customer and stores them as part of the customer's profile information. Tags you've entered using the My Tags box on product pages will appear on your Amazon profile page as links under the My Tags heading. When you click on one of them, Amazon locates all the items you tagged with that term and returns a list of results.

Note that on product pages, just above the customer reviews section, there is a Tags Customers Associate With This Product area with a Search Products Tagged With box at the right-hand side. This search incorporates all the tags entered by all customers who have used the My Tags feature. Going back to the above example, if you search on the tag *Mother's Day* in this box, you'll get a list of products tagged with the phrase *Mother's Day* by all Amazon customers.

Use the Your Tags feature to tag your books with words and phrases you think Amazon customers are likely to search in the Search Products Tagged With box. To create a tag, enter your desired word or phrase in the Your Tags box and click the Add button. Repeat for all the tags you wish to enter. Amazon displays a list of tags other customers have already applied to your book and books similar to yours; you can use these as a starting point, but don't miss the opportunity to apply more specific tags that only someone who's read your book would think to use.

For example, if Quaker life or culture feature prominently in your story you can tag your book with "Quaker," "Quaker life," and "Quaker culture" so that people looking for stories that feature Quakers will be able to find your book. Consider tags that touch on the time period or geographical location of your story, your protagonist's profession,

historical events included in the narrative, and so on.

Also employ tags to overcome limits imposed by your book's genre classification. Your book may be officially classified as romance, but if it's also historical fiction you can tag it "Historical Romance." Fictionalized accounts of historical events can be tagged with the names of historical figures, battles, settlements, and the like included in the book.

Try to think outside the box a little with your tags, but don't be misleading. You may think it's a good idea to tag your sci-fi book with "espionage" because you believe many customers will search for books with that tag, but if espionage isn't prominent in your plot, readers who buy the book based partly on that tag will be disappointed.

The Help Others Find This Product—Tag It for Amazon Search feature is located just below the Your Tags box in the Tags Customers Associate With This Product area on product/book listing pages. Tags added this way are incorporated into general Amazon product searches: searches entered into the Search Amazon.com box, which appears at the top of every page on Amazon's site. Click the Suggest link to access the submission form.

Because unscrupulous people can manipulate the tagging system to make their products appear in the result set for virtually any search, Amazon verifies the validity of any tags entered for Amazon search. Along with your suggested tag, you must also enter a brief reason for why you are suggesting the tag. If the Amazon verifier determines the tag is valid, it will be added to the product in question. If not, it won't. Either way, you will be notified via e-mail.

Tagging your book for Amazon search is a more powerful technique than tagging via the My Tags feature. The Search Amazon.com box is right at the top of every page on Amazon's site and therefore gets more use than the Search Products Tagged With box, which is buried far down in each product page. Also, when customers search using the Search Amazon.com box, they're able to select a product category from a drop-down list. Doing so returns a smaller, more specific result set. Your book may appear higher up in the list of results than it would in a result set from a Search Products Tagged With search, which isn't designed to employ categories.

Note that your book will already be tagged with the author name(s), book title, and the main genre(s) in which it appears in Amazon store listings, so it's not necessary to add these tags yourself.

Tagging With Keywords on the Internet

⏰–⏰⏰⏰	FREE!
🎈🎈	NO CONFIDENCE!

Tags and keywords can also be used to help Internet search engines find Web content you've authored: your website, your blog, your online press releases, and so forth. People who create their own Web pages using HTML can incorporate tags in the metadata and keywords sections of their pages' HTML header code. Those who use fill-in-the-blanks forms to create online content can add tags and keywords

in the Tags, Keywords, or Labels box which is typically provided as part of the form, but such forms usually place a limit on how many words or characters will be accepted.

On most create post forms for blogs, there's a large box provided for composing blog entries and a second, smaller box directly beneath the large box for adding labels, tags, or keywords. You type in the words and phrases you'd like to use as tags, separated by commas, and when you save the blog entry the tags are saved as well.

OpenPR and PRLog provide a similar box for entry of keywords/tags on the page you use to enter your press release details. Most fill-in-the-blanks Web page templates have the feature, but you may need to search on tags or keywords in your provider's help files to find out where it is and how to use it.

Tagging really does make a difference in search results, so take advantage of every tagging opportunity available to you when creating online content.

Podcasting

⏰–⏰⏰⏰⏰	FREE!–$$$$$
🎈🎈🎈🎈	⚡⚡⚡

Podcasting is creating an audio, or audio and video, recording that people can play on a Web page, in iTunes, or on an iPod. You can record a podcast using the media player software that came with your computer, or buy a program designed specifically for that purpose. A specialized program can range from freeware to a very expensive high-end computer recording studio. Some of the programs are designed for maximum simplicity but offer few controls and options. High-end programs offer a wide variety of recording, editing, and sound-mixing options but are harder to use.

Audio podcasts can be added to your author website for visitors to download and play in iTunes, on their iPod, or on their computer's default media player. If you provide a media player widget, visitors can listen to or watch your podcasts right on your site, no iPod or media player needed. You can also list your podcasts in the iTunes store.

A complete primer on podcasting is outside the scope of this guide, so if you're considering podcasting but don't know much about it, you'll need to find a more thorough discussion of the topic elsewhere. A good place to start is the Podiobooks website, podiobooks.com, which includes exhaustive tutorials, a mentoring program, and a lively member discussion where you can connect with and learn from your more experienced peers.

Many articles, tutorials, and community discussions about podcasting can also be found on Apple's website in the iPod+iTunes support section. You can also do an Internet search for "how to podcast" to find more information.

Here, the topic of podcasting is limited to content: what to put into a podcast to help promote your books.

In the days before video iPods existed, podcasting started out as a way for performers, DJs, and talk show hosts (as well as wannabes in every one of those categories) to create their own radio shows that could then be offered to the public in recorded form instead of being broadcast over the radio. Many podcasters still follow this basic format today, blending commentary, interviews, and music in an audio-only podcast. Others approach audio podcasting as a kind of spoken blog, and record themselves talking about the same things they might otherwise write about in a blog.

When video-capable iPods came along, program types common to movies and TV became a part of the podcasting universe: skits, movie trailers, music videos, TV talk shows, documentaries, and full-length films. Different formats will be suitable for different authors, but in every case you'll need to include your name, the name of your book, and website address at the beginning and end of the podcast.

Nonfiction authors and fiction authors whose books required a lot of research can make good use of the radio talk show, TV talk show, or documentary format with podcasts about the topic(s) covered in their book. How-to programs are popular, as are interviews with subject area experts. Subject area experts are only an Internet search away and are usually flattered by a request to be interviewed for a podcast.

Authors can also read excerpts from their books—providing a kind of audiobook sneak peek—create entire podcast audiobook versions of their works, or stage scenes from their books to create podcast advertisements in the format of a radio spot or movie trailer.

YouTube

♩ – ♩♩♩♩♩	FREE! – $$$$$
🎈🎈🎈🎈	⚡⚡⚡

YouTube is an online repository of film clips submitted by site visitors. There are copies of clips recorded from TV shows or movies, music videos, movie trailers, funny or amazing advertisements, and lots of videos produced by members of the general public. YouTube visitors can search for the kinds of clips they'd like to see (for instance, karaoke, cats, or battle of the bands), and then rate and review the clips after watching them.

You can promote your books with YouTube in the same ways you would using a video podcast, but the finished video is uploaded to www.youtube.com instead of iTunes or your website. You can link to the video from your blog or website, or embed the video clip in a page on your author site or blog.

Detailed directions for how to shoot, edit, and upload your video are beyond the scope of this guide, but help and tutorials are available in the Help area on YouTube's site.

The main advantage of YouTube over a video podcast that only appears on your site or the iTunes store is that videos loaded to YouTube are ranked by popularity in real time, on a constant basis, according to viewer ratings. The more popular your video becomes, the higher it climbs in the search results when users search for clips on the site. If viewers like your clip, it will get increasing exposure. Funny, shocking, weird, and instructive videos seem to perform best.

Book Trailers

⏱–⏱⏱⏱⏱⏱	FREE!–$$$$$
🖱🖱🖱🖱	⚡⚡⚡

A book trailer is a promotional tool you can use to raise awareness of your book, and hopefully sell more copies. It can be very much like a movie trailer, or preview, such as you'd see in a movie theater), or a mini movie that stands on its own and may only reference the book indirectly.

The ultimate goal with any book trailer is to pique the viewer's interest enough that she will want to learn more about your book and/or you, the author. Creating a book trailer is essentially creating your own advertisement for your book.

This section assumes the reader is not savvy with audio and video editing tools, and explains how to get a quality result with minimal fuss and the flattest possible learning curve. The basics of how to select and use a mini digital video camera will be covered, so you'll be getting enough information to use digital video in your trailers if you wish. However, this section primarily focuses on how to create book trailers using simple, free tools and online services intended for absolute beginners, and for which the use of a digital video camera is optional.

Of course, someone who's a whiz with digital video and audio can create a much snazzier trailer, but such skills don't necessarily make for a better finished product. We've all seen very slick, flashy ads that grab and hold the viewer's attention, yet don't succeed in getting the viewer to the remember the name of the product being promoted. As in most advertising, a strong concept is much more important than fancy execution.

Movie Trailer Approach

The movie trailer approach aims to give the viewer a preview of the book in much the same manner as a movie preview shown in the theater or on TV. This type of trailer provides an overview of the book's plot, ideally giving just enough information to make the viewer want to learn—and read—more.

Alternatively, this type of trailer may be totally conceptual, giving away little to none of the actual plot but conveying a sense of the book's mood or theme. Just think about teaser-type movie or TV show previews you've seen which don't spell out any plot points but hint at what kind of viewing experience you can expect from the movie or show (for instance, a scary, funny, or offbeat story.

Mini Movie Approach

This type of trailer tells a self-contained story. It may be a filmed or slide show version of an excerpt from the book, or it may reference the book only indirectly, aiming instead to demonstrate the qualities of the author's work in general (for example, humor or scariness).

What Belongs In Every Book Trailer

There are some key pieces of content every book trailer must contain, if it's to be an effective book promotion tool:

- Book Title—with link to a free, online excerpt

- Author Name—with link to author website/blog

- Where-to-Buy Link(s)—list each available format (trade paperback, Kindle, etc.) and a link to where the viewer can buy the book in the stated format for each.

Any links you list in the trailer won't generally be clickable, and it may not even be possible for the viewer to copy and paste them. You can't assume the viewer will manually copy or type a link into his browser, either. If the site where you're posting your trailer allows you to provide a brief description of the trailer, include a clickable link to the free excerpt and at least one clickable Where to Buy link, if possible. If the description won't allow you to include clickable links, include the full text of the Web addresses you wish to include. These won't be clickable links, but they can easily be copied and pasted into the viewer's browser.

First, Zero in on Your Concept

The first step in creating a book trailer is deciding which kind of trailer you want to create: a movie preview or a mini movie that will stand on its own. Given that your finished trailer should have a run time of somewhere between two and four minutes—the shorter, the better—let the type and complexity of your book be your guide.

Nonfiction books lend themselves well to the movie preview approach. All you need to do is lay out the subject matter of your book in a way that conveys what's unique or especially desirable about your take on the subject. On www.indieauthorguide.com, there are links to some good examples of the different types of book trailers described below.

Novels can be a little trickier to promote. If the plot of your story is fairly simple and immediately intriguing, it should be pretty easy to communicate that plot in a trailer. Consider *Jaws* by Peter Benchley and *Jurassic Park* by Michael Crichton. Both have plotlines that are easily summed up in a single sentence:

- killer shark terrorizes beach community at the height of tourist season

- billionaire uses DNA engineering to bring dinosaurs back to life for a theme park

Look at their movie trailers (search "Jaws movie trailer" and "Jurassic Park movie trailer" on YouTube to find them), and notice how the entire plot is neatly encapsulated by each.

Now consider a story with a much more complicated plot that isn't so easy to convey. In that case, rather than try to lay out the plot, you may want to go with more of a teaser approach. Teaser-type trailers have flashes of provocative, intriguing imagery and narration or dialog, but don't give the viewer a clear idea of the plot. Look up the movie trailer for *The Matrix* to see what I'm getting at here.

Other trailers grab the viewer's interest by sharing entire scenes, or chunks of scenes, from the movie. Again, the viewer doesn't get a good picture of the overall plot, but the style, tone, and enough content is presented to generate interest.

Browse around YouTube and the Web for as many examples as you can find (search for "book trailer"). While checking out trailers, be on the lookout for ideas you'd like to borrow for your own trailer and any perceived shortcomings you'd like to avoid. Watching movie trailers can also be a great source of inspiration. YouTube has plenty, as does the movie review site Rotten Tomatoes.

Second, Write an Outline

Before creating a book trailer, it's a good idea to develop a written plan for it in the form of a storyboard or beat outline that lays out the specific images and text you want to display in the trailer, in order.

Some authors may prefer the "pantsing" method—making things up as they go along and deciding what works or doesn't by trial and error—but that system is much more time-consuming and prone to delays brought about by indecision. If you don't begin with a clear-cut plan, it's very easy to continue to tinker and experiment with your trailer indefinitely.

...Or a Script

Most book trailers are created from scratch, using content shot and/or assembled by the person creating the trailer. An exception to this is the case where the trailer will be created using a template-based animation program like those from Xtranormal.

Xtranormal is a website that offers three different animated movie creation programs, all of which include a variety of canned backgrounds, characters, and animations the user can assemble in a totally custom configuration, ultimately producing a full-motion animated cartoon with the characters speaking lines input as text by the user.

If you want to create this type of trailer, you will have write a full script of the scene(s) you want the animated characters to act out in your trailer, but you won't need to supply any additional content because the site does that for you. Xtranormal offers a free online version of its software called "text-to-movie," which allows you to create your trailer entirely online. There's also a downloadable basic version of its State software that offers a few more features and options but must be installed on your computer's hard drive. Finally, there's the premium, paid, online showpaks option. You can find links to the Xtranormal website

and a sample Xtranormal book trailer on www.
indieauthorguide.com.

Third, Assemble Your Content

If you're not using a tool like those from Xtranormal, you will need to gather some content
for your trailer. There are four types of content
you can use: video, audio, text, and still images.
Whichever type(s) of content you choose, you
must make sure you're not infringing anyone's
intellectual property rights.

Pictures and video you shoot yourself are
fine, so long as you get signed releases from every person whose face appears in the pictures or
video, granting you their express permission
to use their likeness in your trailer. Artwork
you create yourself is also fine, so long as it's
entirely original.

With the exception of audio you've written,
performed, and recorded yourself, you can't
use audio recordings in your trailer without
getting a written license, or permission, to do
so from the current rights holder.

Purchased clip art, stock photo, stock video,
and stock audio collections are an excellent,
low-cost resource for content to use in book
trailers. The user is granted a license to use the
content provided in such a collection when he
pays for it, and with the important exception
of packaging that content for resale, the license
for use is virtually unlimited. Just check the
terms of use or end user license agreement that
comes with any such collection to be absolutely
clear on its acceptable terms of use.

You can also find lots of individual free and
low-cost licensed digital video, audio, and still
image files at iStockphoto. There are countless
other online providers of this type of content, but
iStockphoto is the only one for which I've received
personal recommendations from authors who've
used, and been satisfied with, the service.

Yet another option for free content that's
legal for you to use is to search the Internet for
"public domain music," "public domain video,"
"public domain audio," "public domain photos," etc. Public domain material is content for
which the original rights have expired. Such
material is made available to the general public
for free use.

Assemble all the content you intend to use
in a single folder on your computer, along with
your written outline if you've created one.

Using a Mini Digital Video Camera

Many authors like to include some full-motion
video in their trailers, to more closely emulate
the look and feel of movie trailers. This is now
exceedingly easy to do, using a mini digital
video camera.

Mini digital video cameras are small, light,
simple to use, designed with upload to the Web
in mind, and can be fairly inexpensive. They
come with a pop-out USB adapter built right
into the chassis of the camera, and come with
preinstalled software that makes getting your
digital video downloaded to your computer or
uploaded to sites like YouTube and Facebook
(assuming you have user accounts) as easy as
plugging the USB adapter into your computer and following a few on-screen prompts.
There's also usually some video editing software built into or bundled with the camera,
though quality, feature set, and ease of use
varies from brand to brand.

Unlike traditional video cameras, mini
digital video cameras store every video you

shoot as a self-contained digital file, either to memory onboard the camera or to a memory card. The files are playable on your computer or online as is, no editing or converting the video to a special format is required. Once a video you've shot is on your computer, all you need do to view it is locate it on your hard drive and double-click to play.

Getting videos off the camera or memory card and onto your computer is easy. If your video is stored to the camera's onboard memory, just plug the camera's built-in USB adapter into your computer, thereby launching the camera's installed software, and follow the prompts to transfer files to your computer.

If the video is stored to a memory card, pull the card out of the camera, insert it to your computer, and either follow the prompts in the Files and Settings Transfer Wizard (your computer should automatically display) or simply cut, copy, paste, drag, and drop the files where you want them as you would with any other file. It's just like transferring pictures from a digital still camera.

If the prospect of learning how to edit digital video makes you nervous, you can avoid that problem by simply shooting your video clips and downloading/uploading them as is, without editing. For example, if you want part of your book trailer to feature five seconds of footage showing horses running in a field, you can just go to a place where horses are running in a field, find the best location from which to shoot them, and shoot several five-second segments. Each one will be stored as a separate file, so you can simply upload them all to your computer and select the best one for inclusion in your trailer. Be aware that most cameras have

a built-in microphone; you'll have to mute it if you don't want your trailer to include ambient noise picked up while shooting.

You can get good results this way, but you'll have to plan each segment carefully and you'll probably need to shoot multiple takes of each segment so you'll be sure to have something you like when it's time to assemble your trailer. I highly recommend trying the video editing software that comes with your camera; you may have to read through a tutorial or learn how things work through trial and error, but the skills you'll gain will enable you to achieve much better video segments.

You've probably heard of or seen the Flip Mino, but there are plenty of other options out there. After doing a lot of comparison shopping, and based on the specific features I wanted (large built-in memory, ability to expand memory using SD memory cards, ability to take both full-motion video and still pictures, ability to zoom, reasonable price), I ended up going with the Kodak Zi8. There are models available from Samsung, Sony, and plenty of other companies, too, so take your time comparing prices and feature sets before buying.

Pay particular attention to user reviews of the provided software you'll have to use to transfer your videos from the camera to your computer, as well as the software provided to edit your videos and get them uploaded to the Web. If you intend to use your camera for book trailers, ease of transfer and upload/download will be a critical concern.

Fourth, Pick Your Trailer Creation Tool
Slide show book trailers aren't all that different from the slide shows businesspeople cre-

ate for making presentations at work, and the ones conference speakers rely on when making a presentation. They can contain video, audio, still images, text, and animations.

This is the easiest type of trailer to create, through the use of various online services. You can create a slide show book trailer very quickly, easily, and for free at any of the following sites (search for site names online or go to www.indieauthorguide.com for links):

Animoto—You upload your content (for example, files containing pictures, video, and audio), enter any desired lines of text, and specify the order in which the content and text items should appear. Then Animoto analyzes the content and creates the video for you by inserting simple transition effects and adding your desired audio (if applicable). The free version allows for creation of trailers up to thirty seconds long. The paid version allows for longer videos, provides access to licensed content from Animoto, and certain other benefits.

OneTrueMedia—You upload your content, select from among transitions and animations provided on the site, and OneTrueMedia outputs everything as a video file to be used online, for free. You can also purchase copies of your video on DVD.

SlideShare—You create your trailer as a PowerPoint or Keynote presentation file on your computer, then upload it to SlideShare to have it converted into a video file that will automatically play your slideshow when the user loads it. SlideShare can also convert OpenOffice, MS Word, MS Excel, and many other types of files into video slideshows, and the service is totally free. See this page for more information about SlideShare.

Screenjelly—This free service allows you to make a video by capturing anything taking place on your computer screen. It's a great tool for people who have made a slide show or video on their computer, but their program doesn't allow for easy upload of the finished product to the Web.

To use Screenjelly in this scenario, you'd create your video or slide show as per usual in your program, then play the video or slide show while running Screenjelly to record the video as you watch it.

Finally, Create Your Trailer

You'll need to sign up for a (free) account at most of the sites listed above, and it's also a good idea to take a look at each site's tutorials and/or instructions, but they're all very easy to figure out simply by jumping right in and experimenting, too. It can be a lot of fun to play around with the different features and options on the various sites.

Just as studios do for their movies, many authors like to create multiple versions of their book trailers to appeal to the widest possible audience. For example, one trailer for a supernatural romance may emphasize the love story while another highlights the supernatural/thriller aspect.

What to Do With Your Trailer

All the services described here allow the user to share the finished video through multiple online channels. See each service's FAQ or Help/Support pages for more information about the specific steps involved in sharing your trailer online. The most common and useful online outlets for your trailer are YouTube, Facebook, your author website or blog, your Amazon Author page (if you offer a book for sale there), and any of your online community profiles that allow for the inclusion of video.

YouTube

Register for a free YouTube account, ideally under your author or imprint name. Fill out your profile so that anyone who likes your trailer(s) and clicks through to learn more about you can easily find your brief biography and links to your author website/blog and/or online excerpts from your book(s). Then upload your trailer using the simple online upload form, and you're good to go.

Each YouTube member is assigned a personal "channel" on the site. This means every video uploaded by a specific user is linked to that user's account on the site. If you have more than one video/trailer on YouTube, any user who clicks through to view your profile will find links to your other video(s)/trailer(s) there.

For each uploaded video, YouTube will automatically create and display Share and Embed Code—which enables anyone who views your trailer to share a link to it or embed the trailer itself on his own site or blog.

YouTube also includes an automatic interface to the RealPlayer video download tool by default. This is a great feature for trailers created with services like OneTrueMedia, which enable online sharing of the finished video but don't provide a file download of the finished video.

Facebook

Every Facebook user has a Videos tab available in their Profile, and it's a great place to share your book trailer(s).

Author Site/Blog

Most blogging services and fill-in-the-blanks websites allow the user to post, or embed, a finished video to a website or blog by copying a block of code provided by the site, then pasting it in the desired location on your site or blog.

If you don't maintain your own author website or don't have the type of website that allows you to paste code into its pages, at least add links to your trailer(s) so people who visit your author site can view the trailer(s) on YouTube, Facebook, and any others.

Amazon Author Pages, Online Community Profiles

Amazon Author pages allow for video uploads, as do many online community profile pages. Wherever you're online trying to get the word out about your book, if video uploads are allowed, get your trailer(s) posted.

Promoting Your Trailer

Once you have your trailer posted everywhere you want it online, start promoting.

Tweet about it, but don't go overboard. A few well-spaced tweets will be much better received than a never-ending stream of pleas to check out your book trailer.

Write a blog post about the process of creating and distributing your trailer, and include the trailer itself in the post.

Write the same kind of article as a guest blog on someone else's site, or as a pay-per-post article on sites such as eHow, Associated Content, or Squidoo. Again, include the trailer itself in your post if the site allows it, and if not, at least include a link to the trailer on another site.

If you're using the free BookBuzzr widget (and you absolutely should be), be sure to add a link to your trailer there, as well.

Social Media For Authors

◔–◕◕◕	FREE!
🖱🖱–🖱🖱🖱	⚡⚡–⚡⚡⚡⚡

What is social media all about, and why should authors care?

Social media are various means of communicating back and forth with groups of people. Something as simple as an e-mail with a reply request sent to multiple people simultaneously technically qualifies as social media, but when people use the term they're generally talking about specific websites and technologies that make it easy for people to hold online conversations in groups. Currently, the best known of these are probably Facebook and Twitter, but even online bulletin boards and discussion groups qualify, as do comment forms at the end of blog posts and other online articles. Pretty much anything that gets a conversation going online falls under the social media umbrella.

As for the question of why authors should care, it's all about author platform. Your platform is your collection of strategies and methods for interacting with your readership and potential readership. The most effective and engaging authors, in terms of platform, are those who welcome a conversation with the public. Authors who invite the public to communicate with them personally via Twitter, Facebook, their blogs, and online discussion groups and communities are generally seen as accessible, friendly, and interested in knowing what's on their fans' minds.

Authors with such qualities not only succeed in reinforcing their relationship with an existing readership, they also have a much easier time drawing new readers. I'm sure anyone reading this can think of at least one instance in which their exposure to a previously unfamiliar author online prompted a purchase of the author's work. Meaning the purchase was not due to the content of the work itself, but merely because the author seemed like a genuinely warm, amusing, or interesting person. Sometimes consumers make a purchase just to support an artist they believe in.

Most Popular Types of Social Media

This section covers specific strategies for getting started with, then getting the most from, the following major social media.

- Twitter
- Online Communities
- Online Reader Communities
- Online Comment Forms/Discussion Groups
- Facebook

What About MySpace?

While some people like MySpace as a social media outlet for authors, I don't recommend it, for several reasons. First, over the years it's become primarily geared to, and optimized for, musicians. Second, its audience skews predominantly young—most of it college age or younger—it's become sort of an online nightclub, in that sense. Third, people don't generally go there looking for authors; if you go to MySpace right now and do a search on the term *author*, you'll get a seemingly random list of members who have the word *author* somewhere in their content, but they themselves may not actually be authors. Third, the site features prominent banner ads on every member page, and members have no control over the content of those ads.

Having said all this, I know some authors are very happy with the promotional opportunities available at MySpace. If you'd like to check into it before making up your mind, some additional resources are provided on www.indieauthorguide.com.

Social Media Ground Rules

No matter which social media sites or services you intend to use, there are certain ground rules and guidelines that will serve you well.

1. Make your user name the same as your author name, whether that's your legal name or a pen name. When people go searching for you, the author, on the Web, they won't be able to find you very easily if you have accounts under various nicknames scattered all across the Web.

2. Be judicious in the amount, and type, of information you share. Always remember that the purpose of your social marketing efforts is to grow your author platform. Put your best foot forward, and don't post any words, photos, or videos that you wouldn't want everyone from your grandmother to your boss to see or read. You're trying to foster a certain image, and many months or

even years of careful effort can be undermined by a single thoughtless post.

3. Social media can become a major time waster very quickly, particularly in the case of sites like Facebook that constantly bombard users with invitations to online games and clubs. Budget your social media time, and use it wisely. Online games may be fun, but they're not necessarily the best use of your limited author platform time investment.

4. Remember that people are literally watching your every move on Facebook. Social media sites like Facebook tend to keep a running transcript of your activities on your home or profile page on the site. If you're there to establish yourself as an author, but your profile is filled with almost nothing but updates about this or that online game you've been playing, it can make you look like a flake who has nothing better to do all day than play games. You're there to present yourself as a Writer-with-a-capital-W, or Author-with-a-capital-A, so try to keep your site activities relevant to your "brand" and on point. If you're already using social media for personal or family communications, or would like to do so, it's a good idea to set up separate accounts for your personal and family uses.

5. Beware of exposing others beyond their comfort level. Never post photos or videos in which other people are identifiable without first getting permission from ev-

eryone in the photo/video, or in the case of minor children, from their parents. If the site you're using allows you to tag people in a photo, video, or post (meaning, to list the names of people appearing in the photo/video or referenced in the post), don't do so without the other party's permission. Many people on social media sites are there to maintain private networks consisting only of personal friends, family members, or co-workers, and they may view tagging as an invasion of their privacy. While their profiles and information may be marked private, if yours is marked public, anything you post is publicly viewable. You may think there's nothing sensitive about a relatively tame bachelorette party photo you've posted, but everyone visible in that photo may not agree. Better safe than sorry.

6. Beware of libel. Social media sites tend to become very comfortable and chatty the more you use them, and this can be a danger where libel is concerned. You may think you're just chatting with an online friend about this or that celebrity or other person you don't much care for, but never forget that anything you post online, even discussions held in supposedly private areas of a site, can be exposed to the public at any time through hacking, subpoena, or technical glitches. Again, if you wouldn't want your comments repeated in public, it's best not to make them in the first place.

7. Beware of workplace fallout. Many an employee has been fired for reasons re-

lating to their use of social media. You probably already realize the use of social media on company time is something of which your boss will not approve (unless using social media is part of your job), but you may not realize your boss doesn't have to catch you in the act to know what you're up to. Most posts on social media sites are date- and time-stamped. So if you were supposed to be working on that new account at 10 A.M. on Monday, but your boss finds a lengthy series of posts on your Facebook Profile date-stamped on Monday and time-stamped between the hours of 10 and 11 A.M., you will have some explaining to do.

Another common story is that of an employee who bad-mouthed his boss or co-workers or spilled privileged company information online and was subsequently fired. In some cases, companies have even gone so far as to take legal action against these ex-employees, so be careful about what you're putting out there.

8. Keep secure and safe. Keep your log-in information for any social media sites you use secure. Check on, and update, your privacy settings for each social media site regularly, as sites may be redesigned from time to time and available privacy settings/policies may change. Don't ever share personal information that could allow strangers to find you in the real world (for example, your home address, work address, or phone number). One exception to this general rule is if you're setting up a social media ac-

count to promote a retail business, in which case you may want to share the address and phone number of the business. Block any users who send you unwanted, threatening, or otherwise inappropriate material, and report them to the site.

9. Be a genuine contributor, not just a promoter. The essence of social media is authenticity: people connecting with one another to share their ideas, support, opinions, and resources in the spirit of community and helpfulness. People and companies who attempt to co-opt social media for purely promotional reasons, offering nothing of value to the community, are certain to fail because as a rule, nobody volunteers to hear advertising messages. Most of us are willing to hear advertising messages in exchange for something we perceive to be of value, however, so the key to success with social media is to offer something of value. Ideally the community will perceive your something to be so valuable that they'll happily support you in return, whether by purchasing your books or sending more fans your way.

What you offer is up to you to determine. It may be your time and attention, links you've collected for online resources, downloads of your work (or portions of it), contests and activities with prizes on offer, informational articles, podcasts or videos, or anything else your community both wants and perceives to carry value.

The important thing is that most of the time you spend on social media, you're giving something to the community with no strings attached. Then, when the time comes for you to put out a call for support, the community will gladly have your back. It's time-consuming, sure. But it also generates a loyal and strong fan base to which paid advertising cannot hold a candle. You may be a fan of brands like Nike, McDonald's, or Anne Rice, but in the social media world you can actually be a friend to brands and people, and carry on conversations with those brands and people. It's a relationship that's far less fickle than the ones we have as consumers of a brand.

Twitter

🕐–🕐🕐	FREE!
🖱️🖱️	⚡⚡

Twitter allows users to send messages, sort of like texting or instant messaging, but with a strict 140 character limit, with the option to send your message to either an individual or your entire group of Twitter followers, and with the caveat that by default, every message you send is publicly viewable on the Twitter site. There's a private messaging option that allows users to send private messages to specific individuals, but even those messages are searchable on Google so don't count on that privacy.

At first glance, Twitter doesn't seem like a very useful service. You've no doubt heard stories about people using Twitter to post nothing but messages about what they ate for breakfast, that they just got a bad haircut, or other minutiae that would only interest their mothers, but don't let such anecdotes dissuade you from using Twitter because it's an incredibly useful social media tool.

The way Twitter works is simple. It's kind of like an online discussion board, but message length is limited to 140 characters and you get to choose whose messages you'll see. You decide whose messages to see by following other users, and likewise, other users who want to see your messages can follow you.

The display of messages, or tweets, posted by people you're following is called your Twitter stream or tweet stream. (See Figure 11-6.)

Figure 11-6

Following is a one-way street: The tweets of a user who opts to follow you won't display in your Twitter stream unless you decide to follow that user in return. So you're never forced to wade through tweets in which you have no interest, your Twitter stream will contain *only* the tweets of people you've chosen to follow.

The people you'll find are worth following are those who post comments or links of interest to you. And there are lots of authors and publishing folk on Twitter, most of whom are posting links to interesting articles and valuable resources on a daily—or even hourly—basis. It's like having a whole army of like-minded individuals scouring the Web for you every day and reporting back to you with links to the good stuff. Twitter can also be a very useful promotional tool; more on that later in this section. First, let's take a look at how to get a Twitter account set up.

Setting Up a Twitter Account

Go to the Twitter home page and click the Sign Up Now button. (See Figure 11-7.)

Figure 11-7

You'll be taken to an account creation page, where you'll enter your real name, your desired user name, your desired password, your e-mail address, and certify your agreement to the site's terms of use. You'll also have to fill out a CAPTCHA form, which is there to prevent spammers from abusing the site. "Let others find me by my e-mail address" is selected by default, but you can deselect it by clicking the check box. (See Figure 11-8.)

Remember that ideally, your user name should be your author or pen name, but there can be good reasons to go with something else. My Twitter user name is *indieauthor* because it's a name that instantly conveys what I'm all about and why I'm on Twitter. Since my Twitter profile also includes my real author name, people who search for me on the site under my author name can still find me.

THE INDIE AUTHOR GUIDE

Another good reason to go with something other than your author or pen name is that your author/pen name is very long. Remember that users get only 140 characters to work with; if your user name takes up a lot of that space, you might not get many retweets.

Completing Your Profile and Settings

On your Twitter home page, click the Settings link. You'll be taken to your Settings page, which has menu links for your account, password, mobile, notices, profile, design, and connections pages. On each, there's a Save button you'll use to save any changes. (See Figure 11-9.)

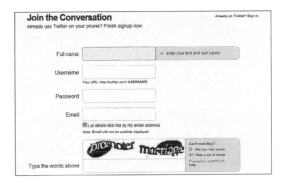

Figure 11-8

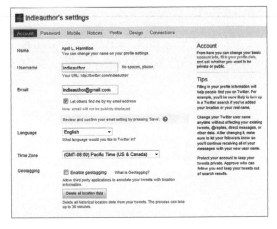

Figure 11-9

On the Account page, set your time zone and preferred language. If you like, you can enable geo-tagging of your tweets. There's also an option here to Protect My Tweets, which won't allow anyone to follow you (and see your tweets) unless you've approved them to follow. This isn't a good option for authors who are on Twitter to grow their author platform, since it presents an unnecessary obstacle for potential new followers.

The Password link takes you to a page where you can change your password. It's self-explanatory.

On the Mobile page, if you like you can enter information about your cell phone so that you can tweet via text message from your phone. You can also specify whether or not you want people to be able to look you up on Twitter by searching on your phone number, and whether or not you want Twitter to send a copy of any tweets you receive as a text message to your phone, but I don't recommend doing so. Once you're following a dozen or more people, your cell could be ringing off the hook with text messages from Twitter, and if your calling plan charges you per text message, it gets very expensive very fast. (See Figure 11-10.)

Figure 11-10

On the Notices page, you can specify your communication preferences. (See Figure 11-11.)

On the profile page, you can enter a very brief bio and a Web page link. These will display on your Twitter profile page. (See Figure 11-12 and 11-13.)

On the Design page, you can choose a background to appear on your Twitter home and profile pages. (See Figure 11-14.)

The Connections page displays information about any outside sites or services to which you've granted access to your Twitter account. On a new account this tab won't list anything, and lots of Twitter users never add a single connection.

Your Account and Settings are now complete.

Home Versus Profile Page

Your Twitter home page displays a text box you can use to enter and send tweets along with your Twitter stream: all the tweets from people you're following. Your profile page displays your profile information and all the public tweets you've sent. Both pages contain links for any lists you've created (more on Lists later) and a sampling of people you're following. Having these items on display makes it more likely that your followers, or anyone viewing your home or profile page, will check out some of the people you're following and possibly decide to follow them as well.

Using Twitter as a Promotional Tool

You can also use Twitter to promote yourself and your work by tweeting about a new blog post you've written, an award you've won, a conference you'll be attending or speaking at, or some such newsworthy item. But as with all forms of social media, if you're smart you'll make sure most of your tweets contain useful or amusing information or

links, and you won't overdo it with the promotional tweets.

Figure 11-11

Figure 11-12

Figure 11-13

Figure 11-14

Any time you decide someone you're following is no longer tweeting enough comments or links of interest to you, you can "unfollow" that person. Conversely, any of your Twitter followers can unfollow you at any time as well. The person being unfollowed will not receive any notification of the change but may eventually notice you are no longer following her because she will no longer be able to send direct messages to you.

Finding People Who Are Worth Following

Begin by visiting the websites and blogs of people who interest you. If they're on Twitter, chances are they'll have a Follow Me on Twitter link right there on the page. Just click it to follow.

Next, go back to Twitter and use the Search box in the right-hand column of your home page to do a keyword search on subjects of interest to you (e-books, self-publishing, and book promotion, perhaps). This will turn up lots of tweets containing the word(s) you've searched for.

If you see any tweets that look interesting, click on the user name of the person who posted the tweet in question. This will take you to that user's profile page. If it seems most of the person's tweets are worth seeing, click the Follow link on the page to follow.

Another strategy to try is doing an Internet search for "Writers on Twitter," "publishers on Twitter," "authors on Twitter," and the like. There are lots of Web pages containing lists like these.

What and How to Tweet

Remember that you want to make your tweets interesting or amusing enough that others will want to follow and retweet you. As a general guideline, try to limit personal/observational tweets (for example, "Having one of those days—who invented Mondays, anyway?") to no more than one-third of your total volume of tweets—ideally, less. Fill the remainder of your tweet volume with useful or amusing information or links.

To get a feel for how tweets are typically constructed and what sorts of abbreviations are used for long words, browse other users' tweets on their home and profile pages. Just as in text messaging, people often use acronyms (TTFN for "ta ta for now") and phonetic spelling ("sez" instead of "says") to cut down on message length; however, excessive reliance on such shorthand can be distasteful to professionals who use the site. Construct your messages in correct, plain English whenever possible. Use of emoticons (smileys faces) is also common, but again, use them sparingly.

Link Shortening Services

Because links can be long and you're only allowed to enter 140 characters in a tweet, you may want to use a link shortening service to shorten any links before including them in your tweets. Two such services are www.bit.ly and www.is.gd. Using them is simple: Just paste in the long link, click the Shorten or Compress button, and voilà! The site presents you with a new, shorter version of the link to copy and paste into your tweet.

Referencing Other Twitter Users

Reference other Twitter users, or direct a tweet to a specific user, by typing in their user name preceded by the @ sign. For example, if you wanted to reference me in a tweet or direct a tweet to me, you would do so like this:

@indieauthor Thanks for sending me that link.

Using this sort of reference to direct a tweet to a specific user is called "sending an @ message." Note that this is not the same as sending a direct message, which is explained below.

You'll notice that as you type a tweet into the text box on your home page, the character counter just above the right side of the box counts down, letting you know how many characters you have left. When you get within ten characters of the 140 character limit, the counter digits turn red to alert you. Whenever possible, keep your messages well beneath that 140 character limit to make it easy for people to retweet your messages (see next section).

Retweeting

Remember that Twitter users only see the tweets of people they're following. If you get a tweet from another user, we'll call her Jane, which you think would be of interest to any of your followers who don't also happen to be following Jane, you can repost, or retweet, Jane's tweet so all of your followers will see it. After doing so, you'll find the original tweet has been labeled to show you retweeted it, as well as the number of times the tweet has been retweeted by others. (See Figure 11-15 and 11-16.)

Figure 11–15 and 11–16

The retweet may inspire some of your followers to check out Jane's profile page, where they can view all the tweets Jane has sent out, and if they like what they see, start following Jane. (See Figure 11-17.)

Figure 11–17

When one of your followers retweets one of your tweets, you have the same opportunity to attract new followers. This is how Twitter follower networks grow.

There are two ways to retweet, or RT, a message on Twitter. The first is to copy the tweet, paste it into the text box on your home page, type RT, leave a space, then type the @ sign in front of the other user's name where it appears at the front of the message, shorten the message as needed to make it fit within the 140 character limit, and click the Send button.

For example, if I tweeted this:

> The e-book publisher panel at TOC looks great [link]

The RT would look like this:

THE INDIE AUTHOR GUIDE

RT @indieauthor The e-book publisher
panel at TOC looks great [link]

The second way is easier, but it doesn't allow you
to edit the tweet before sending it out as a RT
to your followers: Simply mouse over the lower
right-hand corner of the tweet you want to RT
and click the Retweet link. You'll be prompted to
confirm the RT; click Yes. (See Figure 11-18.)

Figure 11-18

To see how the RT looks to your followers, click
on your Profile Page link, which lists all your
outgoing tweets.

Direct Messages

Anyone you're following can send private, or
direct messages to you, and you can send direct
messages to other users as well. The direct
message privilege is only there for people
whom you are following, it doesn't work in
reverse. The system is set up this way to prevent spammers from following everyone in
sight and filling up users' direct message
pages with unwanted advertising messages.
(See Figure 11-19.)

Direct messages, or DMs, can be viewed and
sent from your direct message page. Click the
Direct Messages link on the right-hand side of
your home page, above the search box, to access
your DM page.

The page includes a handy drop-down list
of people you follow and frequently message.
To send a DM to anyone on the list, just select the name from the drop-down. It will be
inserted at the beginning of the message box

on the DM page. Now type in the rest of your
message and click Send.

Once again, I caution you that while direct messages do not appear in public Twitter
streams, you should not assume they're totally
private. Anyone with knowledge of how to do
advanced searches on Google can search Twitter users' direct messages.

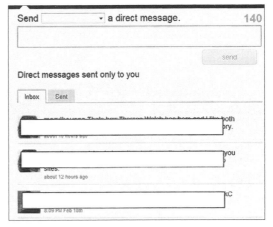

Figure 11-19

Twitter Lists

You can group some or all of the people you
follow into lists, based on categories of your
own devising. For example, if you follow certain people for tweets related to your hobby
of restoring classic cars, you can create a list
called "Classic Cars" (or whatever else you
like) and add the applicable followers to that
list. Presto, a Classic Cars link is added to your
Twitter home page. (See Figure 11-20.)

Now the tweets of people on that list can
be viewed as usual in your Twitter stream, or
you can view a page that only contains tweets
posted by the people on your Classic Cars list
by clicking the Classic Cars list link. It's a
handy way to filter tweets by category or sub-

ject. You can make your lists private, viewable only to you, or public, viewable to anyone on the Twitter site.

Figure 11-20

Furthermore, anyone who checks out one of your public lists and likes what he sees can follow that list, regardless of whether or not he also follows you. Following a list adds that list link to the follower's Twitter home page, but does not automatically add all the tweets on it to the user's Twitter stream.

Common list categories for authors and publishing folk are based on book genres, functional areas of publishing (literary agents, editors, authors, designers), subject area experts (e-books, sales, and promotion) or industry events.

Creating a list is easy. Just click on your home page, then click on the New List link in the right-hand column, under the Search box. This will open a List pop-up. Name the list, enter a description, and specify whether you want the list to be public or private. (See Figure 11-21.)

To add someone to a list, go to the user's home page. You can do this by clicking on their user

name anywhere it appears in your Twitter stream, or by looking them up in your list of followers or via the Search box in the right-hand column.

Figure 11-21

On the user's home page, there are two little drop-down menus displayed just above the user's Twitter stream, to the right. The first of these is labeled Lists. If you click to open it, it will display all your lists with check boxes. To add this user to a list, just click on the list to which you'd like them added. You don't have to follow a user to add them to a list. (See Figure 11-22.)

Figure 11-22

Twitter User Options Menu

The other drop-down menu has a picture that looks like a little gear on it. This one contains options to mention, follow/unfollow, block, or report the user. If the user is following you, it will also have an option to direct message the user. (See Figure 11-23.)

Reporting the user notifies Twitter that you think the user is in violation of site policies (for spam). Blocking the user prevents the user from following you but does not prevent the user from viewing your profile page/Twitter stream. Follow/unfollow are self-explanatory.

Clicking the Mention button will return you to your home page and automatically begin a new @ message tweet in the text box there by placing an @ sign and the user's name at the start of the box. Complete the message as you like and hit Send.

The Direct Message link works the same way, but it takes you to your Direct Message page.

Hashtags

Hashtags are something you'll see on Twitter a lot. A hashtag is any word preceded with the # sign (for example, #POD, #ebooks, #Kindle). Their purpose is to make a tweet easier to find in searches of the site.

This function is very useful for running Twitter chats. If a group of users all agree to log-in to Twitter at 4 P.M. PST on a certain day to tweet about e-book pricing, they can make it easy to follow one another's tweets on the subject, and filter out all other tweets, by including a previously agreed-upon hashtag, such as #ebookprice, in all of their tweets. Now, to view only the tweets pertinent to the chat, users in the chat can use the Search box to search for all tweets containing #ebookprice. They'll have to

rerun the search frequently to keep catching new tweets, but the process is simple.

Just for kicks, try doing a Twitter search on a hashtag version of a popular search term, like #Wii. You'll be amazed at what a powerful tool this can be.

Twitter Adjuncts

After you're comfortable with Twitter, you may find yourself wishing it offered some additional functions such as statistics showing how many people have clicked on links in your tweets or a built-in link shortener, or that it were easier to see your Twitter stream, outgoing tweets, DMs sent and received, and other information at a glance. At that point, you'll want to look into using a Twitter adjunct program like HootSuite, TweetDeck, or Seesmic. Several are listed on www.indieauthorguide.com.

Most are free but each one is a little different in terms of layout and functionality. Entire books have been written about each one. If you think you're at the point where you're ready to try one, I suggest you ask tweeting friends for their recommendations, then go to the adjuncts' site(s) and check them out yourself. You can also do an Internet search on adjunct names to find blog posts and reviews about them.

Online Communities

🕐–🕐🕐	FREE!
👣👣	⚡⚡

Online communities are Web-based clubs and discussion groups. This is where your nonwriting interests can come into play as part of your marketing efforts. Such groups are great places to promote your work, but I do not recommend joining any online community purely for the sake of promotion. To do so would be an abuse of the group, and more likely to generate ill will than sales anyway. Rather, I suggest making fuller use of the unobtrusive marketing opportunities inherent in any communities to which you already belong.

First, edit your user profile to include links to your author website and/or blog. Revise your biography to make brief mention of your books, if desired, but don't rework your biography into a sales pitch. Also edit your signature, adding a link to your author website (or blog if you don't have an author site), or a link to the product sales page of the book you're promoting. Once set up, the link will appear in every one of your posts to the discussion group. If a given community doesn't offer the signature feature, get in the habit of signing all your posts with your name and the desired link.

Some community sites provide an Insert Link button in the window where you compose your posts. In that case, highlight the text you want to make into a link, click the button, and type or paste the desired link into the provided pop-up window. See the HTML Primer in this book for more information about how to create links manually. Be sure to test your link after your post is up, and edit the post as needed if the link doesn't work. If all else fails, you can simply include the full text of the Web address in your post. It's less elegant and a lot less convenient for the user, who must copy the link and paste it into their browser, but it's better than not including a link at all.

Now use the presence of your link as motivation to become more involved in online community discussions. Take every opportunity to contribute to those discussions in a meaningful way. If people find your posts interesting or amusing, they're likely to click your link in order to learn more about you and your work. Don't post solely as an excuse to get your link displayed in a discussion, however. Your motives will be obvious and your posts will be ignored. Be willing to give back to the community in exchange for the opportunity to display your links.

Avoid gratuitous mentions of your books, but in cases where there's a legitimate reason for doing so, germane to the discussion, be sure to make your book titles hyperlinks to their respective product sales pages. If you can't use hyperlinks, include the product page Web addresses at the bottom of your post, under your signature. Again, be unobtrusive.

Online Reader Communities

🕐–🕐🕐	FREE!
🎈🎈	⚡⚡

Online reader communities are groups dedicated to books and reading. They allow (and encourage) reader-members to maintain a virtual bookshelf, on which they list books they've read, are reading, or plan to read, along with any comments or reviews of those books.

Such communities also have discussion groups formed around specific books, genres, authors, topics, or similar categories. Some of them (GoodReads, LibraryThing) offer author pages as well, a bibliography, and information area for author members. On-site messaging and friending are additional features commonly found on reader communities.

Reader-members belong to these communities and participate in them because such communities are a valuable source of unbiased book reviews, as well as havens for book lovers in general. It's important to bear this in mind when you join and start participating in reader communities. Members of such sites can be even more sensitive to promotional messages than users of other social media, and if you step over the line, you're more likely to inspire boycotts than purchases.

However, it's a good idea to join the major reader communities, if only to get your author page set up as an informational resource for members. From there, feel free to get involved in the various groups and discussions to the extent you are sincerely interested in them, but don't try to promote anything in groups or discussion areas unless you're specifically invited to do so. For example, some reader communities may have discussion threads entitled, "Authors: Tell Us About Your Book!" or something similar.

Also check the sites for reviewer groups which accept free review copies of books from authors. You can usually find them by searching the site for the term "review copies." If that doesn't turn up a match for your book, try the site's help file, or look for a groups listing page. If you decide to participate in such a group, be prepared to have an honest and totally unbiased review of your book posted to the site, and don't even think about reacting badly to a poor review on the site. Your membership on the site doesn't grant you any kind of preferential treatment, and you must treat sincere member reviews with respect.

Goodreads has a suite of tools authors can use to promote their work without alienating site members. Authors can blog on the site, post excerpts of their work, set up giveaways ,and even form their own discussion groups.

Several communities are listed on www.indieauthorguide.com.

Online Comment Forms/ Discussion Threads

⏱–⏱⏱	FREE!
🖱🖱	⚡⚡

A great deal of the traffic on my author website and blog comes from my use of online comment forms/discussion threads, either directly or indirectly. People who find my remarks interesting or amusing will often click on the link embedded in my user name when I post comments, and some comments have even drawn the attention of journalists who've gone on to contact me for interviews. Those interviews, in turn, have generated even more traffic. Online comment forms and discussion threads provide authors with a free low-time-commitment promotional opportunity that's tough to beat, but most authors don't see them as a promotional opportunity at all. The key to success in this area, as with all social media, is authenticity.

Whenever you have a spare half hour or so, scan popular media websites in search of articles related to writing, publishing, or any other topics of particular interest to you. By popular media websites, I mean the sites of print magazines, TV news networks, newspapers, blogs, and e-zines (magazines that exist only online, such as *Salon*, *The Huffington Post*, and *Slate*). Alternatively, do periodic Internet searches on topics of interest to you to locate articles about which you'll probably have something to say.

Most sites offer online comment forms or discussion areas at the end of their articles, where readers can respond to the article and discuss it with one another. If you feel you can add anything worthwhile or have a strong opinion about the article, use the comment form to enter your remarks. Most forms allow commenters to enter a name and a website link, and this is where the subtle promotion opportunity comes in. Enter your author name (the name under which you publish or plan to publish) in the Name field, and include a link to whatever it is you're promoting in the website field. This may be a link to your website or blog, to a page where your book is available for purchase online, your Twitter or Facebook profile, or anything/anywhere else you'd like to direct anyone who views your comment and decides to click your link.

Avoid any outright salesmanship in your comments: Don't mention your books, or even the fact that you're an author, unless it's germane to the topic of the post to which you're responding. Look at the comment form or discussion thread as a micro writing sample opportunity rather than a promotional opportunity, and you won't often go wrong. Anyone who's moved to click on your link might become a fan, and anyone who chooses not to click your link won't be left with the impression that you're a spammer. Of course, articles about writing and the publishing industry often provide legitimate reasons to talk about a book or author website/blog in a comment form, so put a little extra effort into seeking out those articles or discussion groups.

Unfortunately, spammers have gotten wise to the power of online comment forms and discussion groups too, and it's become a favorite vehicle for posting baldfaced advertisements. This is why it's so critical to avoid even a hint of salesmanship in your posts. The link must be incidental, and a totally opt-in experience for anyone viewing your comments.

If your comments draw the attention of journalists seeking an interview or quotes from you, make sure that in exchange for your participation the journalist will include a link to your site, blog, or book in the published article. After the article runs, add a link to it on the about or press page of your author site or blog, and promote the article on Facebook, Twitter, and any other sites where such announcements are appropriate.

A comment I posted at *Business Week's* site got the attention of Michael Brush, a regular columnist for *MSN Money*. He was writing an article about Barnes & Noble and wanted to get my perspective as an indie author. I was only quoted twice in the article, very briefly in both cases, but the day the article was published my website traffic went through the roof. Quite a few of those site visitors checked out my press page and online novel excerpts, and book sales followed.

Facebook

⏰ – ⏰⏰	FREE!
🎈🎈	⚡⚡

Facebook (FB) is a site that's set up to help users easily connect with past and present family, friends, classmates, and associates. It also offers various search tools that make it easy for you to find people who share your interests, live in the same geographic region as you do, went to the same school(s) as you, lived in towns you've inhabited, and more. It also offers lots of great, easy ways to share information about yourself (and your books!), interact with your profile visitors, and even set up dedicated pages and groups, which can be used to form online clubs/discussion groups or can serve as information hubs about a person, product, or organization.

Getting Started With Facebook

People have written entire books about how to use all the various features of Facebook, and with good reason. The amount of content and the number of options available can be overwhelming, and FB has a maddening habit of frequently redesigning the site. Here, I'll only aim to present basic information about how to get an account set up and then go on to use specific features that relate to author and book promotion. Note that everything here is based on the FB site *as of this writing*, and the site changes frequently.

On Facebook, there are profile/user account pages and fan pages. The type of page that's right for you depends on your goals and plans.

Set Up a Facebook Account

Go to the Facebook site (www.facebook.com), fill out the onscreen form, and click the Sign Up button to create your account. FB site terms of use specify you must register your Facebook account under your real (or pen) name, not a book or business name. On Facebook, fan pages are used for book, business, and other commercial profiles; I'll explain how to set up fan pages later in this section.

Complete Your Profile

While logged in to FB, click the Profile link at the upper-right corner to access your FB Profile. This is the page people will see when they visit you on FB.

Anatomy of Your FB Profile Page

Note that your profile page is divided up into sections. (See Figure 11-24.)

Figure 11-24

Although the setup sometimes changes, there are certain components that are always present. The ribbon along the top contains three icons at the left, a sitewide search box near the middle, and links to Facebook home, your FB Profile, and the Account menu.

The three icons are, from left to right, friend requests, messages, and notifications. Friend requests let you know when someone has asked you to friend them on Facebook. Messages are communications from any Facebook friends, groups, or fan pages to which you belong—these messages are private and don't show up on your wall. Notifications let you know if anyone has written on your wall, responded to a post you made on someone else's wall, or changed their profile information.

The search box allows you to search all Facebook content. The Home link takes you to a page that displays your FB News Feed.

The left-hand column is where your picture or desired image goes, along with a personal quote or snippet of information if you opt to provide one (many authors use this space to post something like, "Author of [book title], now available on Amazon" or something similar). Beneath that is a selection of some personal information items that you have chosen to display, pulled from your Info section—more on this is coming up.

The largest part of your profile is your wall, where you can post brief messages of your own (see the "What's on your mind?" box in the screenshot, below the tabs. To post a message to your wall, just type it in the box and click Share. (The same process is used to post a message to the wall of a Facebook friend.) By default every post you make to your own wall is visible to anyone on Facebook, but you can click on the little lock icon next to the Share button to change the privacy setting on a post-by-post basis. Be sure to make your privacy selection *before* you click the Share button. (See Figure 11-25.)

Your profile also contains advertising targeted to each FB user based on the content of his or her profile and wall (these are on the right).

The bottom of the page contains various links to Facebook site pages (including the Help Center) and a Chat notification box. This feature allows you to instant message any of your friends who are currently online. Note that the text of these real-time chats will not be saved or displayed on your profile page or wall, but the text will be saved on FB's own servers so don't assume your FB chats are totally private.

Editing Your FB Profile

Once on your profile page, you can use the Edit My Profile link under your profile picture at the upper-left corner, or click the Info tab to access your profile information. (See Figure 11-26.)

Your information will be mostly blank here when you first sign up. Click on the Edit Information link next to the little picture of a pencil near the top of the page to enter as much information about yourself as you'd like, bearing in mind that this information will be displayed to the general public, (I'll discuss privacy settings

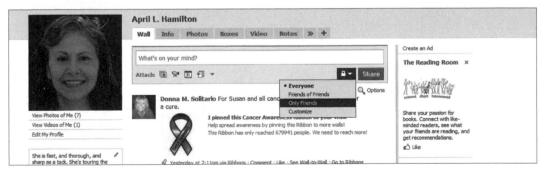

Figure 11-25

later). Click the Save Changes button in each section to save your changes.

To upload your photo, or change an existing photo later on, mouse over the profile picture field to bring up the Change Picture link. Click on that link and follow the prompts to upload your desired image.

Select the photo/image to upload from its location on your computer, check the box certifying you have distribution rights and the image is not pornographic, then click the Upload Picture button. If the picture is not an acceptable size or file format, you'll have to edit the picture outside of Facebook to meet FB requirements, then reupload it.

Some authors, like me, use a standard author photo everywhere online. Others use an image related to a book, event, or site they're currently trying to promote, and change the image as needed.

Check Out Your Account Settings

On your profile page, click the Account link at the upper right. The drop-down menu offers several choices. (See Figure 11-27.)

Edit Friends is for adding or removing Facebook friends. More on that later.

Account Settings is for changing things like your user name, password, e-mail address, and the like. This is also where you can specify your preferences for notifications, telling Facebook whether or not to send you an e-mail notification when someone new adds you as a friend, you're tagged in a post or photo, or someone posts something on your wall.

Figure 11-26

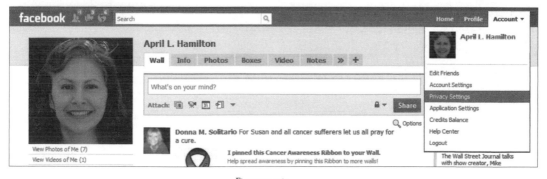

Figure 11-27

Privacy Settings is covered in the next section.

Application Settings is for changing your preferences with respect to any FB applications you use. FB applications, or apps, are little computer programs that run right on the FB site. Many of them are games, but there are also polls, birthday reminders, and much more.

When you first set up your account, no apps will be enabled so you won't need to do anything. In my experience, most apps are major time gobblers and when your list of friends gets to be up into the three digits, you can quickly become buried in app requests. I advise against using game-type apps at all, unless you have a great deal of time to devote to them.

Help Center and Logout are self-explanatory.

Adjust Your Privacy Settings

Click on Privacy Settings to display the privacy menu. This section of Facebook changes frequently and it's vital for you to be aware of how your information is being shared on and off Facebook. Read all the privacy options carefully, look for updates and press releases from Facebook, and look for user feedback elsewhere online to make sure your information is used only in ways you're comfortable with. (See Figure 11-28.)

Figure 11-28

Go into each submenu here and set your desired preferences, but don't forget your pur-

pose in joining FB in the first place. I keep most of my Profile and Search items totally public, to make it easy for people to find me on FB and give them access to all the information and content I'm sharing there. Contact Information and Block List and many other items are explained right on the menu. Application and websites settings allow you to grant permission for FB apps and outside sites and programs to access your FB Profile and potentially, to post to your wall.

Friending on Facebook

Friending someone on Facebook basically means inviting them to follow your Facebook updates and offering to follow theirs in return. If you both agree, you will each show up in one another's FB Friend list and each of your updates/wall posts will appear on the other's wall/live feed. Your group of FB friends becomes your FB community.

To get started, on your profile page, click on the account drop-down menu and select Edit Friends. The Edit Friends menu contains a Friend Finder e-mail tool, a list of friend suggestions, a Search for People tool, and a Find People You IM tool.

The Friend Finder (aka, Find People You E-mail) is a tool you can use to have Facebook scan your e-mail address book to find anyone you've e-mailed who's already on Facebook. You can choose to friend only those contacts you wish, the tool will not automatically attempt to friend or invite everyone in your e-mail address book. The Find People You IM tool works basically the same way, but it searches your instant messaging networks instead of your e-mail address book. Friend suggestions are generated by Facebook based on information you've provided in your profile. FB may also suggest friends of people you've already friended, based on common interests entered into their profiles. The Search for People tool is self-explanatory.

To Friend, or Not to Friend?

This may seem like a no-brainer, but it's not as straightforward as you might think. While you've come to FB to build a fan base of friends, that doesn't mean the wisest course is to just start friending anyone and everyone on the site.

Friending is something that's done on a mutual, opt-in basis on FB. This means that while you can put in a request to become another user's FB friend, they get to choose whether or not to approve your request. Conversely, when users put in a request to become *your* FB friend, you decide whether or not to approve *their* request. This system is in place primarily due to privacy concerns, since many FB users elect to share their FB posts and content only with people they actually know in real life or have known online for a very long time.

A secondary reason for this setup is that the sharing of information between FB friends is a two-way street. Once you're FB friends, the other person's wall posts appear on your profile's live feed and vice versa.

When you receive a friend request, it's a good idea to click on the user's name and view his profile/live feed. If the person who made the request or many of his existing FB friends frequently post profane or otherwise potentially offensive messages, pictures, links, or videos to the user's wall/live feed, it's probably best not to friend him because once you do, that stuff will start showing up on *your* wall/live

feed. If you want to friend someone but don't want to see their updates, you can choose to hide them on your wall.

There are plenty of spammers and scammers on FB, too, and checking out user profiles before friending people will shield you from most of them.

Friend requests don't have to be refused outright, however, they can simply be ignored. When you select this option to respond to a friend request, the requestor doesn't become your FB friend, but they are not explicitly rejected, either. They just never get a response to their request. You can also friend someone, but set a limit to which parts of your profile they can see.

Home Page Versus Profile

Every FB user has a home page and a profile page. The profile page is what people will see when they look you up on Facebook, so it's mostly geared to display information *you* want to share with *others*. The home page, on the other hand, is an FB-generated page that's geared to display FB information and links *FB* wants to share with *you*.

Instead of the live feed seen on your wall, your home page contains a news feed, listing wall posts culled within the past twenty-four hours from all the pages you're connected to (friends, groups, fan pages) based on your activities on FB. The point of this is to display posts that may be of particular interest to you but which have fallen off the live feed on your wall. For example, let's say you frequently visit a fantasy football league FB group page (more on group pages later in this section). If a post is made there, FB will add it to the news feed on your home page, to help you stay in the loop with what's going on with this group. The news feed will also include posts made by FB friends with whom you frequently interact.

In addition, the home page contains links to all the most commonly used FB user functions, such as messages, photos, groups, who's online, and more.

Facebook Fan Pages

A Facebook user profile must be created under the name (or pen name) of an individual. If you want to set up a profile for a book, business, or other commercial entity, you can, but only in the form of a Facebook Fan Page.

In its Help section, FB responds to the following question, "Why is a fan page a better solution than a personal account for artists, businesses, or brands?"

Personal accounts are optimized for individuals, not artists, businesses, or brands. Facebook Pages allow artists, businesses, and brands to showcase their work and interact with fans. These pages come preinstalled with custom functionality designed for each category. For example, a band page has a music player, video player, discography, reviews, tour dates, and a discussion board that the artists can take advantage of. Third-party developers will also build an array of applications that they will compete for page admins to add to their pages. Facebook pages are also not subject to a fan limit and can automatically accept fan requests.

FB Fan Pages look virtually identical to FB user profiles, but there are some key differences.

First, as explained above, fan pages have preinstalled functionality keyed to the type of fan page.

Second, instead of friends, fan pages have fans.

Third, fans don't have to be approved by the person who runs a fan page; if you want to become a fan, you just click the Become a Fan button. The fan page administrator/creator can limit membership by age or country, but that's all.

Fourth, communication on fan pages tends to be mostly one-way: You post information to your fans and they're free to discuss it on the fan page by commenting on your wall posts and content uploads. Think of it this way: Where a profile page is set up for you to interact with a mix of family, friends, and fans, a fan page is set up for you to share information with fans, and for your fans to interact with each other.

Finally, where FB profile pages have a friend limit of five thousand, there is no limit to the number of fans a fan page can have.

Should Authors Have Profiles or Fan Pages?

You can use the Artist, Band, or Public Figure option to create a fan page for yourself as an author. You can have both a regular FB profile and a fan page, but doing so will double the time you have to spend posting to FB and interacting with fans or friends, so it's generally a good idea to choose one or the other. There are some pros and cons to consider here.

While a fan page doesn't place an upper limit on the number of fans you can have, it also doesn't require you to approve fan requests so fan pages are easily targeted by spammers and other undesirables. You'll need to keep on top of moderating the content of your fan page (deleting objectionable posts, blocking unwanted fans) on a near-daily basis.

While visitors to a fan page don't generally expect the same level of one-on-one interaction with you they'd find on a profile page, you're not likely to gather many fans without first having the level of personalized one-on-one interaction that usually takes place on profile pages. You may wish to start with a profile page and then switch to a fan page if/when you get so famous, or accumulate so many friends, that it's impossible to continue with the personalized exchanges typically reserved for profile pages. In that case, you'll have to alert all your friends to the existence of the new fan page and get as many of them as possible to become fans before you delete your profile.

Another option favored by many authors is to maintain a profile for yourself as an author, then create fan pages for each of your books or for the books' protagonists. There will be some additional upkeep demands if you choose to go this route, since you'll have multiple pages to maintain.

Setting Up an FB Fan Page

If you already have a FB account, log-in to FB, then scroll down to the bottom of the page and click the Advertising link. The Advertising menu page is displayed. (See Figure 11-29.)

This is the centralized dashboard for all your advertising and promotional activities on FB. But we're talking about fan pages, so to get started, click on the Pages link in the left-hand menu.

You'll see a message that says "You have not created any pages" and a link labeled Create a Page. Click the link to display the Create New Facebook Page page.

If you're not already an FB member, you can access the Create New Facebook Page page by going to the Facebook home page and clicking on the Create a Page for a Celebrity, Band, or Business link, just below the Sign Up button. (See Figure 11-30.)

As shown, Local > Other Business is selected by default, but you want to select either Brand, Product, or Organization, in the case of a fan page for a book, or Artist, Band, or Public Figure, in the case of a fan page for yourself (as an author) or for a fictional character from your book. In the example below, I'm creating a fan page for my book, *The Indie*

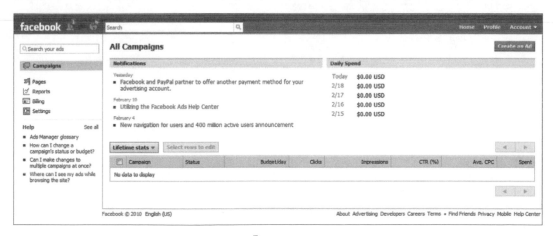

Figure 11-29

Author Guide. The book won't be released for a few months, so I don't plan to make the page public or start promoting it until closer to my book's release date.

Note that the Brand, Product, or Organization drop-down does not offer an option for Book, so you'll have to leave the drop-down set to its default (Products) value. Also note that I've checked the Do Not Make Page Publicly Visible at This Time option box, so I'll have time to tinker with my Fan Page before allowing anyone on FB to see it. (See Figure 11-31.)

When I click Create Page, I see my new fan page. (See Figure 11-32.)

Completing Your Product/Author Information

My fan page looks and works a whole lot like a regular profile page. When I click the Edit Information link, I get access to the same kinds of fields present on a FB user profile, but there are far fewer of them and none of them ask for personal information. A fan page for a person (author) does have most of those fields, however.

As with a regular profile, you can complete as many fields as you like and leave the rest blank. Since the product type of fan page was designed with products other than books in mind, the fields may not seem immediately applicable to a book.

Also like a regular profile, there's a space for you to upload a picture or photo. For my fan page, this is where I'll put a picture of the cover of my book. For an author page, this is where an author photo belongs.

Using the Features of Your Fan Page

The first thing you'll notice about your fan page is the invitation to link it to your Twitter

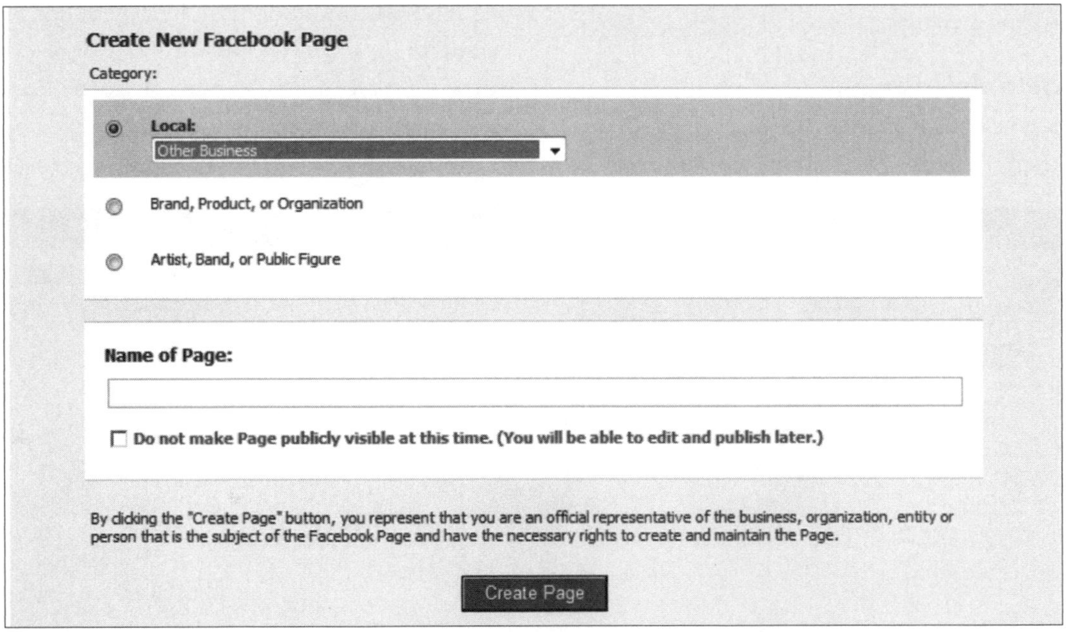

Figure 11-30

account, right up there at the top. If you have a Twitter account, linking your fan page to it will automatically post a tweet anytime you add new or updated content to your fan page.

Think carefully before you enable this feature for linking to a personal or author Twitter account if the fan page is for a specific book. It's not safe to assume everyone who follows you on Twitter does so because they want to get a constant stream of information and updates about one of your books. If you've set up a separate Twitter account just for the book however,

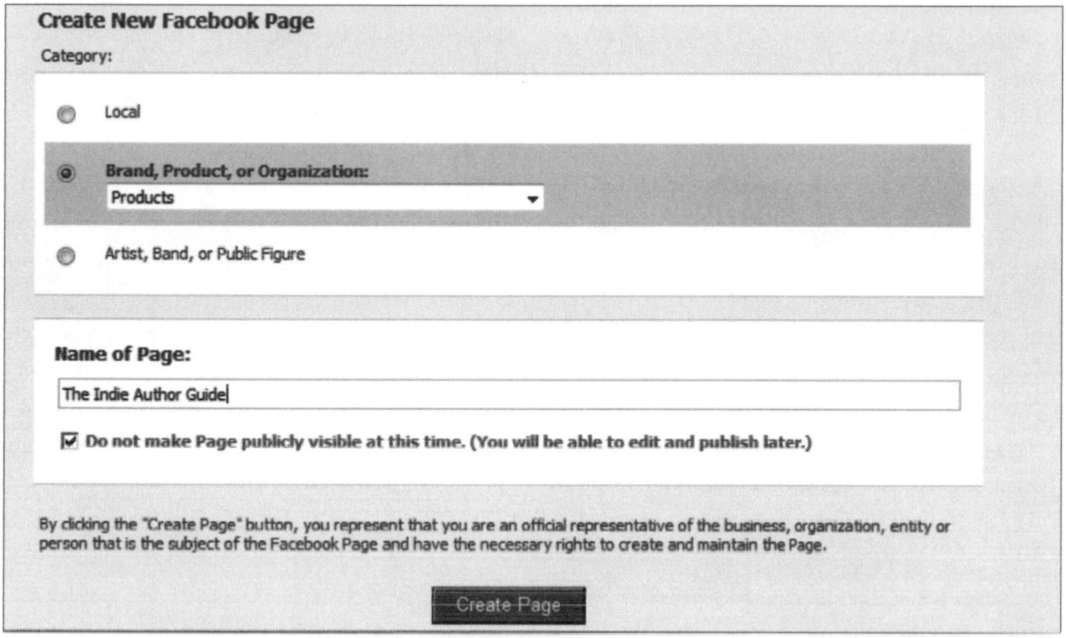

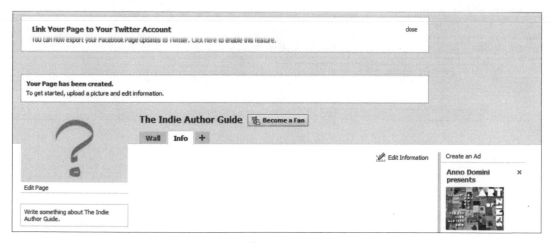

Create New Facebook Page

Category:

○ Local

◉ **Brand, Product, or Organization:**
Products ▼

○ Artist, Band, or Public Figure

Name of Page:

The Indie Author Guide

☑ **Do not make Page publicly visible at this time. (You will be able to edit and publish later.)**

By clicking the "Create Page" button, you represent that you are an official representative of the business, organization, entity or person that is the subject of the Facebook Page and have the necessary rights to create and maintain the Page.

Create Page

Figure 11-31

Link Your Page to Your Twitter Account   close
You can now export your Facebook Page updates to Twitter. Click here to enable this feature.

Your Page has been created.
To get started, upload a picture and edit information.

The Indie Author Guide   🖼 Become a Fan

Wall   Info   ✚

✏️ Edit Information   Create an Ad

?

Anno Domini presents   ✕

Edit Page

Write something about The Indie Author Guide.

Figure 11-32

you'll definitely want to link it up with your fan page.

By default, my new fan page only has two tabs: wall and info. I can click the + tab to add more items. (See Figure 11-33.)

All of the available tabs can be put to good use in promoting either a book or an author, so don't limit yourself to a fan page that's essentially a wall and nothing else.

Use the Photos tab to post pictures of yourself at events, as well as pictures of your fans. Some authors use this tab to display pictures of their fans holding a copy of their book. To include pictures of your fans, just ask fans to post the photos to their own FB Profiles and tag your fan page (by title) in the photos. Doing so automatically displays their photos in your Fan Page Photos tab.

Use the Links tab to share links to reviews of your book, author interviews, your author web-site and blog, articles and guest blog posts you've written, and any other relevant online content.

Use the Events tab to notify fans of upcoming events and appearances. These may be in-person signings or talks, podcast interviews, radio interviews, or any other event or appearance you'd like to invite fans to attend/listen to, or in which you'd like fans to participate. You can also use this tab to alert fans to book, article, or story releases, or to spearhead an Amazon rush, in which you get as many people as possible to all buy your book on the same day on Amazon.

Use the Notes tab to post general information and communications to your fans. Some authors use the Notes section as a blog, and others set it up to pull in the RSS feed of their existing blog. You can find more information about exactly how to do this in FB's help pages. There are also some relevant links on www.in-dieauthorguide.com.

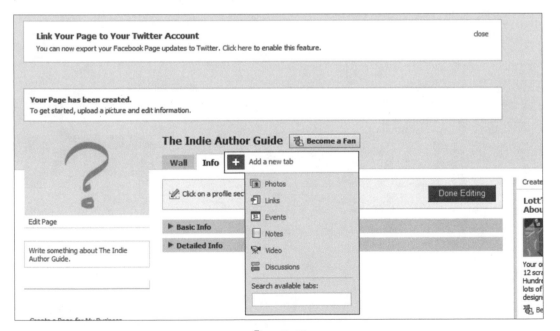

Figure 11-33

Use the Videos tab to post book trailers, instructional videos, a video blog for your fans, or video of any live appearances.

Use the Discussions tab to start a mini discussion board right on your fan page. It will work a lot like the wall of your fan page, but it will be threaded, meaning that people who click on the Discussions tab will be able to view and select from a list of topics. Responses will be contained within each topic, rather than posting in real time, one on top of the other, constantly pushing each other down and off the page.

Promoting Your Fan Page

Remember that you can't friend people from a fan page; people must come to your fan page and click the Become a Fan button themselves.

If you have an FB profile, make a few, well-spaced posts to your wall about the new fan page, inviting your FB friends to come check it out and become fans. Tread lightly here, though. Don't just post a stream of fan page promotional messages for days on end. Instead, conduct business as usual on your profile, but include a post about the new fan page maybe once every few days (or less, if you only post to your profile infrequently) for the first couple of weeks after the fan page goes live. You want to get the word out about your fan page, but you don't want to alienate existing FB friends.

If you're on Twitter, post a few well-spaced tweets about the page.

Post links to the page on your author website and blog. You might even want to write an entire blog post specifically about your fan page: what it is, what it has to offer, and why you've created it.

If you belong to any writer communities, share the link to your fan page, but again, be careful not to come off as a spammer. Present the fan page as a resource for those you're inviting to it. Here's where availing yourself of all those tabs pays off, since every tab can provide useful information and resources, or at the minimum, amusement to your fans.

Keep Building Your Fan Base

Nobody will want to come back to your fan page unless you're regularly updating it with new information and content.

Get the ball rolling on the Discussion tab by posting some provocative questions you know people will want to discuss. Questions about e-book pricing and favorite authors or books are a safe bet, as is posting an invitation for fans to pose specific questions about you or your book for you to answer.

If you don't have the time to blog on your fan page, or don't want to use the Notes tab as a blog, make sure the Notes tab is pulling in the RSS feed for any preexisting blog of yours—provided it's either specifically about the book/author the fan page was created for, or contains posts of interest to fans of your page. For example, I'll be pulling my Indie Author Blog RSS feed into my Notes tab; even though the blog isn't exclusively about *The Indie Author Guide*, it covers topics of interest to the book's target demographic of indie authors.

Be patient. You can't expect to build a huge fan base over night. Keep promoting the page whenever the opportunity arises, and keep adding and updating content so fans have a reason to keep coming back and to recommend your page to their friends.

For more information about fan pages, see Facebook's help pages.

Facebook Groups

Yet another function FB offers is Facebook Groups. An FB Group Page is set up, and works, almost exactly like a fan page, with a few differences.

Where all fan pages are public, with all their content viewable to anyone on Facebook, a group can be set up as private (its content viewable by members only) or public.

Groups can also be set up such that only FB friends of the group's founder and its members can join the group, but this option is far too limiting for a group intended to grow and strengthen an author's platform; you want to reduce barriers to membership, not erect new ones.

A group's Info tab is customized to contain information and links relevant to the group, as opposed to a product or person. You must be a Facebook member to start a group.

The group's founder and members can invite fellow Facebookers to join the group, and just as with friend requests, the recipient of the invitation can join, decline, or ignore the invitation. Facebookers can also search FB Groups on their own and join any public groups they like by clicking a Join button on group pages of interest to them.

The other major difference between the two page types is cultural. Where communication on a fan page is generally one-way (you communicate information to a group which then communicates mostly amongst themselves), communication is two-way on a group page. The founder of the group is also a member, and must participate in group discussions, events, and activities to the same extent expected of any other member.

Groups Versus Fan Pages

If you're already heavily involved in online communities or other social media and have concerns about your time and effort availability, a fan page is probably a better choice for you than a group. On the other hand, if you're just starting out with author platform and looking for an easy, free way to get a full, interactive, one-stop, bells-and-whistles online community going without hiring a Web developer to build a site for you, setting up a Facebook Group may be just the ticket.

The major limitation here is that only FB members can join your group; it won't be open to the general public like a custom-built website. Still, Facebook is hugely popular among the general public in developed nations all over the world.

Forming a Facebook Group

To form a Facebook Group, log in to FB and click on the Home Page link. On the home page, click on the Groups link in the left-hand column. This will open the Groups page, which includes a handy Create a Group button at the upper right. Click that button and you're off to the races, creating your group page and filling out its information the same way you would for a FB user profile or fan page.

Promoting Your Facebook Group

Inviting Facebookers to join your new group is as easy as clicking the Invite People to Join or Share buttons on the right-hand side of your group page.

You can also send personal invitations to FB friends, post on your own wall about the group, and post on FB friends' walls, too. But as always, be cautious in your promotional efforts. Keep any promotional posts on your own wall well-spaced among other posts of interest to your FB friends, and if you're considering sending out personal invitations or posting on a FB friend's wall, be sure the group is something the recipients of your message/invitation will truly be interested in hearing about. Otherwise, you risk looking like you're only on FB to sell something, which is tantamount to spamming. When in doubt, don't post.

Offer information and resources to group members, actively participate in group discussions and events, hold contests, and link to your group from your other sites and blogs.

Communicating With Your Group

The group administrator/creator can send messages to up to five thousand of the group's members, to be delivered to each group member's Facebook in-box, but cannot send messages to individual members from the group page. Use the Message All Members link on your group page to send a message to the members of your group.

Don't overdo it with these messages, however. Facebookers don't appreciate excessive FB messages any more than everyone else appreciates excessive e-mail. The best use of this feature is to send a brief newsletter to group members no more frequently than once a month. You can also alert group members to any important changes to the group.

Facebook Events

If you have an upcoming event to promote (a book signing, public appearance, online chat, book launch, or Amazon rush), use Facebook Events to publicize it on Facebook. You can use the Events tab in your profile, fan page(s), and/or group page(s) for this purpose. If you create the event in your profile, all your FB friends will receive a notification about it in their live feeds, so it's a great, unobtrusive way to get the word out to your community without coming off as pushy.

Paid Advertising On Facebook

Remember that Paid Ads area on the Advertising Menu page? That's where you can set up targeted, pay-per-click advertisements for your books, classes, events, or anything else you're selling. Your ad can be targeted to Facebook users based on their age, gender, keywords used in their profiles, geographic location, and much more. If you're trying to promote something for which the target audience is fairly narrow, this can be a very cost-effective means of advertising since the ad is only displayed to the people most likely to be interested in your product, and you pay only when someone actually clicks on your ad.

Link Tracking Networks

🕐–🕐🕐🕐	FREE!
🎈🎈🎈	NO CONFIDENCE!

Link tracking networks are online services that allow people to submit links to websites and online articles they wish to recommend. Like YouTube, these sites provide a search mechanism and constantly update popularity rankings. The most-submitted links get promoted to the service's front page, where they may be picked up by major media outlets. Link submissions also raise the linked page's rank in Internet search results.

Some services also provide a membership option, which allows users to rate other users' submissions and may also allow the user to maintain a personal centralized list of favorite links on the service's site. Anytime a user adds a link to her personal list, it counts as a vote in favor of the link. Digg, Del.icio.us, Technorati, StumbleUpon, and Furl are some of the many services, and new ones spring up all the time.

In order for your Web content to be eligible to receive votes in the form of submitted links, you have to add a widget to your pages and blog entries. You must supply a widget for each service for which you'd like to be eligible, and this requires a bit of HTML knowledge. Each service provides a block of HTML code for its voting widget, which you can paste into your site pages or blog, but you will have to customize the code to make the widget look and act the way you want it to.

When a visitor clicks the widget, he is taken to the associated service network and is prompted to fill out a brief form describing your page/content. If you become a member of a given service, you will be able to check the popularity of your links on that service whenever you like.

Most marketing types will tell you to join every one of these networks and actively solicit link-submission trades with other online promoters, but they're not as effective as they once were. While it's true that a lucky page can take off in popularity one day, skyrocket to the front page of the link-tracking service's site, and go on to be picked up by a major news outlet, the marketplace is so flooded with link-tracking networks that the odds against any given page rising to the top are getting longer and longer.

With the glut of tracking networks out there it's less and less likely a given major news outlet will happen to pick up a story off the front of a tracking service site to which you subscribe on the day your page happens to be highlighted there. The proliferation of tracking networks also makes it that much less likely your content will get enough votes on any one of them to truly increase its visibility on the Web overall. Now that these networks are so commonplace, advertisers have found ways to manipulate them, further reducing their value. Finally, some networks make those page widgets into a double-edged sword: Users can vote for or against your content. If you attract a Web troll with an axe to grind, he can make a career out of burying your content.

Personally, I don't feel link-tracking networks are worth the time and effort. Still, if you have basic HTML skills, feel free to experiment with them. They may work for you, and if they don't, you can remove the voting widgets from your pages.

Link Trading

🕐	**FREE!** — $$
👆👆	⚡

Link trading is just what it sounds like: offering to put other writers' links on your site in exchange for their agreement to add your link to their site. This is a quick, easy, cost-free way to increase your exposure while providing the same service for other writers. A link trade instantly grants each author visibility to the other author's online audience.

WORKING AMAZON

The Amazon Author Page and blog were covered previously, but they're just the tip of the Amazon iceberg.

Amazon Customer Reviews

🕐-🕐🕐🕐🕐	$–$$$
🎈🎈	⚡⚡

Positive customer reviews of your book on Amazon are one of the best ways to raise your book's visibility on the site, because customers can (and often do) sort search results by Average Customer Review.

This type of sort is a simple sort, which means all the items with an average customer review rating of 5 out of 5 stars appear at the top of the list, followed by all the items with 4.75 out of 5 stars, followed by all the items with 4.5 out of 5 stars, and so on down to the bottom of the list, where items with no reviews will appear. Review count is used as a secondary sort within each customer rating level.

For example, imagine your young adult science fiction novel only has two customer reviews, but both are five-star reviews. Let's say that under this heading there are 2,500 books listed—but only fifteen of them have an average review rating of 5 out of 5 stars. When a customer sorts a list of young adult science fiction titles by Average Customer Review, your book will appear

on the first page with all the other books that have an average rating of 5 out of 5 stars. Your book's position within the group of 5 out of 5 star books will be determined by review count: Those with more reviews appear higher in the list, those with few reviews appear lower.

The Average Customer Review sort is one place where the little guy (or in this case, indie guy) can actually have an advantage over best-selling mainstream books. First, as review count goes up, average customer review rating tends to go down. This is because no book can please everybody, and many best-sellers eventually fall victim to reader backlash, especially if they've been heavily hyped.

Some authors try to raise their standing in the Average Customer Review sort by creating a bunch of dummy Amazon accounts specifically to enter lots of 5-star reviews for their books, but this is a mistake. Since the dummy accounts won't have significant activity other than entering five-star customer reviews for your books and those of your friends, their validity will be suspect. Furthermore, anyone who cross-references the dummy accounts' activity can probably figure out you're the one behind them. Any hint of fraud will instantly cancel out the positive impression you hoped to make, and in fact will have the opposite effect; after all, if the books were any good why would the author go to such lengths to trick people into buying them?

Instead, solicit reviews from friends and family who have Amazon accounts, and also refer to the Editorial Reviews topic in the Traditional Tactics section of this chapter for information about soliciting reviews from Amazon Top Reviewers. Don't request this favor from family members whose Amazon user name includes their last name if that name is the same as yours, since many people will rightly conclude (or at least suspect) the review is from a relative and call its validity into question.

Also, don't solicit reviews with strings attached, such as a demand for a guaranteed five-star rating. You can request that friends and family members only post a review if they enjoyed the book, but with reviews solicited from others you must be willing to graciously accept the posted review, whether good or bad.

Amazon Listmania! Lists

●–●●●	FREE!
●●●	⚡–⚡⚡

Amazon customers can make lists of their favorite books and products. The lists are displayed, on a rotating basis, on Amazon search results pages where the search results include items from a created list.

The Listmania display box offers three options: You can view a complete list by clicking on the list title, you can click the Create a Listmania! list link to create a list of your own, or you can use the Search Listmania box to search for items other customers have included in their lists. When viewing a complete list, you can also view remarks the list author made about each item in the list.

Having your book added to a Listmania list can significantly increase its visibility on Amazon. Since search results are ranked by best-selling by default, your book will probably be buried many pages down in most search results.

However, if your book is part of a Listmania list appearing on the first page of search results, it becomes accessible from that first page. Moreover, the fact that a customer put the book on a list stands as a recommendation, making it that much more likely other customers will give it a try.

Before you go off and create a bunch of lists with your book in them, note that the name of the list author is displayed right along with the list. It's considered poor form to create lists with your own books on them, and your promotional intent will be transparent to the list viewer. Call once again on those friends and family members with Amazon accounts, again granting a pass to those whose user names make their relationship to you apparent.

The Amazon Rush

●–●●●	FREE!
●●●	⚡–⚡⚡

An Amazon Rush is a coordinated effort to get the maximum number of book sales on a specific day. You announce your Amazon Rush date well ahead of time, and keep reminding your followers about it from time to time in an unobtrusive way leading up to the big day. Then, on the appointed day, if all goes to plan your book will start rocketing its way up the various Amazon best-seller lists. There are advantages to this beyond that initial spike in sales.

First, the higher your book appears on various best-selling lists, the more likely it is to be seen (and purchased!) by people who have otherwise never heard of you. These sales help to keep your book well-ranked, which keeps its visibility high, which keeps it well-ranked—and the cycle repeats.

Second, this strategy can quickly vault your book ahead of well-known mainstream best-sellers. And if Jane Doe's book is selling better than Dan Brown's, for instance, plenty of consumers will think Jane Doe's book is worth a closer look. And again, the cycle repeats.

Third, indie books appearing high in Amazon's major best-seller list categories (fiction and literature, nonfiction, reference) can and often do attract the attention of literary agents and publishers, as well as journalists and bloggers.

Form a Web Promo Ring

⏱–⏱⏱⏱	FREE!
🎈🎈	⚡–⚡⚡

Since so many Internet promotion techniques involve accumulating reviews, clicks, ratings, and the like from others, consider forming a Web promo ring with other writers for members' mutual benefit. Members can agree to whatever promotional exchanges they like: Adding books to Listmania! lists, writing Amazon reviews, trading links, rating podcasts and YouTube videos, submitting links to link tracking networks, and so on.

The keys to success with such a group are open communication and consensus: Every member must be able to freely express her comfort level for various promotional activities without fear of criticism, and no member should be pressured to do anything she doesn't want to do. The group should decide at the outset which activities will be undertaken, rejecting any that are objectionable to any member.

It's tempting to allow subsets of members to participate in promotional activities other members don't like, but doing so will splinter the group and give rise to resentments, especially if subset groups go on to enjoy greater success than other ring members. Start with a base assumption that you are responsible for all your own promotion, and view any shared promo ring activity as a bonus.

FIGURE OUT WHAT'S WORKING FOR YOU

When you promote, your ultimate goal is to sell books, but you're also trying to raise awareness about you and your books in general. You're shooting for some vague familiarity, which may grow into name recognition, which may blossom into sales. But how do you know which of your promotional efforts, if any, are paying off? In a word: statistics.

Website Statistics

⏱–⏱⏱	FREE!–$$$
🎈🎈🎈–🎈🎈🎈🎈	NO CONFIDENCE!

There are many website statistics services out there, ranging from freeware to moderately priced software. Google Analytics and StatCounter are two that are free. Do an Internet search for "hit counter" or "site statistics" to find more options. They all work essentially the same way: You sign up for an account, and the service generates a small block of HTML code you can copy and paste into Web pages you want to track for statistics reporting. The block of code is invisible on your pages, and it works entirely in the background.

Recall that most blog and template-based website services allow at least limited use of HTML, and since the provided block of code is to be pasted exactly as is and in its entirety, you don't need to know anything about HTML to accomplish this feat. Open the page or form that allows you to enter HTML on your page, paste the statistics code block into the form, and save your changes. That's all there is to it. If you're adding the code to pages you've authored yourself, follow the service's directions for where to paste the code.

Many of the services that offer simple fill-in-the-blanks template-based websites and blogs include hit counters or limited statistical reports on members' sites, and most hosting services also provide statistics for their customers' sites. Where available, statistics can be accessed from your user control panel or dashboard. These rarely match the level of detail and the amount of information provided by a dedicated statistics service, however.

Website statistics can tell you who's visiting your website or blog, what sites they came from, how long they stayed, which pages or articles they viewed, how often they came back, and more. The statistics don't name names, of course, but they do distinguish individual site visitors by user IP address, which is the unique identifier assigned to a specific computer or Web server. Statistics provide a kind of virtual paper trail from your promotional activities to your website, thereby enabling you to see which activities are bringing the most visitors to your website.

The Came From report lists the websites from which site visitors came. Numerous subreports are typically available within this category, and clicking on individual entries allows you to drill down into more detailed information about the user: her location, browser type, time of visit, duration of visit, and more. Website statistics can tell you almost anything you want to know about your website visitors.

Scanning entries in the Came From report tells me at a glance which of my online promotional efforts are generating the most traffic for my author website, and that information makes it easy to decide whether or not to continue with a given effort. For example, if I've used a comment form at a certain site and found it didn't generate a single site visit, I won't continue to post there.

The Came From report also informs me when someone else provides a link to my site. If there's a Came From entry with a Web address that's unfamiliar to me, I know someone has posted a link to my site somewhere, and someone else followed that link. I can visit the website shown in the Came From listing to see where the link to my site was posted, and in what context. (Hopefully it said, "Check out this excellent site," versus, "You won't believe what an idiot this writer is…") If the context is positive, I try to find contact information for the person who posted the link and e-mail to say thanks, as well as to offer a link exchange if she's a writer. If the context is negative, I decide whether to attempt some damage control or just leave well enough alone and hope the post soon sinks into obscurity.

The Popular Pages report tells you which pages on your site receive the most traffic. This information is helpful two ways: first by identifying the most effective pages on your site, and second by identifying the least effective pages. You may learn that all your hours of work to set up and maintain a podcast page were for naught, in which case you may choose to delete that page from your site and stop putting time into it. On the other hand, you may decide to look at the most popular pages on your site and try to find ways to make your podcast page more like the popular pages.

The Popular Pages report also tells you which pages on your site should be used as the basis for links in your comment form sign-offs, profile pages, discussion group signature lines. For example, if you typically sign off with a link to your About Me page, but find statistics are telling you that visitors who land on that page promptly click a link to go elsewhere, you may want to start linking directly to a more popular page.

The more frequently you check your site statistics, the more quickly you can adjust your promotional strategies to avoid wasting time, money, and effort, or to capitalize on buzz. However, because every statistics service is different, I can't go into great detail about the various reports and options available. In using different statistics services, I've found the best way to figure out what data is available, and what the data means, is to click on all the various reports and compare them.

Sales Statistics

🕐 – 🕐🕐	**FREE!**
🕐	**NO CONFIDENCE!**

Your publisher will provide sales statistics on your books, either in the form of periodic reports or an online reporting service. If your book is sold on Amazon, you can also watch for upward movement in your book's sales rank on your author bibliography; any sudden, dramatic jump usually points to sales, but you'll need to check an actual sales report to be sure. I use the sales ranks shown in my bibliography as a kind of flag, alerting me to the need to check my sales statistics.

Since it's impossible for you to know who is buying your book and what enticed them to buy it, sales statistics are of limited use. However, a sudden spike in sales following a specific promotional effort on your part probably means that effort was successful. You can also use site and sales statistics to correlate the timing of sales with visits to your blog or author site, if you have sales links for your books on a specific page.

KEEPING THE PROMO TRAIN ON TRACK

Keeping the promo train on track boils down to a two-word strategy: Don't stop. Don't stop trying different promotional techniques, don't stop checking your progress, don't stop doing the things that work, don't stop building on your successes, and don't stop looking for opportunities to promote yourself and your work.

Put More Irons in the Fire

Beware of putting all your promotional eggs in one basket. Employ as many different promotional techniques as you reasonably can at all times, but be realistic about how much time, money, and effort you have to give. It's better to give 100 percent to just two promotional activities than to give 10 percent each to ten different activities.

Setting aside a designated block of time each week to focus on promotion can help if you're feeling overwhelmed by the number and scope of promotional strategies available to you. Once-a-week checkups have the added benefit of giving you a set frame of reference for comparing the relative success of different promotional activities, allowing you to see how many website hits or book sales you had per week over time for each different activity. Such insights make it easier to decide where to increase your efforts and where to pull back.

You may have to invest some time, money, and effort in acquiring new skills or improving existing ones, to beef up your promotional arsenal. It's time, money, and effort well spent, as it will pay off for years to come. With all the free tutorials and help available online, anyone with a computer and Internet access should have no difficulty scraping together basic knowledge of HTML, graphics, and photo editing, or even acquiring some advanced skills, if time permits. An HTML primer is provided as an appendix to this book, for a start.

Cultivate and Maintain Contacts

This point is pretty self-explanatory. Cultivate positive relationships with writers, readers, reviewers, journalists, and people in the publishing industry whenever the opportunity presents itself. You don't have to try to be a best friend to all of these people, you just want to do your best to leave a positive impression.

Maintain lists of contact information for everyone you meet along the book promotion road and categorize them by type of contact. You may have a list of other writers with whom you've traded links, a list of publishing industry contacts, a list of people you've solicited for editorial reviews, and a list of writers with whom you exchange drafts for peer review. See Appendix A-1, Worksheets, for some useful tracking tools to use here.

Each list is a potential mailing list for future announcements, but don't be too cavalier about sending them. Blanketing your contacts in frequent unimportant announcements will waste their time and irritate them. Limiting your announcements to events or news that will truly be of interest.

An announcement about the publication of a new book would be appropriate to send to your reviewer list and possibly your publishing industry list. A new website, or website address change, is something to share only with your link-trading list. Recent publication of an article pertaining to writing merits an announcement to your writer list. Winning an award, getting a publication contract, optioning one of your books to a movie producer, or earning a best-selling list slot are all things you may want to share with your publishing industry list.

Document Everything, Store Every Document

Again, the headline says it all. Save copies of every bit of promotional material you create, as well as every e-mail exchanged with your contacts, and back up your files regularly.

Many of your promotional materials can serve as templates to be reused for future projects. Reusing the same basic design and layout for flyers, Web pages, and so on not only saves you time, but supports the goal of consistency in your marketing campaign.

Save copies of your pithiest and most clever comment form posts and discussion group posts by copying them and pasting them into a Notepad (.txt) or a word processing document. The saved texts can be developed into blog posts, articles, or talking points for public appearances. It may help to maintain a single "document" for each major topic covered (that is, writing technique, publishing, contests, reviews and reviewing, and so on), then paste copies of any online posts pertaining to each topic into the appropriate document.

Be Genuine

Perhaps the biggest problem facing any promotional effort in this day and age is the general public's cynicism; while everyone buys things, no one wants to be sold on anything. Thanks to infomercials, telemarketing, spam, and junk mail, salespeople are almost uniformly viewed as conniving scam artists who will do anything to make a buck. In this environment, it doesn't matter how fantastic or needed a new product is, the seller will have a hard time getting consumers to listen to him. Plagiarizing journalists and lying memoirists haven't exactly improved the situation for writers, either.

Honesty, consistency, and time are the only means at your disposal to combat this problem. Potential buyers are looking for any reason to lump you in with the hucksters, so don't give them any. Never be dishonest or even misleading in your promotional materials or any of your communications, and avoid hype. You must absolutely be the real deal, aboveboard in all your dealings, respectful and open in all your communications, and willing to give back as much as you take when it comes to opportunities and assistance. While the ultimate goal of your promotional effort is to sell books, think of yourself more as someone with information and stories or abilities to share than as a salesperson.

twelve} Making the Transition From Indie to Mainstream

Increasingly, aspiring authors are utilizing indie authorship as a proving ground to get a foot in the door of the mainstream trade publishing world. Trade publishing acquisition decisions are dictated to a large extent by risk avoidance; a successful self-published book, whether it's successful in terms of sales or buzz, is a low-risk acquisition opportunity. There's no question about how a given self-published book will perform in the marketplace, because it is already *in* the marketplace.

While it's rare for a self-published book to reach the same sales heights as mainstream bestsellers, mainstream publishers know this and do not measure self-published books by the same sales yardstick that they use for their own books. Numbers merely in the hundreds can make a strong impression with a mainstream publisher if you can demonstrate a steady and growing stream of sales or downloads, particularly if you also have a strong author platform and large fan base.

Large is a relative term, but a figure I often hear quoted at writer and publisher conferences is a documented audience of at least five thousand. This does not mean you must be able to show you've sold five thousand copies of your book, nor even that your blog, website, or e-mail newsletter has five thousand subscribers. If the cumulative total of your online followers, subscribers, and unique website/blog page views approaches or exceeds five thousand, you have a fan base to be reckoned with as far as mainstream publishers are concerned.

Of course, selling the rights to have your self-published book re-released in a new, mainstream edition is only possible if you still own those rights or can buy them back from whoever currently holds them. The fact that you've published the book at all does not make its publication rights worthless, as aspiring authors are often led to believe; concern over first publication rights is an artifact from trade publishing of yesteryear. So long as you haven't signed over some or all of the publication rights to a vanity or subsidy press, or any other entity, you can enter into a contract to have your self-published book re-released by a publisher at any time.

Still, being able to meet mainstream publishers' unofficial requirements doesn't necessarily mean you and your book will benefit from such an affiliation.

CAN A PUBLISHER HELP YOU REACH YOUR GOALS?

To answer this question, you must first identify your goals for both the specific book, and for you as an author. After giving the matter careful consideration, you may find your goals aren't what you initially thought they were.

Most authors would reflexively answer that their goal for the book is maximum sales, and their goal as an author is maximum public acceptance of their art or authority. But if they were to dig a little deeper and think about *why* they want to maximize sales or acceptance, they would likely find different, underlying goals for which these surface goals merely provide the means to an end.

For example, you may want big sales numbers not primarily for the money those sales generate, but because those sales reflect a widening spread and acceptance of your art or message. In other words, upon reflection you may realize that having a large and appreciative readership matters more to you than the dollar amount of royalties earned from that readership.

When I self-published the first edition of this book, getting its contents out there to the widest possible audience of self-publishers and aspiring authors was far more important to me than hitting any specific earnings target because my reason for writing the book in the first place was to help facilitate and grow a true indie author movement.

Though it may not be immediately apparent, your reasons for writing and publishing your book may be equally detached from monetary matters. Similarly, the goal of wide acceptance may have more to do with a desire to bolster an existing career, or facilitate the change to a new one, than it does with a desire for fame in and of itself.

Now consider the goals of a typical trade publisher: maximum earnings, maximum consumer acceptance of their products, and brand reinforcement with every title they release. An individual author's goals are never likely to align completely with those of her publisher, unless perhaps the author is also a stockholder in the company. So the question of whether or not a given publisher can help you reach your goals isn't dependent on *shared* goals, but *complementary* goals.

The big profits a publisher hopes to realize from a book may dovetail nicely with an author goal of maximizing readership for example, but there may be other, better ways for the author to enlarge his readership. Offering free downloads of an e-book edition, for example.

Give careful thought to your goals; it's important that they align with those of your intended publisher to the extent that both parties are motivated to see the other's goals accomplished.

IS YOUR BOOK A GOOD CANDIDATE?

Mainstream trade publishers, by and large, want to publish books with the widest possible appeal within their intended markets. They also want to publish books that will enhance their stature within the publishing industry.

For these reasons, a manuscript that's offbeat, hugely divisive, controversial, or difficult to classify will be a tough sell to a mainstream trade publisher. Manuscripts directed at a very narrow segment of readers (for instance, fans of a specific indie rock band as opposed to fans of indie rock in general) are likewise difficult to move in the mainstream trade publishing arena.

Your book must have the potential to appeal to tens of thousands of readers, and a potential even greater than this is better. It must also have the potential to reflect positively on the publisher, or at the very least, it must *not* have the potential to reflect negatively.

ARE YOU A GOOD CANDIDATE?

Some authors elect to self-publish because they feel very strongly about maintaining absolute control over their work. They want to have final say on their book's cover design, interior layout, and similar matters. They want to decide how and where their books are sold. They don't want to be told what to cut from their manuscripts or how to approach their author platform. This does not necessarily mean such authors are megalomaniacal, it just means they have a very specific vision for their work and careers, and are dedicated to seeing that vision realized. But they are not good candidates for mainstream publication because mainstream publication is always a collaborative effort in which numerous decisions are made by committee.

To work well with a publisher, you must be willing to take both direction and correction. You cannot be so protective of your work that the editing process is likely to become a heated battle of wills. You must be supportive of the publisher's efforts on your behalf, meaning that you are able and willing to participate in any marketing and promotional activities the publisher wants to extend for your book.

You must have a realistic idea of what the publisher can, and will, do for you and your book. A self-published author whose book is doing respectably but not spectacularly isn't going to spark a bidding war, won't receive a six-figure advance, and won't be sent on a glamorous three-continent book tour at the publisher's expense. Such an author cannot assume a mainstream publisher will release her book in every available format (hardcover, trade paperback, audiobook, e-book, and Kindle), either. If your expectations are unrealistic, working with a publisher is sure to bring disappointment.

TARGETING PUBLISHERS

An indie author's easiest and most likely path to crossover success is with an independent niche publisher. Such publishers aren't beholden to the same corporate powers-that-be that conglomerate publishers answer to. Since they tend to serve specific market segments, they are also generally more receptive to unsolicited queries. If you can find a publisher that specializes in your type of book, or in books for your intended audience, and your self-published book is performing respectably, the publisher will probably welcome the opportunity to consider your book for its catalog.

It's important to be on the same page with your intended publisher in the philosophical sense, so that's another factor to take into account when deciding whom to approach. If you feel strongly that e-books are the wave of the future and a key market segment to capture, you don't want to partner with a publisher that isn't fully committed to releasing its titles in e-book formats. If you are staunchly against Digital Rights Management (DRM) but your intended publisher slaps DRM on all its digital offerings, it's not a fit. (To find out more about DRM, go to www.indieauthorguide.com.)

The Writer's Market series of books can assist you in identifying publishers well-suited to both you and your book. You can also check out www.writersmarket.com.

Another way to find likely matches is to look up books that have something in common with yours (whether it's subject matter, intended audience, or something else). Note the publishers of those books, do a little online research to learn more about those publishers (check out their mission statements and catalogs), and if any seem like a good fit, query them.

You may need to check the company's staff or about us page on their website to get the specific name and address or e-mail address of the person to whom your should direct your query. That information is also available in the Writer's Market series of books.

Querying

This type of query is very different from a query for an unpublished manuscript. The latter type of query aims merely to convince the recipient that the manuscript is worthy of a full read. A query for a self-published book aims to convince the recipient that the book has already achieved some measure of success (making it a low-risk acquisition), and that the book would perform even better if it were added to the publisher's catalog.

Open by stating that you have self-published a book that's performing well and aligns with the publisher's catalog. Give the title and genre of the book, then provide a thumbnail sketch of the book's achievements to date, both in terms of sales (or total downloads in the case of an e-book or podcast audiobook made available for free) and buzz. Include information about your author platform (that is, what kinds of platform activities you've undertaken to date), and the size of your existing audience. Close by politely asking if the recipient

publisher would consider adding the book to its catalog, and if so, to whom you can send a copy for further consideration.

The length of your query should not exceed a single page. Be direct but respectful, and keep it brief.

WHEN TO BRING IN AN AGENT

It's both wise and easy to bring an agent onboard when a publisher is ready to make you an offer. You need a seasoned pro looking out for your interests, and you won't have much difficulty attracting one when the time-consuming and unpredictable work of making the sale is already done. The main benefit an agent brings to the table is industry-specific knowledge and experience. Some are very collaborative in the marketing and promotion areas too, but that's not typical. They know if what's outlined in a proposed contract is standard for the industry, which specific areas of a publishing contract are most commonly renegotiated, and what constitutes a red flag in a contract offer. An agent has insider knowledge that can save you a lot of time and trouble, and benefit you financially as well.

The ideal agent under these circumstances is one who already has a relationship with your intended publisher and is therefore already familiar with that publisher's standard contracts. Begin your search for candidates by looking at books in the publisher's catalog of titles. Dedication pages will often acknowledge the author's agent, but when they don't, you can go to the author's website and look for representation information there.

Do some research on your top two to three candidates. Check out their websites. Do

Internet searches on the agents' names and those of their firms. If possible, e-mail authors whom the candidates represent to inquire about the author's satisfaction with the agent's actions on the author's behalf. When you're satisfied that you've zeroed in on the best candidate, contact the agent and let him know you have an offer forthcoming from Publisher X and would like his assistance in negotiating the deal.

If he's interested, he'll send you a copy of his standard representation contract. Read it carefully and, if possible, have an attorney experienced in publishing contracts review it for you as well. Pay particular attention to the clauses which lay out the agent's compensation percentage and specify whether or not your relationship with the agent is limited to this one book. One-off deals are the norm for most authors nowadays, but some agents will request a first-look privilege on any new works you produce within a set period of time from the date the contract is signed. If such a clause exists in your intended agent's contract and you're uncomfortable with it, ask to have that part of the verbiage stricken before you sign.

WHAT TO EXPECT IN THE DEAL

The publisher will begin by offering a standard, boilerplate contract. Your agent will review it and forward a copy of it for your review. While the agent may make note of any obvious red flags, it's really the author's responsibility to determine if any part of the offer contained in the contract is questionable or unacceptable to him.

Read the contract very carefully and be sure you understand everything it says. You can ask your agent for further information or clarification as needed. If anything looks questionable, run it by your agent to see if she agrees with you. You may also wish to have an attorney specializing in publishing contracts review it, to advise you on any items that should be stricken from, or added to, the contract before you sign it.

Remember, the publisher's intention is for this contract to govern control over your book for the rest of its commercially viable life. Many authors feel so lucky to get a first contract offer that they're reticent to question any part of it, but there's no harm in asking for reasonable changes and accommodations before you agree to sign on the dotted line. That's why this stage of the process is called contract *negotiation*. The worst that will happen is the publisher will say no; they will not withdraw the offer entirely.

Once the contract is signed by both you and your agent, and returned to the publisher, your advance, or the first installment of it (if applicable), should find its way to your agent in anywhere from six to eight weeks. Your agent will take his cut and send the remaining proceeds to you.

WHAT TO EXPECT IN THE PROCESS

The publisher will likely intend to release a revised version of the book, with a new cover that matches the publisher's branding and a fresh edit, at the minimum. If more extensive revision is planned, you will likely have discussed, and agreed to, the publisher's desired changes before any contract was offered. In that case, the contract will include deadlines for delivery of revised chapters from you. Take those deadlines seriously, because missing any

THE INDIE AUTHOR GUIDE

of them can render the contract null and void and make you responsible for returning any advance monies received to date.

You will be assigned to an editor, who will receive your revised chapters, review them, and send back any notes for desired changes. The editor will also act as your main contact with the publisher and will make introductions to staff members in other departments, such as marketing or production, as necessary.

You may or may not be consulted on the book's new cover design—either way, it'll be addressed in the contract. Authors don't typically get a vote in this area, so don't feel slighted if that's the case for you.

You may or may not be made privy to the publisher's marketing plans for your book, if indeed there are any (this is something you should inquire about *before* signing with a publisher if it's important to you), but you *will* be given its release date.

As an indie author you should already be well versed and comfortable in book promotion; regardless of any marketing the publisher intends to do, develop your own parallel plan for the book and run it by your agent and editor. Both will probably have ideas and suggestions to further strengthen the plan.

After you've delivered the last of your manuscript draft or responses to notes from your editor, turn your attention to setting your marketing plan in motion so you'll be ready on your book's release date.

CAN YOU STILL SELF-PUBLISH OTHER WORKS?

It's fine for authors to have a mix of self-published and mainstream-published works in their bibliography. If your contract with an agent or publisher has a first-look clause for future works, you must honor that clause. (A first-look clause means the agent or publisher is entitled to see, and potentially sign or make a contract offer for, a given work before you offer it for sale or representation to anyone else, or self-publish it.) But if the publisher doesn't want to take it on, you're free to shop it around to other publishers or self-publish it.

appendix A } Worksheets

This appendix contains worksheets you can copy (you may want to enlarge them), three-hole punch, and keep in a binder for easy use and reference. They've also been made available for free download as 8 ½" × 11" (22cm × 28cm) sheets in PDF format on the Indie Author Guide website. (www.indieauthorguide.com).

You may wish to use tabbed dividers in your three-hole binder to organize the different sections/worksheet types.

In order to fill out some of the worksheets, you will need to get pricing and product/service information from the websites of the service providers you'd like to compare. You will also need a calculator for the worksheets that involve cost calculations.

While record keeping is generally a chore, it's an important one. You can't expect to maximize your efficiency and effectiveness as an indie author unless you're performing all the calculations and keeping all the records represented in this appendix. However, if you have a different way of accomplishing the same ends that works better for you than using these worksheets, don't feel obligated to use them. The worksheets are intended to make your life as an indie author easier, not to create pointless busywork for you. Use the worksheets that make sense for you, and skip those that don't. Also feel free to adapt the worksheets to computerized spreadsheets or accounting programs with which you're already familiar.

So long as you're doing these calculations and keeping these records, it doesn't matter exactly how you do it.

You can download printable copies of the worksheets at www.indieauthorguide.com and www.writersdigest.com/article/indie-author-worksheets.

A-1. SHOPPING FOR SERVICE PROVIDERS

This worksheet will help you do at-a-glance service/feature comparisons among publishing and print service providers.

1. Enter the names of up to four providers you'd like to compare in the Provider row.

2. Check off the boxes indicating available services/features of each provider.

3. Use the blank spaces in the far left-hand column to write in any services/features not already listed in the worksheet. A blank version of the form is also provided, in case you need to create a custom list of services/features to compare; for example, the blank form will be useful for comparing the availability of a range of trim sizes (4" × 6.5", [10cm × 17cm] 6" × 9" [15cm × 23cm], A5, A4, and square), binding types (saddle-stitched, coil-bound, perfect bound) or e-book formats (Kindle, Sony Reader, .mobi) if these items are important to you.

Provider >				
Setup Fee	❏	❏	❏	❏
ISBN	❏	❏	❏	❏
EAN	❏	❏	❏	❏
Bar Code	❏	❏	❏	❏
Editing	❏	❏	❏	❏
Interior Layout	❏	❏	❏	❏
Cover Design	❏	❏	❏	❏
Hardcover	❏	❏	❏	❏
POD	❏	❏	❏	❏
E-Book Release	❏	❏	❏	❏
iPhone App Release	❏	❏	❏	❏
Min. Print Run Discount	❏	❏	❏	❏
Amazon U.S. Distribution	❏	❏	❏	❏
Barnes & Noble Distrib.	❏	❏	❏	❏
Expanded U.S. Distrib.*	❏	❏	❏	❏
Expanded Foreign Distrib.*	❏	❏	❏	❏
	❏	❏	❏	❏
	❏	❏	❏	❏
	❏	❏	❏	❏
	❏	❏	❏	❏
	❏	❏	❏	❏
	❏	❏	❏	❏

*catalog listings to make your book available for order by brick–and–mortar stores and libraries

INDIE AUTHOR GUIDE: SHOPPING FOR SERVICE PROVIDERS				
Provider >				
	❏	❏	❏	❏
	❏	❏	❏	❏
	❏	❏	❏	❏
	❏	❏	❏	❏
	❏	❏	❏	❏
	❏	❏	❏	❏
	❏	❏	❏	❏
	❏	❏	❏	❏
	❏	❏	❏	❏
	❏	❏	❏	❏
	❏	❏	❏	❏
	❏	❏	❏	❏
	❏	❏	❏	❏
	❏	❏	❏	❏
	❏	❏	❏	❏
	❏	❏	❏	❏
	❏	❏	❏	❏
	❏	❏	❏	❏
	❏	❏	❏	❏
	❏	❏	❏	❏
	❏	❏	❏	❏
	❏	❏	❏	❏
	❏	❏	❏	❏

A-2. COMPARING PUBLISHER/PRINTER UP-FRONT COSTS

This worksheet will help you do at-a-glance, up-front fee comparisons among publishing and print service providers. Remember that up-front fees are just one piece of the total cost puzzle however; also be sure to complete worksheets A-3 and A-4 for each provider.

1. Enter the names of up to four providers you'd like to compare in the Provider row.

2. Within each Provider column, enter the fee charged by each provider for each item listed in the far left column, or zero (0) if there is no charge for the item.

3. Bundled Items: Enter the fee for the entire bundle next to one of the items included in the bundle, then enter bundled next to all the other items included as part of the bundle.

4. Reduced Royalty Items: Some service providers offer certain services in exchange for keeping an extra percentage of the author's royalty. For example, if your standard author royalty with a given company is 25 percent, they may offer an expanded distribution option to get your book into more sales outlets in exchange for your acceptance of a reduced royalty rate of 22 percent. For these items, enter the extra percentage of royalty the provider will keep (in the example just given, it would be 3 percent).

5. Author Copies: Some providers include a quantity of author copies as part of a bundled package; if this is so for any of the providers you're comparing, enter the quantity of author copies to be provided. Do not enter per-copy cost for you to order copies here, this worksheet is only for calculating/comparing up-front fees.

6. Use the blank item slots in the far left-hand column to write in any additional fee items not already on the form. A blank version of the form is also provided, in case you need to create a custom list of fee items to compare.

INDIE AUTHOR GUIDE: COMPARING PUBLISHER/PRINTER UP-FRONT COSTS				
Provider >				
Project Setup				
ISBN				
EAN				
Bar Code				
Editing				
Interior Layout				
Cover Design				
Amazon US Distribution				
Amazon UK/Canada Dist.				
Barnes & Noble Dist.				
Expanded U.S. Dist.*				
Expanded Foreign Dist.*				
E-Book Release				
iPhone App Release				
Expanded U.S. Distrib.*				
Expanded Foreign Distrib.*				
TOTALS				

Catalog listings to make your book available for order by brick-and-mortar stores and libraries

INDIE AUTHOR GUIDE: COMPARING PUBLISHER/PRINTER UP-FRONT COSTS				
Provider >				
TOTALS				

A-3. CALCULATING PER-COPY PRODUCTION COST

There are two calculations you need to do to here. First, you need to figure out what your service provider will charge per copy of the book produced. The next table is for calculating "per-copy production cost"; the equation for this is:

(# OF PAGES X PER-PAGE FEE) + PER-COPY FLAT BINDING FEE = TOTAL PRODUCTION COST PER COPY

Note that when counting pages, you must count the front and back of each page. In other words, if you were to tear a page out of a book and hold it in your hands, you'd actually be holding two pages of content from the book: one page of content on the front and one page of content on the back. Blank page sides must also be included in this count.

This is a critical calculation you'll want to do early on, because high per-copy production costs are often the deal breaker that will prevent you from working with a given service provider.

Three copies of the table are provided so you can compare costs for up to twelve service providers on a single page.

INDIE AUTHOR GUIDE: PER-COPY PRODUCTION COSTS				
Provider >				
Per-Page Fee				
x Number of Pages*	x	x	x	x
= **Page Printing Fee**				
+ Per-Copy Flat Binding Fee				
= **TOTAL PROD. COST PER COPY**				

Provider >				
Per-Page Fee				
x Number of Pages*	x	x	x	x
= **Page Printing Fee**				
+ Per-Copy Flat Binding Fee				
= **TOTAL PROD. COST PER COPY**				

Provider >				
Per-Page Fee				
x Number of Pages*	x	x	x	x
= **Page Printing Fee**				
+ Per-Copy Flat Binding Fee				
= **TOTAL PROD. COST PER COPY**				

*Remember that the front and back of each page of a book count as a page when doing these calculations, even if one side of a given page is blank.

A-4. CALCULATING AUTHOR COPY COST

Next, you need to figure out what you will have to pay per author copy you order. This is necessary because some providers have surprisingly high shipping fees, especially for shipments outside the United States, and if you intend to hand sell many copies or order many for promotional and giveaway purposes, those fees can become prohibitive.

This can be another deal breaker for authors intending to order a lot of author copies, so it's another calculation to do early on, before you commit to service provider.

Four copies of the table are provided so you can compare costs for up to twelve service providers on a single page.

INDIE AUTHOR GUIDE: AUTHOR COPY COST				
Provider >				
Production Cost Per Copy				
+ Shipping Cost Per Copy*	+	+	+	+
= **TOTAL COST PER AUTH. COPY**				

Provider >				
Production Cost Per Copy				
+ Shipping Cost Per Copy*	+	+	+	+
= **TOTAL COST PER AUTH. COPY**				

Provider >				
Production Cost Per Copy				
+ Shipping Cost Per Copy*	+	+	+	+
= **TOTAL COST PER AUTH. COPY**				

Provider >				
Production Cost Per Copy				
+ Shipping Cost Per Copy*	+	+	+	+
= **TOTAL COST PER AUTH. COPY**				

Provider >				
Production Cost Per Copy				
+ Shipping Cost Per Copy*	+	+	+	+
= **TOTAL COST PER AUTH. COPY**				

If you're ordering a quantity of books, you will have to divide the total shipping cost by the number of books ordered to determine shipping cost per copy.

A-5. CALCULATING NET AUTHOR ROYALTY PER COPY SOLD BY BOOKSELLERS

Next, if you'll be selling through any bookseller outlets, whether online or brick-and-mortar, you need to finish up your service provider comparisons by getting some idea of what your net author royalty will look like per copy sold, based on the per-copy production costs you've calculated for each service provider candidate in worksheet A-4. The other key factor in this calculation is the retail price you set for your book. In doing these calculations early on you can accomplish two very important things.

1. Eliminate any service providers whose per-copy production costs are so high that working with them will force you to price your book higher than a comparable mainstream-published book.

2. Zero in on the lowest retail price you can set while still earning an author royalty of at least 15 percent—a royalty comparable to what mainstream-published authors earn—or ideally 20 percent or higher.

The worksheet can also be useful for doing what-if calculations to forecast your author royalty in cases where the service provider offers expanded distribution options in exchange for a higher discount, or bookseller percentage, which signifies what percent of your retail price the bookseller will keep on each sale.

The worksheet has enough spaces to compare up to eight service provider/pricing scenarios.

INDIE AUTHOR GUIDE: NET AUTHOR ROYALTY PER COPY SOLD BY BOOKSELLERS				
Provider >				
Proposed Retail Price				
x Bookseller Percentage*	x	x	x	x
= **Bookseller Cut**				
Proposed Retail Price				
- Per Copy Prod. Cost	-	-	-	-
Provider >				
Proposed Retail Price				
x Bookseller Percentage*	x	x	x	x
= **Bookseller Cut**				
Proposed Retail Price				
- Per Copy Prod. Cost	-	-	-	-
Provider >				
Proposed Retail Price				
x Bookseller Percentage*	x	x	x	x
= **Bookseller Cut**				
Proposed Retail Price				
- Per Copy Prod. Cost	-	-	-	-
- Bookseller Cut	-	-	-	-
= **TOTAL PROD. COST PER COPY**				

Standard is 40 percent, or .40 in this calculation.

A-6. CALCULATING NET AUTHOR ROYALTY PER COPY HAND SOLD FOR MAIL ORDER

Many authors make the mistake of thinking their net royalty on mail-ordered copies of their books is equal to selling price minus the price the author paid for the book, but this leaves some expenses out of the equation. This worksheet will help you take the added expenses of order fulfillment via mail order into account.

First, there's the shipping expense incurred for the service provider to ship the books to the author. This expense is included in worksheet A-4, Calculating Author Copy Cost, so if you take your calculated Total Cost Per Auth. Copy from that worksheet, the service provider's shipping expense will already be included here.

Next, there's the packaging expense. You must acquire padded envelopes, or possibly small boxes and packing peanuts or other padding material, to pack up your books for shipment to mail-order customers. Generally, you'll have to pay for these items.

Then comes the shipping expense involved in getting the books from you to your mail-order customers. This may vary from shipment to shipment, but you can get an estimated average to work with on your postal or shipping service's website. In the United States, the U.S. Post Office Web address is www.usps.gov. The Web address for United Parcel Service (UPS) is www.ups.com, and FedEx is www.fedex.com. These are just the three largest shipping service providers in the United States; there are many more, and it may pay to do some hunting around online for more providers to compare.

Provider >				
Total Cost Per Author Copy				
+ Packaging Cost Per Copy	+	+	+	+
+ Avg. Shipping Cost Per Copy	+	+	+	+
= Total Cost Per Copy Sold				
Selling Price				

Provider >				
Total Cost Per Author Copy				
+ Packaging Cost Per Copy	+	+	+	+
+ Avg. Shipping Cost Per Copy	+	+	+	+
= Total Cost Per Copy Sold				
Selling Price				

Provider >				
Total Cost Per Author Copy				
+ Packaging Cost Per Copy	+	+	+	+
+ Avg. Shipping Cost Per Copy	+	+	+	+
= Total Cost Per Copy Sold				
Selling Price				
- Total Cost Per Copy Sold	-	-	-	-
= Author Royalty Per Copy Sold				

A-7. CALCULATING NET AUTHOR ROYALTY PER COPY HAND SOLD IN PERSON

You can't do this calculation until you've settled on a publishing services provider and one or more sales venues (such as conferences and speaking/signing events) because you must know your actual cost per author copy and the actual costs associated with each particular sales venue.

The costs associated with different hand-selling situations will differ. For example, hand-selling copies to people at work won't carry any additional expense since you'd already be going to work, but traveling to a brick-and-mortar store to do a reading and signing will.

It's not possible to provide a one-table-fits-all set of calculations for hand selling in person. The expense items listed in the worksheet provided here won't apply to every situation, but they provide a good starting point to get you thinking about, and including, all the expenses incurred in hand selling. You may want to use the worksheet to help you decided which hand-selling events will be most cost-effective for you, before committing to any.

Columns are provided for you to compare or track expenses for two different hand-selling events. Enter the appropriate expense in the row for each expense item, then total them at the bottom of each column. Leave any nonapplicable items blank. It's fine to pencil in estimates before a hand-selling event, but be sure to go back afterward and enter actual expenses in ink. That way, you can keep a copy of the worksheet with actual expenses listed for reference at tax time, or for comparing against other hand-selling opportunities in the future.

If you find the first version of the worksheet doesn't cover the expenses involved in your particular hand-selling situation, use the second or third version supplied, and fill in the expenses that are applicable.

A final note: Remember that if your primary purpose in attending a conference or similar event is to hand sell books, you must record all the expenses incurred for the event in a worksheet like this one. All of those expenses must be deducted from any income you receive while hand selling at the event in order to calculate your true net profit for the event.

Sales Venue/Event >		
Location/Address >		
Date >		
Total Cost Per Author Copy		
x # of Copies Ordered For Event[1]	x	x
= Total Expense For Books		
Booth/Table Rental or Event Fee		
Mileage Expense, if Traveling By Car[2]		
Parking Fees		
Public Transport Expense		
Flight Expense		
Hotel		
Taxis, Other Ground Transport		
Meals or Snacks, Drinks		
Total General Expenses		
Venue Cut, for Store/Library Events[3]		
x Number of Books Sold	x	x
= Total Venue Cut		
Total Gross Income from Book Sales		
- Total Expense for Books	-	-
- Total General Expense	-	-
- Total Venue Cut	-	-
TOTAL EVENT PROFIT/LOSS		

1. *To prepare for the event, you may have to order author copies of your book. Note that while you may not sell all of the books you've bought for the event, you have incurred significant expense in buying them. Your total expense here is based on the total number of books ordered, not sold, because what you must pay when ordering author copies is a fixed expense regardless of how many you actually sell. If you ultimately go on to sell leftover copies later, you will record your income for them in another worksheet, but the expense for ordering them in the first place belongs here.*

   If you sell copies from stock-on-hand, pencil in the number of copies you intend to bring before the event, then write the actual number sold in the worksheet in ink after the event is over and adjust Total Expense For Books accordingly.

2. *The Internal Revenue Service standard for this is $0.55 per mile; this includes gas and vehicle upkeep expense; remember to include all miles for the round-trip.*

3. *When hand selling at a retail store or library, instead of having to pay a booth or table rental fee, you will typically be asked to pay the venue a percentage on each sale (usually 10 to 40 percent). Calculate what this percentage will cost you per copy sold based on the price at which you'll sell the book, and enter that figure here.*

Sales Venue/Event >		
Location/Address >		
Date >		
Total Cost Per Author Copy		
x # of Copies Ordered For Event[1]	x	x
= Total Expense For Books		
Total General Expenses		
Venue Cut, for Store/Library Events[3]		
x Number of Books Sold	x	x
= Total Venue Cut		
Total Gross Income from Book Sales		
- Total Expense for Books	-	-
- Total General Expense	-	-
- Total Venue Cut	-	-
TOTAL EVENT PROFIT/LOSS		

Sales Venue/Event >		
Location/Address >		
Date >		
Total Cost Per Author Copy		
x # of Copies Ordered For Event[1]	×	×
= **Total Expense For Books**		
Total General Expenses		
Venue Cut, for Store/Library Events[3]		
x Number of Books Sold	×	×
= **Total Venue Cut**		
Total Gross Income from Book Sales		
- Total Expense for Books	-	-
- Total General Expense	-	-
- Total Venue Cut	-	-
TOTAL EVENT PROFIT/LOSS		

A-8 CALCULATING YOUR BREAK-EVEN POINT

Here is where you will calculate how many books you must sell to recoup all the up-front expenses incurred in bringing the book to market. The point at which you've sold enough copies to zero out all the up-front expenses is your break-even point, and every book sold after that starts earning you a profit on the book. The worksheet for this is fairly self-explanatory. Just fill in the various expense items, skipping any that are nonapplicable to your situation and using the blank spaces in the left-hand column to add any expense items not already listed, and do the calculations listed on the worksheet.

Note that this calculation will vary depending on how you are fulfilling book orders (whether through booksellers, by mail order, or hand selling), because your net profit/royalty for each different fulfillment type will vary. Therefore, a column is provided for each fulfillment type.

As before, a blank version of the worksheet is provided for fulfillment situations that don't fit the standard three types covered by the first worksheet.

INDIE AUTHOR GUIDE: BREAK-EVEN POINT			
Fulfillment Type >	Bookseller	Mail-Order	Hand-Sold
Total Up-Front Costs (see A-2)			
+ Total Cost of Author Copies to Be Used for Promo, Reviews, or Giveaways (see A-4)	+	+	+
+ Cost to Package & Ship Author Copies Listed Above	+	+	+
+ Cost of Promo Materials (postcards, bookmarks, etc.)	+	+	+
+ Cost of Paid Advertising	+	+	+
+ Cost of Author or Book website	+	+	+
+ Cost of Book Tour	+	+	+
+ Cost of Listings on Showcase Sites	+	+	+
+ Cost to Register Copyright	+	+	+
+ Cost to Set Up Your Imprint or Business	+	+	+
+ Cost for Catalog/Wholesale Listings Not Already Included in Total Up-Front Costs	+	+	+
	+	+	+
	+	+	+
	+	+	+
	+	+	+
Total Up-Front Costs			
Divided by Net Author Royalty Per Copy Sold	B	B	B
TOTAL NUMBER OF COPIES TO BE SOLD TO BREAK EVEN			

INDIE AUTHOR GUIDE: BREAK-EVEN POINT			
Fulfillment Type >			
Total Up-Front Costs (see A-2)			
	+	+	+
	+	+	+
	+	+	+
	+	+	+
	+	+	+
	+	+	+
	+	+	+
	+	+	+
	+	+	+
	+	+	+
	+	+	+
	+	+	+
	+	+	+
Total Up-Front Costs			
Divided by Net Author Royalty Per Copy Sold	B	B	B
TOTAL NUMBER OF COPIES TO BE SOLD TO BREAK EVEN			

A-9. TRACKING SALES

The purpose of this worksheet is to provide you with a place to track your sales from various outlets so that over time you can get an idea of which sales outlets are, or aren't, working for you, and record notes about your sales. For example, you can make a note of it if you are running a coupon or discounted price at the time certain sales took place, or if certain sales are the direct result of a specific promotional campaign or activity.

You will need to make a copy of this worksheet for each different sales outlet, venue, or event where you've sold books in a given month. For example, if you offer both hard copy and Kindle books for sale on Amazon, you would keep one copy of this worksheet for the hardcopy sales and another for Kindle sales, to better track how each format is selling. Also, you'll start a new set each month so keep additional blank copies of the form on hand.

Many publishing services providers and sales outlets provide real-time sales reporting. For these, you can just look up your sales report and copy down the figures shown. For those who don't report sales in real time, you'll need to fill out this worksheet some time after sales have been reported to you.

Some outlets will report sales per day, others on a per-week basis. Either way, enter the number corresponding to the calendar day for which sales are being reported in the far left-hand column. For instance, if Bookseller A reports sales on a daily basis and your first sale in a given month occurs on the 5th, you would enter 5 in the far left-hand column. If Bookseller A reports sales on a weekly basis, and your first sale in a given month occurs on the 5th, but the last day of that week is the 8th, you would enter 8 in the far left-hand column.

It doesn't matter what weekday you want to count as the first day of the week (Sunday versus Monday), so long as you count each week as seven days and are always consistent in which day you use.

INDIE AUTHOR GUIDE: SALES TRACKING FOR MONTH/YEAR: _____

BOOK TITLE: _____

SALES OUTLET/VENUE/EVENT: _____

Day/ Week Ending	Qty Sold	Royalty Earned	Notes
TOTALS:			

A-10 TRACKING EXPENSES

Like the previous worksheet, the purpose of this worksheet is to provide you with a place to track your expenses from various sources so that over time, you can develop an accurate picture of where you're spending money on your book project on an ongoing basis. Once you know that, and have a history of sales tracking for at least a few months, you can determine where you're getting the most bang for your buck in terms of promotional and sales activities.

As with the previous worksheet, you'll want to keep blank copies of this worksheet on hand so you can set up a separate sheet for each category or source of expense incurred in a given month, and to start a new set at the beginning of each month. Here are some common expense category/source examples:

- Author Copies for Promo
- Advertising Giveaway/Review
- Sales/Promo Event Registration
- Travel Expense
- Monthly Fees for Website/Maintenance
- Fees for Catalog/Blog Website Listings
- Association/Club Dues
- Professional Magazine Subscriptions
- Contest Entry Fees
- Class/Workshop Fees
- Up-Front/Promo/Platform Expenses When Publishing a New Book
  (see A-2, A-4)

This is only a partial list; your specific expense items and categories may differ. Consult a tax professional for more information on which expenses will be tax deductible in your specific circumstances. Keep some blank copies of the form on hand, and anytime you incur an expense that doesn't fit the category or source listed on worksheets you're already using, start a new one.

INDIE AUTHOR GUIDE: EXPENSE TRACKING FOR MONTH/YEAR: _____

BOOK TITLE: _____

EXPENSE SOURCE/CATEGORY: _____

Date	Expense	Notes
TOTALS:		

A-11. PROFIT AND LOSS

Here is where you'll total up your monthly earnings and expenses for each month, then total them up at the end of the year for tax filing purposes. This worksheet should be updated with your total royalty and expense figures at the end of each month, according to your sales-tracking and expense-tracking records.

Use the Notes column to keep track of anything you'd like to remember about a given month's sales and/or expenses at the end of the year. For example, if you raised the book's price, offered a discount coupon, temporarily suspended sales, or did a signing event, these will be important things for you to know when you're looking over your monthly and annual totals later on.

INDIE AUTHOR GUIDE: PROFIT AND LOSS FOR YEAR: _____

BOOK TITLE: _____

Month	Expenses	Royalties	Notes
Jan			
Feb			
Mar			
Apr			
Muy			
Jun			
Jul			
Aug			
Sep			
Oct			
Nov			
Dec			
TOTALS:			

TOTAL ROYALTIES – EXPENSES = NET EARNINGS ON THIS BOOK FOR THE YEAR

_____ - _____ = _____

A-12. CONTACT FILES

Use these sheets to keep information about your book- and publishing-related contacts in a single organized location.

A-12.1 PUBLISHERS/PRINT SERVICE PROVIDERS

Company Name	
Company Type	
Address Line 1	
Address Line 2	
Phone Number	
Website	
Contact Name	
Notes	

A-12.2 OTHER SERVICE PROVIDERS

Company Name	
Company Type	
Address Line 1	
Address Line 2	
Phone Number	
Website	
Contact Name	
Notes	

A-12.3 INDUSTRY CONTACTS

Name	
Position/Title	
Company Name	
Company Type	
Address Line 1	
Address Line 2	
Office Phone	
Cell	
Website	
E-Mail #1	
E-Mail #2	
Met At	
Notes	

A-12.4 FELLOW AUTHORS

Name	
Book Title	
Book Title	
Book Title	
Address Line 1	
Address Line 2	
Work Phone	
Cell	
Website(s)	
Blog(s)	
E-Mail #1	
E-Mail #2	
Met At	
Notes	

A-12.5 SPEAKING/SIGNING EVENTS

Event Name	
Event Type	
Event Date	
Event Time	
Location Name	
Address Line 1	
Address Line 2	
Phone	
Hours	
Website	
Contact Name	
Contact E-Mail	
Contact Phone	
Notes	

A-13 AUTHOR PLATFORM ADMINISTRATIVE RECORDS

In this section, you'll find worksheets upon which you can record information pertaining to your author platform activities.

Note that because these worksheets will include website login information, you should keep them in a secure place, apart from your binder of other worksheets.

A-13.1 AUTHOR OR BOOK WEBSITE (see instructions, next page)

1	Website Name	
2	Website URL	
3	Website Registrar Name	
4	Website Registrar URL	
5	Website Registrar Support Phone #	
6	Registrar Site Login	
7	Site Registration Date	
8	Registration Expense	
9	Registration Renewal	
10	Website Host Name	
11	Website Host URL	
12	Website Host Support Phone #	
13	Website Host Login	
14	Hosting Setup Date	
15	Hosting Expense	
16	Hosting Renewal	
17	Site Admin Name	
18	Site Admin Phone/Cell	
19	Site Admin E-Mail	
20	Admin Expense	
21	Notes	

1. Enter the domain name of your website.

2. Enter the website address of your site.

3. Enter the name of your domain registrar (examples: Network Solutions, MyDomain).

4. Enter the website address of your registrar.

5. Enter the support phone number of your registrar.

6. Enter your login name and password for your registrar account.

7. Enter the date on which you originally registered your domain.

8. Enter the price you paid for domain registration; this will usually be a dollar amount per year, for the number of years to which you've committed.

9. Enter the date on which your registration expires and must be renewed.

10. Enter the name of your website host (examples: HostGator, Gate); note that in some cases, this may be the same company as your domain registrar.

11. Enter the website address of your host.

12. Enter the support phone number of your host.

13. Enter your login name and password for your hosting account or Control Panel.

14. Enter the date on which you initiated hosting with this host.

15. Enter the price you paid for hosting; this will usually be a dollar amount per month, per quarter, or per year, for the term to which you've committed.

16. Enter the date on which your paid hosting expires and must be renewed. You may prefer to simply enter monthly, quarterly, or annually, as appropriate.

17. If you've hired a site administrator to run the site for you, enter his or her name.

18. Enter the site admin's phone number.

19. Enter the site admin's e-mail address.

20. Enter the rate you're paying the admin; this will usually be a weekly, monthly, quarterly, or annual figure.

21. Use the space provided to enter any notes about your site.

A-13.2 AUTHOR OR BOOK BLOG

Site/Svc Name	URL	User Name	Password	Notes

A-13.3 ONLINE COMMUNITIES & RELATED MEMBERSHIPS

Site/Svc Name	URL	User Name	Password	Notes

A-13.3 PROFESSIONAL ASSOCIATIONS

Assn. Name	
Assn. Type[1]	
Address Line 1	
Address Line 2	
Assn. Contact	
Contact Phone	
Contact E-Mail	
Dues Amount	
Dues Frequency[2]	
Member Since	
Notes	

1. Enter the type of association, e.g., booksellers, authors, publishers.

2. Enter the frequency with which you must pay dues to this association, such as monthly, quarterly, annually.

A-14 BOOKSELLER REFERENCE AND RECORDS

Company Name	
Company Type[1]	
Address Line 1	
Address Line 2	
Phone Number	
Website	
Contact Name	
Percentage[2]	
Notes	

1. *Online only, brick and mortar only, or online + brick and mortar?*

2. *What percentage of each sale will this bookseller keep?*

appendix B} An HTML Primer

This chapter will give you a good understanding of how HTML works and teach you how to use it to create links, custom-formatted text, and embedded graphics. The information provided will also enable you to create your own web pages from scratch—but only very basic pages. If you want to create and maintain your own author website, I recommend using a web page creation program such as Adobe Dreamweaver or Microsoft FrontPage to get a professional look without having to become an HTML expert. However, even if you use such a tool, you will still need basic HTML knowledge and skills.

HOW WEB PAGES WORK

You've undoubtedly seen all kinds of Web pages, and probably know they can only be viewed in a Web browser. Still, I bet you didn't know that web pages don't really exist *until* they're viewed in a browser, nor that they *stop* existing when the browser moves on to another page or closes. Universal Resource Locators (URLs), or Web addresses, don't actually point to Web pages at all. They point to files containing instructions, or source code, for how to build Web pages. The browser reads the source code and interprets it, then builds a Web page according to the source code's directions in a matter of seconds. It's as if the source code contains a written description of a picture and the browser is a superfast sketch artist. Technically, when we speak of someone creating a Web page, what we really mean is that someone is writing source code the *browser* can use to create a Web page.

You can get a better understanding of what's going on by looking at a Web page together with its source code. Let's use the home page of my website as an example, since I maintain the source code for it myself: www.AprilLHamilton.com/index.html. Open this Web page in your favorite browser and right-click on any open space in it. A pop-up menu will appear, offering you various options. One of the options will display the source code that was used to create the Web page in your computer's text editor.

In Internet Explorer, the option is called View Source. In Mozilla Firefox version 2.0.0.7, it's called View Page Source. In older versions of Firefox there's an option called Page Info, and View Page Source is one of the items included in the Page Info dialog box. In the Mac Safari browser, it's an option under the View menu.

This source code was written in Hyper Text Markup Language (HTML). HTML is one of several languages used to pass instructions to a Web browser. HTML is written as ordinary text, and the text file is saved with a file extension of .htm or .html. These file extensions label the file as HTML source code so a Web browser will recognize it. The source code file is uploaded to a Web server, making it accessible on the Internet.

Anyone who wants to visit my home page does so by either typing its URL into their browser or following a link that contains the URL. Recall that URLs point to source code files; the browser locates the source code file, reads it, interprets it, and creates, or renders, my home page according to the instructions contained in the source file. The rendered page is discarded by the browser as soon as the site visitor closes his browser or navigates away from the page. The next time that same visitor accesses the page, the process happens all over again and the page is rendered anew and includes any changes I've made to the source code since the previous visit.

The Page Load buttons on your browser menu or toolbar (*back, forward, refresh, reload*) direct the browser to dump its rendered page, access the source code file associated with the button, and render a new page based on that source code. The refresh/reload button forces the browser to discard its rendered page, re-read the same source code file, and re-render the page—a useful tool when you're waiting for an e-mail or discussion board post to show up.

Browser Cache

Depending on your browser settings, the source code of pages you've visited may be stored, or cached, on your hard drive up to a user-specified limit of disk space. This speeds up page rendering even further, since the browser can get the source code file from your hard drive instead of having to pull it off the Web, but the pages rendered won't include any source code updates made since the source code was cached. Page caching was an important feature back in the days of dial-up Internet access, but high-speed Internet connections have done away with the need.

Web Page Versus Web Application

ASP, Javascript, VBScript, and PHP are examples of programming languages used to create Web *applications*. As a rule of thumb, any Web page that accepts data input from the user, does something with that input, and then returns some kind of response to the user is running a Web application. For example, a search engine accepts search conditions from a user, searches for Web pages matching those conditions, and returns a list of matching pages for the user to review. HTML, on the other hand, is used to create Web *pages*, like my website home page. Web pages don't accept data input from users and don't do any kind of data processing.

Unlike the programming languages used to create Web applications, HTML is pretty easy for the average untrained person to understand. It's all written in plain English, using everyday words and some abbreviations.

HOW TO CREATE A SOURCE CODE FILE

The best way to learn HTML is to create your own source code file and experiment with it. Look at the following little block of source code.

```
<HTML>

Hello, World!

</HTML>
```

Believe it or not, that little block of code is enough to create a Web page. The first and third lines contain HTML code, and the page content is contained between them. Most HTML code is enclosed in brackets

(<>), and each piece of bracketed code is called a tag. Here's that block of code again, but this time I've added some comments to clarify what each part of the code is telling the browser to do.

The Browser Is No Dummy

You'll notice that the browser didn't have to be told what font to use, what color to make the text, or to make the background of the page

HTML CODE	WHAT DOES IT MEAN?
<HTML>	Begin HTML (Hey browser, render a Web page!)
Hello, World!	Content (Hey browser, display this on the Web page!)
</HTML>	End HTML (Hey browser, stop rendering!)

You can open Notepad (or any plain text editor program, as opposed to a full-featured word processor like Microsoft Word), type in this same block of text, save the file as Hello.html (be sure the file type dialog is set to all files), and presto, you've authored your first source code file.

Recall that HTML is written and stored as a text file; you can open the file in Notepad or any other text editor to make changes to it. Just right-click on the file name, select Open With and choose your text editor. In fact, you can open any source file with an .html or .htm extension in any text editor.

Now you know how to make a basic source file and edit it, but you haven't seen the rendered page yet. Close your file, go to the location where you saved it on your hard drive and double-click on the file to open it again. Any file ending with .htm or .html is recognized by your computer as a Web page, and the file will open in your computer's default Web browser—even though the file is on your hard drive, not the Web.

white. White is the default background color for all Web pages, so if you don't specify a different color (I'll show you how later on) the background of your page will be white. There is also a default font setting which may vary from browser to browser, but is generally Times New Roman. That's the font the browser will use unless it's told to use something else. The size of the font and the black color you see on Hello. html are also default values.

Still, it's a pretty sorry-looking page. It doesn't have a title at the top, it doesn't have any color or graphics ... actually, all it's got is the text, "Hello, World!" That's because the only thing in the content section of the page is the text, "Hello, World!" The source code doesn't tell the browser to render anything else.

USING HTML TO BOSS THE BROWSER

Every HTML source code file must contain, at the minimum, the two tags used in Hello. html: <HTML> and </HTML>. As described previously, these tags tell the browser to start rendering a Web page and to stop rendering the page, respectively.

Tags are typically paired this way, with the first tag of a pair referred to as the opening tag and the second as the closing tag. The first tag of the pair is like an on switch: It turns on an instruction to the browser. The browser will keep doing whatever the first tag of the pair says until it comes to the second tag of the pair, which is like an off switch: It turns off the instruction to the browser. Off tags always start with a forward slash (/) and often, that's the only difference between the opening and closing tag. The basic format, or syntax, for all HTML tags is as follows:

<OPENING TAG> Content to be affected by tag </CLOSING TAG>

The following tables demonstrate tags used to format text and the resulting changes. We begin with the code saved as Hello.html. Add the changes shown in each step to your own Hello.html, save the file, and view the results in your browser.

HTML CODE	RESULTING PAGE	NOTES
<HTML> <FONT FACE="Arial"> Hello, World! </FONT> </HTML>	Hello, World!	<FONT FACE> tags specify a font. You can specify any standard font in FONT FACE tags. Note that in tags, text entered after an = sign must be enclosed in quotation marks.

The definition of standard font varies from browser to browser, but the following fonts are fairly universal: Andale Mono, Arial, Comic Sans MS, Courier New, Georgia, Impact, Times New Roman, Trebuchet MS, Verdana, and Webdings. The next example demonstrates how to apply boldface to your text.

Note how the <B> tags are nested inside the <FONT FACE> tags to apply both the font and boldface. I could've reversed the nesting order or used either pair of tags by itself, too. Next, you'll see how to change the size of your text.

HTML CODE	RESULTING PAGE	NOTES
<HTML> <FONT FACE="Arial"> <B> Hello, World! </B> </FONT> </HTML>	Hello, World!	The <B> tags apply boldface to text.

HTML CODE	RESULTING PAGE	NOTES

`<HTML>`
`<FONT FACE="Arial" SIZE="4">`
`<B>`
`Hello, World!`
`</B>`
`</FONT>`
`</HTML>`
	Hello, World!	I've enlarged the text by adding the SIZE attribute to my FONT tag.
		
		HTML text ranges in size from 1 to 6; 1 is smallest, 6 is largest, and 3 is the default. The text you're reading now is size 2.

FONT FACE and SIZE are contained in a single opening tag, and that single opening tag is closed with a single closing tag of </FONT>. Font face, size, and color can all be grouped together into a single tag, but other text properties, such as alignment, bold, and italics, use separate tags of their own.

Look at how the tags are nested, and how I enter the closing tags in the same order as I entered the opening tags. The closing formatting tags can be put in any order, but I find that I'm less likely to leave any out if I repeat the opening tag order in my closing tags. You may prefer to do something different. Again, remember that any

HTML CODE	RESULTING PAGE	NOTES

`<HTML>`
`<FONT FACE="Arial" SIZE="4"`
`COLOR="Red">`
`<B>`
`<I>`
`<U>`
`Hello, World!`
`</B>`
`</U>`
`</I>`
`</FONT>`
`</HTML>`
	Hello, World!	I've added three more tags, one for italics, one for underlining, and one for font color. Can you guess which is which?
		
		About underlining: In Web pages, underlined text is assumed to be a link, so it's not a good idea to use underlining on plain text.

tag you enter after the = sign must be enclosed in quotation marks, as shown in the <FONT FACE> tag. And by the way, the <U> tag is for underlining, and <I> is for italicizing.

While I've put each tag on a separate line, doing so isn't necessary. If you wanted to, you could write all of the HTML code on a single line. The resulting Web page would look the

same, but it would be harder to read and edit your code. Developers have varying preferences for how many tags to use on a single line.

Using Color in Your Web Pages

There are two ways to set text and background colors in HTML: using named colors and using hexadecimal colors. Named colors are the eight standard hues on the color wheel: white, black, red, blue, yellow, green, orange, and purple. You can set any of these colors just by typing the desired color name in the tag, as I've done in the <FONT> tag on the prior page. Hexadecimal color numbers are used to describe all the other colors you can use on the Web—over 250 of them.

If you didn't use a numbering scheme of some kind, how would you distinguish the slightly different shades of green from one another? The use of hexadecimal numbers ensures every one of the available colors has a unique name, and that those names are known to all browsers. Unfortu- nately for you, hexadecimal numbers are not easy to remember. You can obtain a key to hexadecimal color names online by doing a Web search for "hexadecimal colors," but to keep things simple you can always stick to the eight named colors for text. The eight named colors are a little bright for backgrounds, however (see next section).

Essential Tags—Page Formatting, Links, and E-Mail

The following pages begin with new HTML code to demonstrate tags related to page formatting, links, and e-mail.

HTML CODE	RESULTING PAGE	NOTES
<HTML> <HEAD> <TITLE> Hello, World!</TITLE> </HEAD> <BODY> Hello, World! </BODY> </HTML>	Hello, World!	The <HEAD> tags insert a page header. Since we've added a header to our page, we must tell the browser which part of the page is the main body. To do that, we use <BODY> tags.

The header contains information about the page, such as the page title, author name, keywords, or pieces of Web application code. Nothing entered in the <HEAD> section will be visible on the page, except for the title, which will appear in the browser title bar. The title will be entered in the next example using <TITLE> tags and is always stored in the <HEAD> section.

HTML CODE	RESULTING PAGE	NOTES
<HTML> <HEAD> <TITLE> Hello, World!</TITLE> </HEAD> <BODY BGCOLOR="Purple"> Hello, World! </BODY> </HTML>	Hello, World!	The page has been entitled "Hello, World!" and that title will appear in the browser title bar when the page is loaded. The BGCOLOR attribute in the BODY tag sets the background color of your page.

See what I was talking about when I said named colors aren't good to use for backgrounds? Instead of a color, you can set the background of the page to a graphic file, or image, as I'll explain later.

HTML CODE	RESULTING PAGE	NOTES
<HTML> <HEAD> <TITLE> Hello, World!</TITLE> </HEAD> <BODY> <A HREF=>"http://www.aprillhamilton.com/Hello.html"> Hello, World! </A> </BODY> </HTML>	Hello, World!	See below

The <A HREF=> and </A> tags make the text between them into a hyperlink, underline the text, and change its color into the default hyperlink color for the browser (usually blue). Note the format, or syntax, used:

> <A HREF="[link address]">
>
> [Text To Display As A Link]
>
> </A>

The *target* of a hyperlink is the location to which the user will be taken when he clicks on the link. The target of a hyperlink will usually be displayed in the footer of the browser window when the user mouses over the link. Try this in your own browser.

There are four types of hyperlinks: named anchors, MAILTO:, off-site, and on-site. An on-site link takes the user to another page on the same website. An off-site link takes the user to a page on some other website. A MAILTO: link opens a compose mail form in the user's default e-mail program and prefills the recipient e-mail address. A named anchor isn't actually a link, but the target of a link that takes the user to a different location on the same Web page.

Named anchors are commonly used on Web pages that are very lengthy, to save the site visitor the trouble of scrolling up and down when trying to locate a specific section. Instead, the user clicks on a link at the top of the page, within a sort of table of contents for the page consisting of links, and is immediately taken to the referenced section of the page.

Since named anchors are targets, they must always be paired with hyperlinks. For example, the hyperlink for "I. Introduction" could be paired with a named anchor called "#I," which serves as the target for the link. This is the syntax for the hyperlink:

> <A HREF="#I">

The pound sign (#) tells the browser that the text immediately following is a named anchor, not a regular hyperlink. When the user clicks that link, the browser will scan the page to find the named anchor, I. Once the anchor is located, the browser will scroll down the page until the anchor is at the top of the page, sort of like taking a shortcut.

This is the syntax for creating the named anchor:

<A NAME=" [desired anchor name"></A>

In named anchor tags, text is not typically entered between the opening and closing tag where the text to be affected usually goes. This is because it's typical for anchors to be invisible to site visitors, so the text to be affected is—nothing.

The MAILTO: link allows site visitors to send e-mail to a specified e-mail address. In the table that follows, I've added some more text and made that text into an e-mail link. When the user clicks on the e-mail link text, the browser will launch its internal mail program and preaddress a mail message to the address specified by the link.

E-mail link syntax is basically the same as that used for normal hyperlinks, but the linked address is a little different. Where the hyperlink address is normally a Web URL, the e-mail link address is an e-mail address with a prefix of MAILTO:

HTML CODE	RESULTING PAGE	NOTES
<HTML> <HEAD> <TITLE> Hello, World!</TITLE> </HEAD> <BODY> <A HREF="http://www.aprillhamilton.com/Hello.html"> Hello, World! </A> <A HREF="MAILTO:info@aprillhamilton.com"> E-mail me. </A> </BODY> </HTML></BODY> </HTML>	Hello, World! E-mail me.	See below

Notice the <BR> tag, just above the e-mail link. This is the line break tag, and each one you use inserts one line break in your page. If I left the <BR> tag out, both my original hyperlink and my new e-mail link would've appeared on the same line, one right after the other. As you can see, the <BR> tag is one of those few tags that is used alone, not as half of a pair. No closing tag is required for the <BR> tag.

 tags are useful for controlling line spacing. Text on Web pages is single-spaced by default, but with <BR> tags you can fake wider spacing.

Also, most Web page creation tools, including online forms used to create blog posts and fill-in-the-blanks website templates, automatically format any text you enter as paragraphs, using the <P> and </P> tags, and apply a minimum default spacing between paragraphs. This wouldn't be a problem were it not for the fact that you can't easily customize the default spacing.

When using such tools, every time you hit the enter key to begin typing on a new line, you're indicating the start of a new paragraph—whether you want to or not—and inserting empty space between the previous line and the next one—whether you want to or not. This can be a major pain when you're trying to format text that shouldn't be handled as paragraphs (poems, bulleted lists, mailing addresses to name a few).

To eliminate the problem, you must edit the HTML source. Blogger allows this, and some of the template-based websites do, too. Any Web page creation software will provide access to the source code of your pages as well. In the source code, delete any <P> and </P> tags enclosing the text you *don't* want to be formatted as paragraphs, then simply insert a <BR> tag wherever you want a line break. Problem solved!

ANSI Codes

American National Standard Institute (ANSI) codes are used to tell the browser to render special characters and symbols that don't appear on a keyboard, such as © and ±. Typing an ANSI code into your HTML is like using the insert symbol function in your word processor.

ANSI codes can be entered using a name or number, and are typed into the HTML page like ordinary text. However, when the HTML page is rendered, the browser substi-

tutes the desired symbol for the ANSI name or number. For example, the ANSI name for the © symbol is ©. Let's say you want to display the following copyright message on one of your pages:

Page Content © 2008, Joe Author

The HTML code would look like this:

<FONT FACE="Tahoma" COLOR="blue" SIZE="2">

Page Content © 2008, Joe Author

</FONT>

ANSI name codes always begin with an ampersand (&) and ANSI number codes always begin with an ampersand and pound sign (&#), and both types always end with a semicolon. The ampersand alerts the browser that the following characters are an ANSI code, not ordinary text, and the semicolon marks the end of the ANSI code. A summary table of the ANSI codes you're most likely to need is presented at the end of this chapter, but there are hundreds more. To find them, do an Internet search for "Web" + "special characters."

The Nonbreaking Space

The ANSI code you're likely to use most is the nonbreaking space ( ). In a Web page, inserting a nonbreaking space is like hitting the space bar in a regular document: It inserts a space *without* creating a line break, unlike the enter key. Of course you can hit the space bar when typing text into an HTML page, but by default, HTML only recognizes a single space between sentences or characters, regardless of how many times in a row you hit the space bar. There are times when you need more than one space.

For example, in a normal typewritten document, it's standard to leave two empty spaces between the end of one sentence and the beginning of another. HTML's default spacing allows only one space between sentences, and certain fonts and formatting options appear crowded that way.

There are special HTML formatting codes for creating bulleted lists (see next section), but just as with paragraphs, HTML inserts empty space between the lines of bulleted lists created with list tags. If you want a single-spaced list, you have to fake it by inserting a tiny graphic to serve as your bullet, followed by one or more spaces (using the ANSI code   as needed), followed by the text of your list item, followed by a <BR> tag. This is how I create all my bulleted lists.

Default Bulleted Lists

The basic HTML syntax for creating a bulleted list is this:

```
<UL>

<LI> text of item 1 </LI>

<LI> text of item 2 </LI>

<LI> text of item 3 </LI>

</UL>
```

The resulting list would look like this:

- Text of item 1

- Text of item 2

- Text of item 3

You can enter as many items in a bulleted list as you like, just enclose each list item in <LI> and </LI> tags, and be sure to close the list with the </UL> tag at the bottom. The default

bullet is the black dot, but you can specify an empty circle or a filled-in square in the opening <UL> tag, as follows:

```
<UL TYPE="circle">

<UL TYPE="square">
```

There are HTML tags for creating numbered and outline lists too, but they're a bit more complex. Do an Internet search on HTML + "lists" to learn more.

Graphics in HTML Pages

Web browsers can only display graphics, photos, and art in a limited number of formats. JPG and GIF are universally acceptable, so if you want to keep things simple stick to those two formats. Also, don't use any copyrighted or trademarked images on your pages without the owner's permission. Contrary to popular misinformation, images appearing on Web pages are not automatically added to the public domain. The syntax used to insert graphics in Web pages is:

```
<IMG SRC=" [filename or URL]" WIDTH="
[no. of pixels]" HEIGHT=" [no. of pixels]">
```

Like the <BR> tag, the <IMG SRC> tag appears singly, without a closing tag. Place your cursor where you want the graphic, then use the syntax above to set a pointer to the image and, if desired, specify the exact width and height of the image as you'd like it to appear on your page. If the dimensions of the image to which you're pointing are acceptable as is, just omit the WIDTH and HEIGHT attributes from your tag altogether.

The image will not be stored as part of your source code file, the <IMG SRC> tag merely sets up a pointer to the image. Therefore, any image referenced in an <IMG SRC> tag must be accessible to that tag at all times, meaning that it must be stored somewhere on the Web. People who build and maintain their own websites will usually have a folder on their sites to store all the images referenced by <IMG SRC> tags on their pages, so their pointers will use the file name option. If the referenced image is stored anywhere other than the website of your page, the pointer must be set to a URL address for the image.

If you don't know the URL address of the image, go to the Web page with the image, right-click the image and select Properties from the pop-up menu. Among other details, the image's file format (that is, JPG or GIF), dimensions in pixels, and URL will be shown. Looking at the properties of images can also help you figure out what to enter for HEIGHT and WIDTH in your <IMG SRC> tags, since after viewing properties for a number of images, you'll have a good idea of the average height and width in pixels for small, medium, and large images.

To use an image as a page background, modify the opening <BODY> tag:

> <BODY BACKGROUND="[filename or URL]">

You don't need to specify height or width because the browser will automatically fill up the entire page with your specified background, laying out copies side-by-side if the image isn't large enough to fill the page as is. If you use a background image this way, be sure that the image is very light, like a watermark on paper, and that it's not so busy it will distract the viewer from your page content. Also, be sure that the chosen image is one that will tile, or repeat across and down your page, easily. Abstract, repeating designs usually work best.

Text Headers

A text header is a line or section of boldface text that is slightly larger than, and set apart from, the main body text. Text headers are most often used for page or section titles, such as the title Text Headers, which appears just above this paragraph.

Text headers can be set to a value of 1 through 6, with 1 being the smallest size/emphasis and 6 being the largest size/emphasis. You can set text headers by applying font size and boldface tags also, but many website developers consider it a good practice to use text header tags instead. To set a text header, use this syntax:

> <H[1–6]>text to be made into a header</H>

Add a text header to your Hello.html and experiment with changing the value to see how the appearance of the header changes.

BEST PRACTICES

Here's a review of the best practices, or good habits, mentioned in this chapter and the Author website section of the Promotion chapter, plus a couple more.

Don't use underlining to format Web page text—to the person viewing the page, the text will look like a hyperlink.

Don't use named colors as page backgrounds—they're too bright.

Type your HTML tags in uppercase to distinguish them from other page content.

Don't go crazy with graphics, fonts, sounds, and animations—too much of a good thing will make your pages busy, harder to read, and slower to load, and many Web surfers won't have browsers that support all the bells and whistles.

If you set a graphic as your page background, make sure it isn't too dark, bright, or busy—the text and images you put on top of it may be hard to read or just hard to look at if the background is fighting for top billing.

Don't use copyrighted or trademarked graphics or images in your Web pages without the owner's permission.

Make sure any images referenced by your <IMG SRC> tags will be on the Web and available for display in your page at all times.

Always make a backup of a page before you begin editing it.

Always preview a page by opening the copy saved on your hard drive in a browser window before posting it to the Web.

NAME CODE	NUMBER CODE	DISPLAYS	DESCRIPTION
†	N.A.	†	dagger
‡	N.A.	‡	double dagger
‹	N.A.	‹	less than
›	N.A.	›	greater than
–	–	–	en dash
—	—	—	em dash
			nonbreaking space
¢	¢	¢	cent sign
£	£	£	pound sterling
©	©	©	copyright
®	®	®	registered trademark
°	°	°	degrees
±	±	±	plus/minus
²	²	^{2}	superscript two
³	³	^{3}	superscript three
¶	¶	¶	paragraph sign

&middot;	&#183;	·	middle dot
&sup1;	&#185;	¹	superscript one
&frac14;	&#188;	¼	one-fourth
&frac12;	&#189;	½	one-half
&frac34;	&#190;	¾	three-fourths
&divide;	&#247;	÷	division

SUMMARY TABLES

A summary table of commonly used ASNI codes is presented below.

The next page contains a summary table of all the HTML tags discussed in this chapter, as well as a few that weren't discussed, but whose use is self-explanatory.

Experiment with these tags in your Hello. html file until you're comfortable with them. Also, try viewing the source code of various HTML pages online to see how others are using them, as well as to learn more tags. When you see something you like on an HTML page, view source to see how it was done.

HTML TAG	PURPOSE
<HTML> </HTML>	declare HTML page
<HEAD> </HEAD>	declare page header section
<TITLE> </TITLE>	set a page title
<BODY> </BODY>	declare page body section
<BODY BGCOLOR="[name or hex]"> </BODY>	set page background color
<BODY BACKGROUND="[filename/URL]"> </BODY>	set page background image
<H[1 – 6]> </H>	insert page header
<B> </B>	make text bold
<I> </I>	make text italicized
<U> </U>	make text underlined
<CENTER> </CENTER>	make text center-aligned
<LEFT> </LEFT>	make text left-aligned
<RIGHT> </RIGHT>	make text right-aligned
<FONT SIZE="[1 – 6]"> </FONT>	make text size 1 through 6

<FONT FACE="[font name]"> </FONT>	set text font
<FONT COLOR="[name or hex]"> </FONT>	set text color
  (no closing tag)	insert single-spaced line break
<P> </P>	format text as paragraph
<A NAME="[anchorname]"> </A>	insert named anchor
<A HREF="#[anchorname]"> </A>	link to a named anchor
<A HREF="[URL]"> </A>	hyperlink
<A HREF="MAILTO:[e-mail address]"> </A>	e-mail link
<IMG SRC="[filename or URL]"> (no closing tag)	insert pointer to an image—remember optional HEIGHT and WIDTH attributes

index